ART AND
THOUGHT IN
THE HELLENISTIC
AGE

ART AND THOUGHT IN

The Hellenistic Age

THE GREEK WORLD VIEW
350–50 BC

JOHN ONIANS

with 189 illustrations

THAMES AND HUDSON

For Richard Broxton Onians, Rosalind Lathbury
and Elisabeth de Bièvre

Library of Congress Catalog card number 78-63040

Printed in Great Britain by BAS Printers Limited, Over Wallop, Hampshire

Contents

Prologue **Athens and Atlantis – A Myth of Style and Civilization** 7

One **Fourth-century Attitudes** 17

Dorians, Ionians and the 'Choice of Hercules' · Socrates and Plato · Aristotle · The Philosophy of Hellenism and Hellenistic Philosophies · Fortune and Virtue: Chance and Art · Artistic Naturalism and its Limitations · Art as Deception and the Deceiving Eye · Beauty and the Beast · Town and Country

Two **Art: its Classification and Criticism** 53

Ethos and *Pathos* · Chronological Classification and Criticism · Geographical Classification and Criticism · Stylistic Choice at Alexandria and Syracuse · Stylistic Choice in Architecture · Stylistic Choice at Pergamum · A Stoic Style?

Three **Allegory, Images and Signs** 95

Allegory · Word and Image · Writers and Images · Images as Words · The Power of Sight

Four **Measure and Scale** 119

Measure, Scale and Perception · Large and Small · The Large River and the Small Jug · Attic and Asiatic in Rhetoric and Sculpture · Active and Passive in Artistic Creation

Five **Time and Space** 151

Time, Length and Distance · Sound and Space in the Theatre · Geometry, Geography and Space · Optics and Architectural Planning

Greek Epilogue – Roman Prologue 180

Map of Greece and the Eastern Mediterranean 181
Guide to Further Study 182
List of Illustrations 183
Index 189

1 Quartz ringstone engraved with head of Alexander the Great, late fourth century BC. Alexander wears the horns of Zeus Ammon.

Prologue

Athens and Atlantis
A Myth of Style and Civilization

1 When Alexander the Great was born in Macedon in 356 BC, Plato had been writing and teaching in Athens for forty years. Through Plato's dialogues we can learn much about Greek attitudes just before the Hellenistic period begins, as they bring together a wide range of speakers in discussion with Plato's master, Socrates. Indeed, few passages in Greek literature are more enlightening than the stories or myths contained in the Platonic dialogues – myths in which Plato was able to present his interpretations of the past and his visions of the future. One such mixture of history and fantasy is the myth of Atlantis, referred to in the *Timaeus* and given at length in the *Critias*.

Nine thousand years before the time of Solon, Plato tells us in the *Critias*, there was a great war between those who lived within and without the Pillars of Hercules. The dominant power within the Pillars, that is the Straits of Gibraltar, was Athens; the dominant power without was Atlantis. As the *Critias* is incomplete we know nothing of the war, except that the Athenians won. However, the dialogue does contain a full account of both Athens and Atlantis, including not only descriptions of the social and economic structures of the two powers, but also information on their attitudes to art. Plato is at pains to point out the contrasting qualities of Hellenic culture as represented by Athens and of the non-Hellenic, or barbarian, culture as represented by Atlantis. The deficiencies of the latter and the virtues of the former are seen as the respective causes of the tragic outbreak and inevitable conclusion of the war. Whatever echoes there may be here of tales of a land beyond Gibraltar or of a Bronze Age confrontation between Athens and some Aegean island power, the key notion of an essential opposition between Greek and barbarian culture is clearly based on attitudes that grew up chiefly in Athens after the Persian Wars of the early fifth century.

These attitudes are especially important for us as they were partly responsible for the semi-barbarian Macedonians aspiring first to support and then to identify themselves with the Greek cause. They first inspired the fifth-century king of Macedon, Alexander I, to take Philhellene ('friend of the Hellenes') as his proudest title. They led a successor, Philip, to choose the Athenian-trained Aristotle as tutor to his son Alexander. Finally they brought Alexander to Asia to replace Persian with Greek supremacy there. The myth of Atlantis helps us to understand the effects of Alexander's conquests by suggesting both what the Greeks might have offered the barbarians and what barbarian qualities and achievements most fascinated the Greeks. Yet perhaps the most interesting function of the myth is that it provides us with a key to the artistic culture of the whole period studied in this book, from the founding of the Hellenistic kingdoms to the rise of Rome. For Plato saw that a nation's use of art is integrally related to its political structure and economic organization. Hence the difference in the myth between the art of oligarchic, self-sufficient Athens and that of monarchic Atlantis with its empire. The validity of Plato's observations can be confirmed by comparing his fantasy with historical reality. The Athens which he describes in the *Critias* corresponds in essential aspects of its organization with many Greek city-states

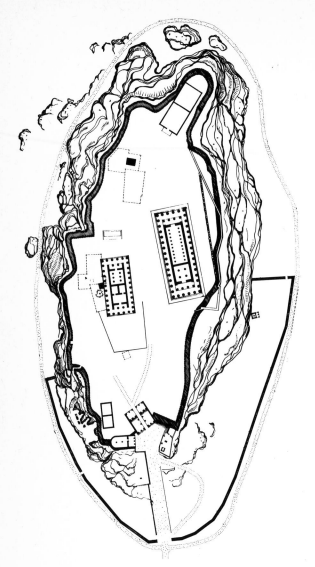

2 Plan of the Acropolis, Athens, on the eve of the Persian invasion in 480 BC.

three of these models that Plato learnt the effects of monarchic centralization and international trade on culture and art. In a sense, too, his Atlantis was to become a reality after his death when Alexander, dominating Athens, taking control of Ionia and conquering the Middle East, laid the foundations of the Hellenistic world.

What then are the characteristics of Athens and Atlantis in the myth told by Plato in the *Critias*? Athens was founded by Athena and Hephaestus who were united in their love of crafts and love of wisdom. The land produced all things in plenty and so was self-sufficient. The state enjoyed a simple distribution of classes, with the warriors, the highest class and guardians of the state, living on the Acropolis around the temple of Hephaestus and Athena, where they worshipped an image of the armed goddess. The craftsmen lived round them on the slopes, and beyond them lived the workers on the land. Neither the classes nor their houses changed from generation to generation. All goods were shared in common, the military class receiving enough for its needs from the craftsmen and the farmers. The Athenians were not mean in their use of natural resources, nor were they ostentatious, but they observed a moderation (*meson*) embodying order (*kosmos*) and appropriateness (*prepon*). With the exception of the site, Plato's ancient Attica bore little relation to fifth-century Athens. But as a self-sufficient *polis*, with a dominant warrior class supported by craftsmen and food producers, it corresponded to Athens and other Greek states as they existed before the expansion of trade and the development of power groups in the sixth and fifth centuries. Until the time of these changes, which resulted largely from the collapse of Greek self-sufficiency, Greek society had remained a conservative one as is witnessed, for example, by the persistence of the Homeric tradition and by the lack of change in architecture. In so far as the aristocracy could take what they wanted from whom they wanted there was even a historical basis for Plato's 'sharing'. The moderation which Plato attributes to the ancient Athenians also existed in practice, though more as a necessity, arising from the intermediate position of Greece between rich Asia and poor Europe, than as a virtue. This is not to deny that the moral emphasis on both sharing and moderation is not Plato's own. Indeed, these qualities and also those of order and appropriateness are essential features

2

before the sixth century and shares with them a restriction of large-scale art to the religious context. Plato's Atlantis, on the other hand, bears a strong resemblance both in its society and in its art to the civilizations of the ancient Middle East, to the rich cities of Greek Ionia, to fifth-century Athens in particular, and also – looking forward in time – to the Hellenistic kingdoms and the Roman Empire. It was from a study of the first of his philosophy of man, deriving from the physical speculations of the Greeks in the sixth and fifth centuries. The order which the Ionians had found in the heavens and the mathematical arrangement which the Pythagoreans had seen in the world had convinced Plato that such stable patterns were vital not only for the well-being of the macrocosmic universe but also for that of microcosmic man.

The opulent diversity of Plato's Atlantis is in strong contrast to his austerely perfect Attica. Poseidon, the founder of Atlantis, was no philosopher or craftsman; he simply controlled nature herself. Having chosen the Atlantic island as birthplace for his progeny, he used his physical power to give it a new form. Round a great hill he dug three circular canals separated by two rings of land. On this hill his children built his temple and next to it the palace where the eldest son and his descendants were to rule as kings over all the rest. The kings of Atlantis continued the spirit of Poseidon in adapting nature to their use, throwing up bridges to link the rings of land and joining the canals with tunnels. They were enormously rich. Not only did they bring in foreign products from the territories they controlled, which included Etruria and Egypt, but they used the precious metals with which their land was lavishly endowed to adorn both palaces and temples. Instead of the single statue of the warrior Athena in Athens, they had a giant representation of Poseidon in his chariot surrounded by a hundred nereids, all in gold and ivory. In the temple of Poseidon there were also statues of men and women of the royal families. Unlike the citizens of Attica who always left their houses unchanged, the kings of Atlantis always tried to surpass their predecessors by adding to the palace. The houses of the ordinary people in Atlantis, instead of being built to the standard of bare sufficiency as were those of the rival state, had exteriors variegated with black, white and red marble. While the Athenians simply fitted into the pattern of the seasons, living on the north side of the Acropolis in winter and on the south side in summer, the inhabitants of Atlantis used the hot and cold springs of the island to supply baths where they could choose what temperature they liked. They were equally remote from nature in preferring the sophisticated spectator sport of the hippodrome to the healthy activity of the Athenian gymnasium.

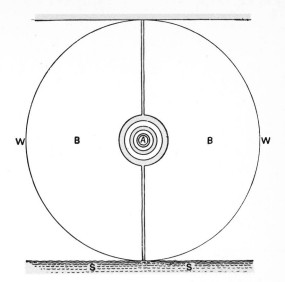

3 Reconstructed plan of Atlantis, after Plato. A = acropolis; B = outer city; S = sea; W = city wall. Shading denotes lay-out of canals.

Atlantis is definitely a barbarian state. The language spoken is not Greek and the territories of its empire are equally un-Hellenic. Typically barbarian is the institution of monarchy, associated by the Greeks above all with the arch-barbarians, the Persians. Other elements of Atlantis probably derive directly from barbarian communities. The Babylonian queen, Semiramis, was famous for building canals and bridges, and particularly for her unnatural hanging gardens. The Egyptians had temples full of portraits and in many cases a pharaoh attempted to surpass his predecessors by the addition of new and ever larger courts and pylons. The gold, silver and ivory interior of the temple of Poseidon at Atlantis is singled out by Plato as especially 'barbaric' and the temple of Solomon at Jerusalem, as described in *Kings*, is an example of what he might have had in mind. Yet although Plato felt that such a political organization and such expenditure were essentially un-Greek he must have been well aware that there had been Greeks who had acquired an authority in their own community and, consequently, control over finance which approached that of an oriental king and who had embarked on similar activities. The Ionian tyrant, Polycrates of Samos, around 530, had challenged nature with his tunnels and other feats of engineering. Pericles was said to have

4 Reconstruction of east cella of the Parthenon, Athens, with Phidias' colossal gold and ivory statue of Athena Parthenos, 447–432 BC.

introduced his own portrait into the Parthenon by getting Phidias to put it on the shield of his statue of Athena. Pericles too had been responsible for the enormous expenditure of gold and ivory on the giant statue itself. In fact, the character of the Atlantean statue of Poseidon is so recognizably similar to that of the Phidian statue of Athena that it seems almost certain that Plato specifically wanted to chasten the Athenians by stressing the latter's 'barbaric' quality. It is significant that the Greek states where the use of art most closely paralleled that in Atlantis were those most famous for their overseas trade and influence, and also those in which single individuals had achieved almost monarchic powers. Plato had correctly diagnosed that such extravagant and arrogant constructions were not so much typically barbarian as typical of such political and economic circumstances.

This point prepares us for the prophetic quality of Plato's work. The most striking parallels to Atlantis are not to be found in previous civilizations, either Greek or barbarian, but in the Hellenistic and Roman worlds. For there, not only did the circumstances described above exist for most of the time from Alexander to Constantine, but they existed against a background of vastly increased wealth such as Plato could only dream about for his vanished land. In the Hellenistic period, as a result of the fragmentation of Alexander's empire into a number of smaller kingdoms after his death, there were not the same resources as during the period when the whole Mediterranean world was under the control of the Roman Empire. Because the Hellenistic monarchies are separated by so short a time from Plato himself, however, their use of art is likely to be more precisely within the range of his imagination. It is indeed particularly appropriate to apply Plato's analysis to the years after 350, when he was writing, since his purpose in composing such works as the *Critias* at all must have been to provide a warning about potential cultural developments. By then, at the end of his life, he might well have been disillusioned by the behaviour of his pupil Dionysius, tyrant of Syracuse, fearful of the expansionism of Philip of Macedon, and all too conscious of the increasing material extravagance of the wealthier Greek citizens.

One characteristic feature of Plato's Atlantis is the richness of the private houses and this too is a feature of the fourth century. Already, before 400, Alcibiades had shocked public opinion by having his house decorated by the Samian painter Agatharchus, and such ostentatious rejection of the principle of 'sufficiency' had become so marked by the time of Demosthenes that the latter could remark in 349 that some private houses were even grander than public buildings. At Olynthus, destroyed by Philip himself in 348, many excavated houses are quite opulent, but they represent only the beginning of a development which can be traced through the Macedonian capital Pella, third-century Priene, Morgantina in Sicily (a town controlled by Hiero II of Syracuse) and second-century Delos, where dwellings are adorned with rich two-storey colonnades. Plato laid particular emphasis on the multicoloured decoration of the houses in Atlantis, and from Olynthus to Delos there is a regular increase in polychromy, especially evident in the use of mosaics. At Olynthus and Pella,

5 Lion hunt. Pebble mosaic from Pella, late fourth century BC.

6 Winged Dionysiac infant riding a lion. Mosaic from the House of the Faun, Pompeii, second century BC.

7 Reconstruction of section of the House of the Hermes, Delos, second century BC.

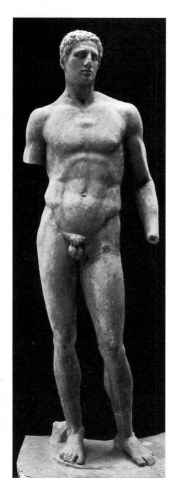

8 Agias, from the monument of the Thessalians erected at Delphi by Daochus II, *c*. 340–330 BC. Probably contemporary copy of bronze original by Lysippus.

where these mosaics appear for the first time in a Greek context, designs are formed of natural pebbles just as they had been in the eighth century at 'barbarian' Gordion in Asia Minor. Around 250 at Morgantina, pebbles are replaced by cut marble tesserae which, in their artificiality and greater brilliance, echo Atlantis more precisely. By the second century large areas of mosaics of increasing complexity are found at Pergamum, at Delos and, eventually, in Italy. The expansion of the originally barbarian device is closely associated with the establishment of Hellenistic culture. Less easy to document is the growth of the use of rich materials and variegated colours on walls, which is a regular feature in the houses of second-century Delos. About 300, in a religious context, the walls of the Kabeirion of Samothrace were covered with painted stucco imitating coloured marble slabs. The shrine, which was heavily patronized by Alexander and his successors, was open to all classes, sexes and races, in contrast to Eleusis, for example, which was reserved for those who were Greek and free, or Olympia where access was even more restricted. Plato would not have been surprised to find that, as in Atlantis, multicoloured decoration was associated with a multinational centre. Nor would Plato have been surprised to discover that the

9 Greek fighting Amazons. Detail of frieze from the Mausoleum, Halicarnassus, mid-fourth century BC.

magnificent river boat of Ptolemy Philopator contained columns which were not only made up of alternating black and white stones, rather like the walls of Atlantis, but were also carved in the Egyptian, that is a barbaric, manner.

It is in the environments of the same third-century Egyptian and Sicilian rulers mentioned above that we find the first dynastic portrait galleries corresponding to that described in Plato's Atlantis. On Ptolemy's river boat there was also a shrine of Dionysus which contained statues of members of the royal family and in the temple of Athena at Syracuse there was a series of painted portraits of the rulers of Syracuse up to the time of Hiero II, probably put up by the latter. A timid anticipation of the dynastic intention of these groups is found in the monument erected by Daochus in the precinct of Apollo at Delphi in the 330s to commemorate his appointment by Philip as tetrarch of Thessaly. This included statues of himself and of his ancestors. But there were no real parallels in Greek tradition for such intimacy between a mortal family and the gods. The source is clearly oriental, particularly Egyptian, practice. Pharaohs and their families were frequently accorded such divine honours. Alexander, as their successor, was said to have been accepted by Amun Ra as his son when he visited the oracle

of the god at Siwa. The Ptolemies readily accepted the tradition. Hence they could be present as three-dimensional statues within the Dionysiac shrine. The position of Hiero in Greek Sicily was naturally more difficult. Thus although he and his ancestors were visible in the temple, the fact that they were represented in paintings rather than bodied forth as sculptures made them seem to claim divine protection rather than divinity.

All these features of Hellenistic civilization which Plato anticipated in his Atlantis, rich private houses, multicoloured architectural decoration and dynastic sculpture, find an even greater development in the Roman world. This is equally true of other elements in Atlantis. In the Hellenistic cities there were, for example, small bath buildings, but the importance attached to baths in Atlantis reminds us more of Rome. The specific emphasis in Atlantis on baths as a source of pleasure, their association with gardens, the construction of different buildings for hot and cold water, and the provision of separate facilities for women all look forward to Roman baths. In the same way the importance attached to horses and to the hippodrome anticipates the Imperial City with its several circus racecourses. The perversion manifest in the decision of the citizens of Atlantis to construct separate baths for horses

13

is paralleled in Caligula's wish to make his horse a senator. The Greeks admired horses to a degree, but they associated such admiration more normally with the barbarians. Consequently we have the many reliefs showing the Greeks, almost always on foot, defeating either the half-horse centaurs, or the horse-riding Amazons or Persians. In Rome there were as many statues and reliefs representing Roman cavalrymen subduing babarian foot soldiers. The Greeks were proud of their victories won by superior skill and human strength over enemies who were helped by horses. In the same way they were fond of setting their simple spear or sword against the Persians' complicated bow and arrow, and of visualizing themselves fighting naked against Amazons or Persians wearing clothes. In complete contrast, the Roman was sure of his superiority over possibly stronger Germanic tribesmen mainly because of his horses and elaborate armour. In Atlantis, horses play such an important role partly because they represent the inhabitants' lack of awareness of the distance that should separate man and beasts, and partly because they were associated with Poseidon and illustrate the control enjoyed by Poseidon's descendants over nature and natural forces. The construction of the baths in Atlantis also makes this last point, but the clearest demonstration of its inhabitants' control over nature is their construction of roads and bridges, tunnels and canals. Such vast works were emulated by Hellenistic kings, as when Alexander almost had Dinocrates hew Mount

Athos into a statue holding a city in one hand and a basin in the other, or when the Ptolemies improved the canal linking the Red Sea and the Nile. These works were far surpassed in their turn by the monuments of Roman civil engineering.

The palace of the kings of Atlantis, to which they each successively added in an attempt to surpass each other, also makes one think of Hellenistic, and especially of Roman, buildings. Most Greek temples were as unchanging in their forms as the houses of Plato's proto-Athenians. Sacred buildings are normally conservative, and what we know of Greek secular buildings before the fourth century does not suggest that they revealed a greater spirit of competitive development. Competition in Greece was normally only between cities. One city might claim a longer or more richly decorated temple than the next. Once built, the temple would remain unchanged, unless destruction by fire, as in the case of the Artemisium of Ephesus, or by the Persians, as in the case of the buildings on the Acropolis, made reconstruction necessary. Only occasionally did a desire for personal aggrandizement stimulate architectural innovation, as in the case of the Alcmaeonid marble façade of the temple of Apollo at Delphi or the startling Pisistratid plan for the Olympieum at Athens. The nature of Greek political life made such association of an individual or a family with a particular structure a rare exception. It was not until the early Hellenistic period, when families and individuals controlled the revenues of whole states and their

10 Dedicatory inscription of Alexander the Great from the temple of Athena Polias, Priene, 334 BC.

ascendancy, both internally and externally, depended largely on the impression of power they could present, that the notion of personal expression through architecture became widespread. Alexander tried in vain to have his name inscribed on the temple of Diana at Ephesus in return for his contribution to its rebuilding, but 10 he succeeded at Priene. From the time that Philip built his family shrine, the Philippeion, at Olympia after defeating the Greeks at Chaeronea in 338, the rival Hellenistic kings competed architecturally for admiration and praise in the old religious sanctuaries. The result was a series of novel and striking buildings such as the Sanctuary of the Bulls at Delos, probably completed by Antigonus Gonatas, grandson of the founder of the dynasty which ruled Macedon 11 after Alexander, and the Arsinoeion, dedicated at Samothrace by the daughter of the first Ptolemy. The series culminated in the Pergamene monu- 184 ments such as the Stoas of Eumenes and Attalus put up at Athens in the second century when the city became a centre for a new cult – that of Attic Hellenism. It is, indeed, the series of buildings including palaces put up on the acropolis of 79 Pergamum itself, as each successive king strove to make his mark, which most reminds us of Atlantis. But we have to turn to Rome to find the most brilliant evocation of the Atlantean spirit. There, the Republican tradition of inscribing on buildings the names of their constructors, even when they were largely state financed, led to great competition in the pursuit of renown through architecture. Under the Empire we have the exact parallel to Atlantis in the expanding group of palaces on the Palatine. The successive homes of Augustus, Tiberius and Domitian were added to each other in order that the earlier ruler should be seen to be surpassed. A rhetorical echo of this theme is heard as Justinian enters Hagia Sophia and declares: 'Solomon, I have surpassed you.'

It is appropriate that we should follow the story through to the end of the Roman Empire because the correspondence with Atlantis continues even there. Plato describes how the citizens of that country managed to bear the burden of so much wealth and power for a long time. Eventually, however, as a result of the repeated dilution of the divine stock with mortal elements, they became corrupted and arrogant in their excesses. So Zeus decided to punish them in

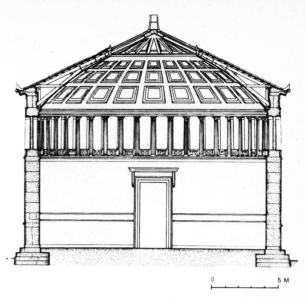

11 Reconstruction of section of the Arsinoeion, Samothrace, 289–281 BC.

order that they should become more careful and wise. The dialogue breaks off at this point leaving us in doubt about exactly what followed. But we gather that the instrument of Zeus' punishment was the simple and virtuous state of Attica. Presumably the victory of virtue over vice in the ensuing war taught the wicked a lesson Some time later the whole continent of Atlantis vanished beneath the waves and only the Egyptians recorded the history of the Atlantic state and preserved it for Solon, the inquiring Athenian, to rediscover. It is not unlikely that behind this account lies the memory of some Bronze Age Aegean commercial community overwhelmed by a more economically backward but stronger mainland power. A similar pattern repeated itself many times in the Bronze and Iron Ages. But it would be interesting to know when a moral lesson was first drawn from the destruction of the rich by the poor. The theme had certainly been explored before Plato. The notion of not trying to dominate nature, which appears throughout Plato's story of Atlantis, is found in the earlier Greek view revealed in Aeschylus' *Persae* that the defeat of Xerxes was a punishment for his arrogance or hubris in subjecting nature to such indignities as the castigation and bridging of the Hellespont and the cutting of a canal through the Athos peninsula. Another model for the victory of poverty over luxury was probably the destruction of Sybaris, in southern Italy, by neighbouring Croton in 510. This is likely to have particularly impressed Plato because Croton was the centre of the Pythagorean sect who, living as an ascetic aristocratic brotherhood, served as a model for his ideal state. The Sybarites, moreover, were interested in the exploitation of nature in their pursuit of luxury. Instead of taking hot baths in winter, like the inhabitants of Atlantis, they planted trees along their roads in order to keep cool in summer.

For most people, however, the conflict of Athens and Atlantis would call to mind most immediately the war between Sparta, aided by her Peloponnesian allies, and Athens at the head of her empire. Plato certainly had the Spartan military aristocracy in view when describing the early Athenians; equally clearly, he modelled aspects of Atlantis, such as the image of Poseidon, on fifth-century Athens. The defeat of Athens by Sparta must have been much the most traumatic experience of Plato's early life. The fusing in Plato's mind of the two models, Croton and Sybaris and Athens and Sparta, must have been greatly facilitated by the knowledge that Sparta had helped to found Croton, and that the Athenians had founded Thurii in 443 near ancient Sybaris, with the remnants of that community and a varied group of people from other Greek cities. The notion that the gods punish men for their arrogance by manipulating human events was already well established, as we can see in the Old Testament or in the Greek myths. In the fifth century this developed into a more humanistic interpretation of historic failures as due to moral defects. Aeschylus' *Persae* leads on to Herodotus' and Thucydides' commentaries on the Persian and Peloponnesian Wars. The philosophic interest in man displayed by Socrates and his pupil, Plato, was generated in them in part by contact with these writers. Plato's philosophy of history as revealed in the Atlantis myth is an extreme abstraction of tendencies in their thought. The authority of all these thinkers for people in the Hellenistic and Roman periods meant that whenever material civilization threatened to collapse the same theme was returned to.

Thus Polybius, the second-century Peloponnesian historian, watched with understanding the victories of Rome over Carthage and the Hellenistic states. His remarks on the Romans have much in common with Plato's on the ancient Athenians, and not without reason. The Italy he first visited in 167 was still largely self-sufficient with a citizen army and an aristocratic government whose leading members, such as the Scipios, showed marked leanings to Stoicism, the Hellenistic philosophy which inherited most from Pythagoras and Plato. Everywhere in the Greek world Polybius saw signs of decadence. On his visit to Egypt he found the once Greek ruling class corrupted by interracial marriage and excessive power and weakly supported by a disorderly mercenary army. He saw only the beginnings of the process by which Rome in her turn took on the attributes of Atlantis. It was the task of the Republican aristocracy to chronicle the change. Foreign trade led to foreign possessions which necessitated first a professional army and finally the institution of monarchic authority in the person of the emperor. From the time of Cato to that of Juvenal the members of the old families watched, cynically predicting the inevitable collapse.

The sharp diagnosis of Tacitus in the late first century AD even isolated Germany as a moral chastener to succeed Plato's idealized Athens. Tacitus was partly right. The barbarian tribes pressed ever harder on the northern frontier until in the fourth and fifth centuries AD they broke through. But another group claimed the role of primitive Athens more self-consciously. These were the Christians, an aristocracy of the poor fighting in a spiritual army. Guided by the teaching of the Jewish tradition as well as by the morality of the Greek ascetics they attacked the trappings, as the barbarians attacked the structure, of the Roman Empire. So it is that Augustine closes our period in the same spirit that Plato began it. Inspired by the fall of Rome in AD 410 he applauded the passing of the City of Man and the coming of the City of God. His City of Man is a direct descendant of Plato's Atlantis, as the City of God is of pristine Athens. The spiritual kingdom of Augustine was only a heavenly dream. But on earth there came into being the medieval Christian world which, though different in essence, corresponded in many aspects with the Athens of Plato's dreams. Trade and international connections diminished and there was a return to self-sufficiency, power was in the hands of a warrior aristocracy, organized asceticism represented the strongest cultural force and art once again found its main function in the service of religion.

Chapter One

Fourth-century Attitudes

Dorians, Ionians and the 'Choice of Hercules'

The myth told by Plato in the *Critias* is more than an account of two cultures based on contrasting principles; it reveals an explicit set of values for the judgment of works of art in terms of both style and subject. Such explicit values are characteristic of Plato's later works, but from the time of Socrates and the Sophists, in the late fifth century, major figures in Greek intellectual life had interested themselves in criticism of the arts. In Xenophon's *Memorabilia* II, i, 21–34 Socrates borrows a story from the contemporary Sophist Prodicus which already embodies some of the critical values of the Atlantis myth. Hercules as a young man has to choose between two ways of life represented for him by two women. The one, Virtue, was tall, erect and dressed in white; the other, Vice, looked taller than she was, tended to fleshiness, used make-up in order to look more rosy and wore a semi-transparent dress. The former ate only when hungry, the latter whenever she wanted; Vice also looked for snow to keep herself cool in summer and when she went to bed put on heavy rugs to keep herself warm. The contrast in these two figures – between the natural and the artificial, the plain and the coloured, sufficiency and pleasure – anticipates many features of the Atlantis myth. Yet there is another important element, that of choice. In the Atlantis myth the differences in the art of Atlantis and Athens follow almost inevitably from the innate characters of the two societies; Hercules, on the other hand, has a free choice. The problem of choice fascinated many Greeks in the hundred

years before the Hellenistic period. Their discussions of the problem are of fundamental importance not only for the Hellenistic period but for all later Western European culture. This is as true of art as of other fields.

Previously the problem of aesthetic choice had hardly arisen. Earlier writers assumed agreement on what constituted a good spear or a beautiful girl, and when it came to objects such as vases and chests, where standards were less familiar, the degree of workmanship and the value of the materials employed were usually recorded. This is true both of descriptions of objects in the Old Testament and of accounts of dedications at Greek shrines in Herodotus. By the late fifth century, however, as Prodicus' story makes clear, agreement on such standards could no longer be taken for granted. The reason for this was apparently that the Greeks, and particularly the Athenians, had become aware that there was more than one way of doing any particular thing and that these options could often be understood as simple alternatives. This was most demonstrable in the opposition between Greeks and barbarians in the Persian Wars and between Athenians and Spartans in the Peloponnesian War. For the Greeks both these conflicts could be reduced to an opposition between the two main Greek cultural traditions, Dorian and Ionian. From the viewpoint of Herodotus, citizen of a Dorian colony in Asia Minor, it was the softness of the Ionians, who were by far the largest Greek group in the area, which made possible the rapid Persian take-over there. Equally, it was the toughness of the Dorian element, the backbone of mainland Greece, which ensured the ultimate

12 West front of the Parthenon, Athens, 447–432 BC.

failure of Persian expansion in that direction. Thucydides could see the later defeat of Athens by Sparta as depending on the same factors. Sparta was a Dorian state and although Athens had not identified herself with the Ionians before the Persian Wars, she had subsequently found it convenient to do so in order to be able to put herself at the head of an Ionian maritime confederacy.

The Athenians claimed to be autochthonous, the aboriginal inhabitants of Attica. This meant that they claimed to represent the population of Greece in the Mycenaean period before the Dorian invasions. Historically, the Athenians do seem to have been protected by the geographical isolation and relative unattractiveness of their land from being driven out by this invasion onto the Aegean islands and the coast of Asia Minor, as had other pre-Dorian groups such as the Aeolians and Ionians. During the pre-Classical period they had been influenced more by their closer neighbours, the Dorians, than by their closer relatives,

the Ionians. The perfection of technique of Attic black-figure pottery was derived from Corinth. The early Archaic limestone sculpture of Athens clearly belongs to the mainland tradition. Dorian influence is seen particularly in the use of limestone technique and Doric forms in all early Athenian architecture. Ionian, or rather Aegean, influence only really emerges in Athens in the late sixth century with the slow introduction of marble for both architecture and sculpture, and the borrowing of such motifs as the rich Ionic *chitōn*, to replace the simple Doric *peplos*, for the standing female sculpture type. When, after the Persian Wars, the Athenians with their fleet found themselves in a position to command the Aegean offensive against the barbarians, they still only made limited concessions towards indentifying themselves with the Ionians. We can perhaps so classify the inclusion of Ionic elements in the Parthenon, begun in 448, but it should be noticed that these occupy subsidiary positions. The Ionic 12 frieze only runs round the cella; it is the Doric

13 West front of the Erechtheum, Athens, after 421–406 BC.

band of triglyphs and metopes that surrounds the whole temple. The Ionic columns of the interior are confined to the back room, while the columns in the chamber containing the cult statue are Doric.

Only when Athenian leadership was in jeopardy, as Athens found herself leading unwilling Ionian allies against the Dorians, did the Athenians use art to assert their Ionian connections decisively. By some genealogical juggling they claimed that Erechtheus, king of Attica, was the grandfather of Ion, ancestor of the Ionians. Euripides wrote a play called *Ion*, drawing attention to this fact. Soon after 421 a new temple, 13 the Erechtheum, not apparently envisaged in the Periclean building plan, was begun on the Acropolis. The site it occupied was that once occupied by the palace of the Mycenaean kings and it had long contained shrines dedicated to different members of the ancient royal house. The decision to build a magnificent temple on this site drew a new attention to the centre of resistance to

the Dorians, and as Erechtheus, the common ancestor of both Athenians and Ionians, figured prominently in the dedication of the temple, the latter also served as a monument to Attic-Ionian unity. The symbolic importance of the Erechtheum is confirmed by the tradition which always denied entry to it to Dorians. It is small wonder that it was decided to build it in the Ionic order, which had until that time hardly appeared at Athens. A final futile gesture of Ionianism was made by the Athenians about 410, just before the defeat of Athens by Sparta and her Dorian allies: Ionic script was adopted for Athenian state inscriptions.

These choices made in fifth-century Athens are the background to the opinions of Prodicus, Socrates and Plato. They demonstrate how, when the Greeks reached that stage of self-awareness which enabled them to choose between a number of solutions to the same problem, such as between scripts for writing, or columns for building, they naturally tended to think in terms of the separate

cultural traditions of the different Greek races. This situation came about because of the isolation of these different groups from each other at least until the sixth century. A sixth-century Aeolian would speak the Aeolic dialect, build in an Aeolian style, use Aeolian pottery and sing and dance to Aeolian music. Minor racial groups tended increasingly to be dominated by major ones as trade developed, but it was only in fifth-century Athens, a society relatively independent of any racial grouping and with wide-ranging international contacts on a political and economic level, that we find anything like liberation from local racial traditions. Yet Athens had still opted for Ionic forms on racial grounds. It was to be the task of the philosophers to break this circle and to introduce moral and other criteria. Admittedly, these thinkers were strongly motivated by hostility to Athenian Ionianism which was so closely linked to Ionian defeat. They also had reason to admire the qualities which had brought the Dorians victory.

Hence Prodicus' 'Choice of Hercules' can be seen to have clear reference to the contemporary situation. Hercules, the Dorian, chooses rightly. The personification of Vice, which he rejects, has attributes which connect her to Ionian and recent Attic sculptural types. Fleshiness is a marked characteristic of Ionian sculptures, and the women who became increasingly prominent in Athenian reliefs of the later fifth century revealed ever more of their charms through their flimsy draperies. The generally more feminine character of Vice, compared to the more manly Virtue, can also be directly related to a contrast between Ionian and Dorian character as seen, for example, in Ionian and Dorian architecture. Vitruvius' notion that the Doric column was based on the male and the Ionic on the female form had probably not yet been formulated, but when statues had been used in place of columns on temples and treasuries, men had been used in the Doric structure of the Olympieum of Acragas and women in the Ionic treasuries of Siphnos and Cnidos as well as in the Erechtheum. That the original meaning of the Greek word for virtue, *aretē*, was manliness, gave added significance to Prodicus' choice of attributes. In the same way Plato gives Atlantis Ionian characteristics, not only in the details which were noted in the prologue, but also by making it the land of Poseidon, the god worshipped at the Panionium,

15 Plato (428–348 BC). Roman copy of an original probably of the fourth century BC.

focus of Ionian loyalties. He also attributed to the ancient Athenians qualities that were Spartan, and so Dorian. Nevertheless, although their frame of reference is still strongly influenced by an opposition between the races, it is important to note that in the stories of both Prodicus and Plato attributes are apportioned not because of their racial associations but because of their conformity to moral values.

Socrates and Plato

Prodicus was unusual among the Sophists in believing that, instead of just teaching anybody any skill they would pay to learn, he actually had a responsibility to influence their choice of skill in the first place. Socrates is probably attacking that whole group of mercenary teachers when in Plato's early dialogue, the *Phaedrus*, he describes the clash between the Egyptian god, Theuth, inventor of many arts, and the Egyptian king,

14 Nike undoing her sandal, from balustrade of the temple of Athena Nike, Athens, late fifth century BC.

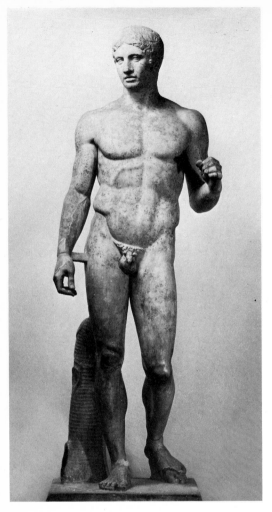

16 Doryphoros, after Polyclitus. Roman copy of an original of the mid-fifth century BC.

Thamous. Theuth suggested that the arts he had discovered, such as arithmetic, geometry, astronomy and writing, should all be given to the Egyptians. But Thamous said that it was the job of one person to invent the arts and of another to decide how useful they were. Writing, for example, which Theuth said would make people wiser and better at remembering, would in fact make them forgetful and dependent on the writings of others for what they should know for themselves. Plato continued to regard the arts with the suspicion shown here, if not with direct hostility, and in the later dialogues he attempts to form some critical principles on the matter. These

principles are founded on his notion of man's relation to the divine. We all have a portion of the divine in us. In the beginning this portion was great, when man was made by the minor gods in the image of their father, the great Demiurge. But it diminished in time, as in the case of the citizens of Atlantis. However, if we wish, we can rediscover the divine element in ourselves by following our natural desire for beauty and goodness. For that appetite is the manifestation of the desire of our small divine element to reunite itself with God. Beauty and goodness are the properties that God built into the Universe and man from the beginning. The two qualities are expressions of each other. As Plato says in the *Republic* 400–1, reasonableness, decorum, gracefulness and excellence of rhythm are all qualities in oratory that follow from the possession of a good character. The same qualities are to be found in drawing and the allied arts, in crafts such as weaving, embroidery and architecture, in the nature of bodies and in plants. These are also the qualities to be pursued by the children in the model state. Poets are accordingly to be forced to represent only good characters. All badness, lowness and unseemliness is to be forbidden both in the representational arts and in architecture.

We cannot analyse here the vague and abstract terms that Plato sees as expressions of the good in the beautiful, but all can be seen as referring to qualities of organization in general, with particular emphasis on regularity, harmony and order. There is no mention by Plato of qualities such as size, richness or value of material and workmanship, which were the terms in current use for the description of works of art in Greek as in other languages. The emphasis placed on this quality of order by Socrates and Plato is particularly clear in a passage of Xenophon's *Oeconomicus* where Socrates asserts that even objects of no intrinsic attraction, such as Phoenician pots, look good when arranged in a regular order. In Plato's *Philodemus* there is a discussion of one particular way of producing order where it is not; this involves putting 'bounds on the boundless' by opposing qualities such as slow and fast, hot and cold, high notes and low notes. The balance of measure against measure and note against note produces proportion and harmony. This last passage leads us straight back to the origin of Plato's arithmetical and geometrical theory of beauty in Pythagoras. The latter's observations on the correspondence between mathematics and music had led him first to see numerical relationships as underlying the whole structure of the world and then to try to impose order on human society and behaviour by applying similar principles to these too.

Plato, however, is not so much taking over an earlier philosophic theory as fitting into a developing aesthetic tradition. The later fifth-century Argive sculptor Polyclitus wrote a book, the *Kanōn* or *Rule*, establishing the proportionate relationships of the different parts of the human body to each other, and carved the Doryphoros to illustrate it. The notion of commensurability was also growing in architecture, as we can see in a series of temples from the mid-fifth to the mid-fourth centuries. This begins with Ictinus' temple of Apollo at Bassae in the Peloponnese, continues in Scopas' temple of Athena Alea at Tegea and culminates in the temple of Athena at Priene, designed by Pythius and dedicated by Alexander

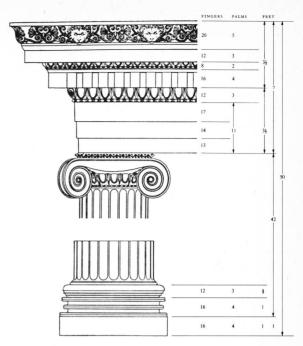

17 Diagram of Ionic order of the temple of Athena Polias, Priene, mid-fourth century BC.

the Great. A large number of elements in the last temple can be measured exactly in terms of complete Attic feet, and accordingly have a rational numerical relationship to each other. In town planning too the grid plan, which is known in both Greece and Italy in the sixth century, reached a high level of geometrical co-ordination in the theory and practice of Hippodamus of Miletus in the mid-fifth century, as we know from Aristophanes and Aristotle. The importance of mathematical order for painting is more difficult to measure: almost no works of the period survive and the nature of painting as a two-dimensional representation of a three-dimensional reality makes it hard to transfer the geometrical proportions inherent in the world into the work itself. However, manifestations of the increasing interest of painters in mathematics are recorded in ancient texts. Vitruvius tells how Agatharchus, scene-painter for Aeschylus in the mid-fifth century, wrote a treatise on the geometrical basis of perspective, and vase paint-

18 Apulian volute krater, fourth century BC.

18 ing shows that perspective developed rapidly at this time. Parrhasius of Ephesus (*c.* 400) is described by Pliny the Elder as the first person to introduce *symmetria* into painting, and Socrates' interest in Parrhasius' ideas is documented by Xenophon who records a conversation between the philosopher and the artist. Pamphilus of Amphipolis (*c.* 350) is described by Pliny as 'the first artist who was erudite in all branches of knowledge, especially arithmetic and geometry, without which he held that an art could not be perfected'. Plato is thus lending his approval to one very important tendency in art at the time, a tendency that developed, as did his ideas, out of the discoveries of the Ionian philosophers.

Most of Plato's other remarks relating to the arts are much more restrictive. In the *Republic* 596 he discusses the three levels of reality: the ideal, created by God; the produced, represented by objects on earth which are poor copies of the ideal; and, finally, the imitated. This last level is the realm of the representational artists who make copies of what they see around them, which is itself only a copy of the ideal. Obviously the artist's activity is not a noble one. He understands the table which he paints less than the carpenter who made it. In the *Republic* and elsewhere Plato makes it clear that if the mimetic artist, be he poet or painter, sculptor or musician, is to have any role it is in the education of the young, and that he can only fulfil this role by representing the true and the good. Homer, for example, should only have shown the gods behaving in a good light, for only good behaviour is truly divine. Still, Plato clearly prefers Homer and the tragic tradition, which he saw as stemming from Homer, as the best form of writing. Thus in *Laws* 657 he says that young children prefer puppet shows, adolescents comedy, adults tragedy and old men the *Iliad*, the *Odyssey* and Hesiod. Only the old have standards and so only the old can judge. The same strain of conservatism is found in *Laws* 656 where Plato deals with music and dance. He recommends following the Egyptian practice. In Egypt music was instituted by the god Isis who knew what was good, and laws were made prohibiting any change or innovation. The same was true of Egyptian painting and sculpture which had remained unaltered for ten thousand years and which were used to present patterns of virtue in temples. This consecration of the arts as holy forms made it impossible for the unhealthy

love of novelty, arising from pleasure in the new and weariness of the old, to have any effect. The Egyptians, we remember, were used as models before for their selectiveness in the use of the arts and they are praised in several other passages, as in *Laws* 819 where Plato commends them for teaching their children mathematics by games. In fact, the Greeks regarded the Egyptians with much the same veneration as the latter in turn received from the Romans.

The favour accorded by Plato to the Egyptians is all the more remarkable when compared with his attitude to other non-Greeks. In the *Laches*, for example, Plato insists that Dorian is the only truly Hellenic, and so respectable, mode in music, in contrast to the Ionian, Phrygian and Lydian modes. Presumably he means that the two last are completely foreign and that even Ionian is corrupted by alien influence, because it grew up in Asia. In the *Republic* 399 he admits Phrygian along with Dorian for its warlike quality but again condemns Ionian and Lydian for being soft and more appropriate to parties, and also Mixo-Lydian and Syntono-Lydian for being sad. We know from other ancient texts that Dorian was considered manly because of its low key note and staid rhythm. Phrygian was a little bit higher and faster. The other modes were closer to the top of the scale and slower, and so were neither invigorating nor manly. The choice of the Dorian mode in Plato's musical criticism thus had much in common with the 'Choice of Hercules'. In the same passage of the *Republic* polychordic and polyharmonic music is also rejected. Although the exact meaning of these two terms is unclear, they evidently refer to a complexity and diversity which Plato always found objectionable. The multicoloured architecture of Atlantis suffered from the same defect.

The surviving information on the opinions of Socrates and Plato covers a period of more than sixty years and the thoughts of the two men are often difficult to separate. Not surprisingly, little uniformity emerges since the artistic context was constantly changing. But the dominant theme is the correlation of moral goodness with physical beauty. It is this which leads both men to accept the growing interest in proportion and other mathematical elements in the visual arts as parallel to the pursuit of regularity and consistency in human behaviour. In the same way they rejected the musical modes which seemed in

19 Grave stele of Thraseas and Euandria, from Athens, third quarter of the fourth century BC.

any way feminine, because of their incompatibility with true *aretē* (manly virtue). They must also have looked with disfavour on the increasing popularity of feminine subjects in art as represented by the Aphrodites of Zeuxis and Praxiteles, and would have shuddered at the thought of the *hetaira* or courtesan, Phryne, one of Praxiteles' models, having a portrait statue at Delphi. One of the clearest glimpses of how Socrates seems to have followed and attempted to influence the contemporary trends in art is provided by Xenophon's account of a meeting between him and the painter Parrhasius. Reflecting recent developments, which are particularly well illustrated in Attic grave art, Parrhasius

24–25

19

agrees that the painter represents not only physical forms but emotions and character as well. Socrates then comments that only good characters and emotions are pleasant to look at, undoubtedly implying that they alone were suitable subjects. Certainly the awareness of Plato and Socrates not only that the subject and style of a work of art are closely connected but also that both together may reflect the character of the artist and affect the character of the audience or spectator is an important development. But their consequent rejection of novelty in art, because it might be as damaging as novelty in human behaviour or in the movements of the heavens, betrays the crudeness of many of their analogies.

20 Aristotle (384–322 BC). Roman copy of an original probably of the fourth century BC.

It is characteristic that Plato should have insisted on the eradication of every trait that seemed a deviation from what he considered truly human, truly male and truly Greek. All these points had inspired his picture of the mythical Athens, and just as they were all denied in his Atlantis, so they were soon to be denied in the Hellenistic world.

Aristotle

Before the Hellenistic world came into being, however, one of Plato's own pupils, Aristotle (384–322), had already come to question many of Plato's assumptions and had formulated an approach to art which was more realistically based on the contemporary situation. In many ways Aristotle still echoes his teacher, as when he advised his own pupil Alexander to behave to the Greeks as their leader and to the barbarians as their master. Indeed, in *Metaphysics* 1078 he repeats Plato's view that the elements of beauty are order, symmetry and limit. But in *Metaphysics* 983ff. he gives a history of Greek philosophy in

terms of his own development in which he is emphatic about the limitations inherent in Plato's point of view. He had, he tells us, first accepted the Heraclitean notion that the sensible world was in a continuous state of flux and had consequently decided that no scientific knowledge could derive from its study. Later he had followed Socrates and Plato in disregarding the physical universe and concentrating his attention on moral questions, finding answers to these in the existence of universals, the 'ideas'. He had, however, subsequently come to realize that all sciences and arts had relied on the use of the senses for their development. As a result he had directed his attention to the sensible physical world, and instead of seeing it as a collection of material copies of 'ideal' forms he had separated out a whole series of factors governing the generation of each object. These he called the efficient cause, the material cause, the formal cause and the final cause. The form that an object took now depended not on some fixed heavenly model but on who made it, what it was made of and what shape it was given; all these depended on its final purpose. It was by an understanding of these causes that an artist was distinguished from a craftsman, a distinction which is still important today. Aristotle did not himself develop this formulation of causality in relation to art, but throughout his work we feel the potential influence of the change in attitude which it represents.

For Plato, the craftsman was bound by a tradition descending from God. All versions of an object should conform as closely as possible to their divine model. Because the arts were originally given to man by divine beings, their first forms were the best. The more remote man became from his divine origin, the more these forms became corrupted by the pursuit of novelty and complication. The tribal arts of pre-sixth-century Greece had largely conformed to this pattern of conservatism. Plato wished to return to a pre-Classical model for his society. He was an aristocrat made cynical by the collapse of Ionian and Attic materialism. Aristotle was the son of a member of the medical guild of the Asclepiadae and had been brought up in Macedonia, a country which was trying to liberate itself from its backward state by making use of all that Greek science, commerce and military experience had revealed. He had no reason to idolize the primitive, which he must have seen at first hand. Instead he almost worshipped science, and not just the useless mathematical sciences valued by Plato, but the technical sciences that could change a person's standard of living. As Theophrastus, Aristotle's pupil and successor as head of the Lyceum, said: 'Nobody would describe the life of the Heroes at the time of the Trojan War as pleasant. That description is rightly preserved for our present way of life. For in Homeric times life was ill-provided and was not equipped with inventions because of the absence of commerce and the immaturity of techniques. But life now lacks nothing in the cultural amenities which promote the enjoyment of leisure' (Athenaeus 511d). Aristotle saw that Greek science and technology had advanced from 600 onwards by a process of analysis and improvement of technique and concepts. His observations were stimulated mainly by a study of the results achieved by speculation in the physical sciences, but they could as easily have been derived from a knowledge of the developments in practical fields, such as the growth of medicine in the Hippocratic period or the improvement in metallurgy through a better control of furnace temperature, which had led to the expansion of bronze casting in the fifth century. Progress in the latter technology, for example, could be said to stem from the isolation and study of the material and motive causes of sculpture.

We can see some of the consequences of Aristotle's opinions in his own discussion of the two arts of drama and rhetoric in the *Poetics* and the *Rhetoric*. Plato had assumed the one true goal of art to be the bringing of man closer to the divine, but for Aristotle the final cause had to be defined for each human activity. Thus in the *Poetics* he was able to discuss the psychological function of drama and, because he was concerned with establishing the material cause in tragedy, he had to discuss carefully what sort of person should be its subject. Similarly in the *Rhetoric*, because he was interested in isolating a formal cause for oratory, he had to discuss the use of rhythm and metre. Questions which Plato would answer by turning to tradition with its limited number of possibilities Aristotle would answer by speculation and argument, which theoretically gave him a much wider range of choice. A precise example of how Aristotle's ideas, if followed, could liberate artistic development by turning previous notions on their head is provided by a simile in the *Parts of Animals*. There Aristotle says that it is clearly silly for the form of a house to be conditioned by the manner of its genesis; rather the manner of its genesis should be conditioned by the nature of the form it should have in the end. In fact, up to this time the forms of Greek temples were precisely conditioned by the way in which the temples had evolved. The stone orders were cumbersome derivatives of wooden prototypes whose original forms had been strictly preserved. The process of rejecting such a rigid tradition had already begun at Athens with the mixing of Doric and Ionic elements in the same building, but it was not until 12 the period after Aristotle that the flagrant denials of the original forms of the Greek orders occur. In the second century Doric entablatures are frequently put on Ionic columns, and horizontal 21 entablatures are bent to form arches.

21 Reconstruction of elevation of the Stoa of Athena, Pergamum, first half of the second century BC.

22 Battle between Greeks and Amazons. Detail of frieze from the temple of Artemis, Magnesia-on-the-Maeander, *c.* 140 BC.

Other remarks by Aristotle shed light on the development of sculpture and painting. In the *Rhetoric* he explains how different styles of speech are appropriate to different subjects and environments. Thus speech in the public assembly should be like *skiagraphia* or shadow-painting (probably a style of painting using strong contrast of light and shade), for the bigger the crowd the further away the spectator or audience. In this context a fine and detailed speech would seem fussy and bad. In the law-courts, on the other hand, the latter type would be quite appropriate. Aristotle's relativism here is clearly opposed to Plato's idea that art should conform to absolute standards and should certainly make no concessions to mass appeal. Aristotle's views have implications which are as clear for subject as for style. In the *Poetics* he distinguishes between history and *poiēsis* (poetry). History tells what happened. *Poiēsis* tells what could have happened. Poetry is thus almost by definition concerned with what did not happen, that is with falsehood and fantasy. The poet should adapt his story and his characters to the effect he wishes to have on his audience. In terms of dramatic poetry, tragedy should imitate people better than ourselves, because this heightens our emotion as we witness their disasters, while comedy should imitate people who are worse than ourselves, because they are more *geloioi* (ludicrous, provoking of laughter). Aristotle clearly feels that similar distinctions can be applied to other arts as he also says that some painters represent men as they are, some as worse and some as better; however, he gives no hint that these various treatments reflect particular differences in the painters' goals. Developing his general concern with psychological effect, Aristotle also remarks that things which repel us in everyday life, such as corpses and lower animals, actually delight us when represented in art. Aristotle's increasing aesthetic tolerance is also found in his view that each age and sex has its own beauty, which represents a development from Plato's apparent conviction that true beauty is embodied only in the young male. All these points illustrate how far Aristotle had moved beyond Plato. The latter had formulated a rigid set of moral and aesthetic ideals as standards which had to be applied to art as to the whole of human life. Aristotle, on the other hand, had not only introduced a more flexible system of standards for real life but had established from a study of the 'causes' of art that the latter was an autonomous activity, almost by definition distinct from life. From Aristotle onwards ethics and aesthetics begin to move apart.

The change of attitude represented by Aristotle is fundamental to the understanding of Hellenistic art. Much that was created in the next two hundred years can only be explained in terms of a new interest in the mechanics of perception or in terms of new expectations and responses in the spectator. Thus developments in relief sculpture can be related to just such a concern for legibility, and an increasing awareness of how distance affects this, as is revealed in Aristotle's remarks on the styles of painting and rhetoric. There is little sign that earlier sculpture was significantly affected by such considerations. The Parthenon 164 frieze certainly lacks the quality of bold light effects recommended by Aristotle for the distant view and instead has the fineness of detail approved by him for close scrutiny. This is not true of most Hellenistic friezes. The frieze on the 22 temple of Artemis at Magnesia-on-the-Maeander, which was a similar distance from the eye to the Parthenon frieze, was executed in a high-relief technique with coarse cutting of detail that would have greatly improved its legibility, while on the large Gigantomachy frieze of the Great Altar of 86 Zeus at Pergamum strong shadows produce clear and emphatic patterns and all figures are outlined with the running drill to make them emerge more distinctly. Nothing demonstrates more clearly the growing importance of the spectator and the increasing acceptance of the limitations of the eye than the tendency to carve only those parts of a statue which would be visible to a normal spectator. In the Classical period standards of internal and absolute perfection required that invisible parts of a statue, such as its back, should be finished as well as the front; but during the fourth century in the series of Attic grave reliefs there is a marked change from the early reliefs, which are fully worked all over, to the later ones where less visible areas, such as the hidden parts of the face and the 23 undersides of stools and chairs, are only sketched out. This trend only accelerated in the Hellenistic

period. It constitutes a decisive rejection of the Platonic contention that a sculptor is trying to copy an ideal chair in the same way as a carpenter is. It relies instead on the notion, found in Aristotle, that the success of artistic imitation is measured only by its effect on the audience or spectator, and that to do more than is necessary to satisfy his sense and psyche is superfluous.

Aristotle was not alone, either, in his concern with the emotional and psychological effect of art. Fourth-century grave reliefs and painted vessels show a consistent interest in the expression and thus the communication of emotion. It was in his discussion of tragedy that Aristotle showed most perception in his study of emotion and, as we shall see in the next chapter, his account of the role of emotion in the dramatic context may well be specifically applicable to the visual arts. Fear, pity and laughter are the emotions most closely connected with tragedy and comedy, but an emotion closer to the hearts of the Hellenistic Greeks was love, and erotic art formed an even more important category in our period. Artists were as susceptible as their public. Apelles, who was particularly proud of the

23 Detail of grave stele from Attica, *c.* 360 BC.

24 Aphrodite, after Praxiteles. Roman copy deriving from the Aphrodite of Cnidos of *c.* 350–330 BC.

physical charm (*charis*) of his work, when he was commanded to paint Alexander's favourite concubine, Pancaspe, in the nude, fell in love with her himself. Fortunately Alexander, acknowledging a power greater than his own, then gallantly presented her to the artist. Praxiteles too was known for his passions and he had already made a naked statue of Aphrodite, an embodiment rather 24– than a personification of love. Its powers were 25 acknowledged by the Cnidians who bought it and erected a shrine which enabled it to be seen from the back as well as the front and which exposed it to such effect that it was supposed to bear the stains of attempted violation. The Crouching Aphrodite, probably by the third-century sculp- 31 tor Doidalsas of Bithynia, must surely have had the same effect and Praxiteles' son Cephisodotus made a *symplēgma* or embracing group which was probably the first of a whole series of studies of sexual assault. Disappointingly few sculptures and paintings of the Hellenistic period survive but the many epigrams referring to such works document the emotional response to art in the period. The increasing importance of these responses is seen in the shift in the classification of epigrams away from grouping by author, form or subject towards a grouping by effect; so that, for instance, it is possible to talk of humorous and erotic genres.

To say that the study of the change in attitudes between Plato and Aristotle is helpful for the understanding of the origins of Hellenistic art is not to imply that these thinkers had a direct influence on artistic developments. We should see these philosophers' dominant positions, in the first and second halves of the fourth century respectively, as being largely due to their expression of points of views widely shared by their contemporaries. This is not to deny their individual contributions but rather to stress that as educators they tended to sum up and draw conclusions from the state of knowledge at the time. Not surprisingly, both their knowledge and their conclusions are based on differences not only of time but of background, and these too are suitably representative. The divergence of their underlying attitudes is thus particularly significant. That of Plato, the Athenian aristocrat, is based on an admiration of earlier societies and on a general conservatism, while that associated with Aristotle, the Macedonian scientist, reveals a great faith in the notions of change and historical

improvement. But Aristotle's attitude also corresponds in important aspects with what we can
infer about later Hellenistic artists, and here it is
perhaps possible to talk of influence. Not only do
Aristotle's own writings on both poetry and
rhetoric include metaphors from the visual arts,
but major writings on the arts are associated with
his immediate followers. Aristoxenus' treatise on
music was the most influential in antiquity and
Douris' work on painting was evidently very well
known. Furthermore, cultural life in Alexandria,
the most important artistic and literary centre of
the Hellenistic world, was dominated by the
Museum, an institution probably founded by
another pupil of Aristotle's school, Demetrius of
Phalerum. There the work of classification and
co-ordination of all fields of human knowledge
begun by Aristotle in Athens was continued. In
the end the development of philosophy and art
should be regarded as parallel. An awareness of
the achievement of the Greeks, apparently un-
aided by the gods, after 600 – an awareness which
was even greater for the half-barbarian Macedonians and for the Greeks who established
themselves in the barbarian East after the
conquests of Alexander – led Aristotle to abandon the notion of philosophy as a religion and,
equally, led artists to reject the idea of art as a
ritual. It also led to a wider recognition of
Hellenism as a unified culture superior to all
others and to an identification of one of its
essentials as an understanding and control of
nature.

The Philosophy of Hellenism and Hellenis-
tic Philosophies

The notion of Hellenism as a cultural rather than a
racial term had been formulated by Isocrates in
the mid-fourth century. 'Athens', he said, 'has
brought it about that the name Hellene no longer
suggests a race but an intelligence, and the title
Hellene is applied rather to those who share our
culture than to those who share our blood.' How
far Alexander may have been directly motivated
by a desire to bring this Hellenism to the rest of
the world is unclear. But the evidence suggests
that he certainly pursued something more than
political control and economic exploitation of the
areas he conquered. All the later accounts of his
achievements agree that he believed that all men
were essentially equal and as such could be

25 Aphrodite, after Praxiteles. Rear view of plaster
cast of previous statue (Pl. 24).

31

26 Battle between Greeks and Persians. Detail of the Alexander Sarcophagus, *c.* 310 BC.

treated as citizens of the world, sharing *homonoia* (oneness of mind) and living in peace under one rule of law. In *On the Fortune or Virtue of Alexander* Plutarch summed up Alexander's civilizing mission as having the effect of making the Indians worship Greek gods and of making the Scythians bury their dead instead of eating them. He also saw the towns which Alexander established everywhere, from Alexandria in Egypt to Prophthasia in Sogdiana, as eliminating the 'wildness' of the barbarians. For Plutarch the process of civilizing and Hellenizing were exactly the same, as Alexander brought Greek civilization to the areas under his dominion by either persuading or forcing people to live in Greek *polis* (city) units.

In seeking to impose order throughout the world, Alexander was clearly putting into practice the underlying political philosophy of Plato and Aristotle. Law should impose the same regularity on human behaviour that we observe in the heavens. Aristotle had said that the whole world is like a household where free persons have the least liberty to act at random; their actions are ordained for them. By contrast, slaves and animals have little common responsibility and do act for the most part at random. When we remember that Aristotle had also urged Alexander to behave to the barbarians as their master, that is to treat them as slaves, we can see that there was a general tendency at the time to oppose barbarians, slaves and animals, all living at random, to Greeks and free men whose actions were ordained by law. Plutarch's remark about Alexander's taking away the 'wildness' of the barbarians by putting them into cities shows us that the one group was associated with life in the country and the other with life in the town. This contrast is here for the first time approaching a rigid formulation and its importance is such for the whole subsequent history of Western culture that later we must examine it further. One of the most important implications of the basic attitude is that individuality is regarded as a defect rather than as a quality. The free Greek, who has his behaviour ordered by law, conforms to a common pattern. The barbarian, slave or animal behaves at random and so differently from everyone else. The aesthetic corollary of this view is that the first group also conforms to a common physical pattern, a normative beauty of face, body and movement. The second group, on the other hand, have no standards to which to aspire. Because they act at random they all look quite different from each other. Indeed, when we look at representations of free Greek males in the Hellenistic period they do all look alike physically and also move in the same controlled way. Moreover, as can be seen from the so-called

26 Alexander Sarcophagus of the late fourth century, when Greeks and barbarians confront each other in battle the Greeks seem calmer in both face and gesture than their opponents and appear more restrained even in death. The Hellenistic approach to all inferior beings, whether women, denizens of the country, barbarians or slaves, is seen in such figures as the

33 Drunken Old Woman, the crudely slumped
28 Barberini Faun, the grinning Scythian from the
92 Flaying of Marsyas and the innumerable servile
27 cripples. The diversity of these figures is stressed as much as is the uniformity of the Greeks.

Evidence that the opposition mentioned above had a great influence on the structure of Hellenistic thought is provided by two schools of philosophy that grew up in the years immediately after Alexander. The founders of both Stoicism and Epicureanism were educated in Athens in the last quarter of the fourth century. It was the

29 philosophy of Zeno, who set up his school in the Stoa Poikile, one of the most prominent buildings of the Athenian Agora, which related most directly to the political vision of the conqueror Alexander. The founder of Stoicism saw the

27 Hellenistic bronze statuette of a hunchback beggar.

28 Barberini Faun. Roman copy of an original of perhaps c. 200 BC.

inhabitants of the *oikoumenē* (inhabited world) as one people, citizens of one *polis* (city) and living under one *nomos* (law). The universe possessed an order with which it had been endowed by the divine mind or world soul. Each human being should order his actions in the same way, for the individual soul was part of the world soul whence it came at birth and to which it would eventually return. Man could only be happy if he learnt to live according to the law of order inherent in nature. He must learn his task and perform it regardless of his personal feelings. Many of the ideas of Zeno and of his successors Cleanthes and Chrysippus derive from Pythagoras and Plato, but the notion of the unity of mankind may well have been inspired by Alexander's achievement and many of the religious aspects of Stoic philosophy appear to be taken over from the newly conquered East. The whole Stoic system was well adapted to the new Hellenistic world and in fact it remained influential right down to the Roman period.

The site of Zeno's school was unusual and probably carefully chosen. The *stoa* or colonnaded porch was the typical secular urban building type developed by the Greeks. Thus not only did the school itself represent a model of organized urbanism but being situated on the Agora it was close to all the activities that should be the occupation of the socially integrated man.

30 Epicurus' choice of environment and location for his school was equally significant. He bought a garden away from the centre of the city. There he preached and practised a philosophy which also relied on an understanding of nature. But the 'nature' of Epicurus was that of the fifth-century Atomists, Leucippus and Democritus. The haphazard movement, collision and conjunction of tiny particles had brought into being the material world which is constantly changing as the atoms separate and come together again in different patterns. Being but a collection of particles which is broken up at death, man is an individual with no responsibilities. Since he has no future after death to live for he should trust his own desires, seeking peace and happiness in their satisfaction without going to excess. This is best done in a garden away from the pressures of the town where society is constantly imposing its demands. The contrast between Stoic order and Epicurean disorder is seen even in the theories of perception of the two schools. While the Stoics

29 Zeno (*fl. c.* 300 BC). Roman copy of a Hellenistic original.

believed that man sees by emitting straight rays from his eyes, the Epicureans argued that each object gives off tiny images of itself which are received by our visual sense often after considerable wanderings; thus stories about monsters originate when these images become broken up and join up with the fragments of other images to which they do not belong. In language too, Epicurus was celebrated for the irregularity of his Greek, while the Stoics, following Aristotle, studied the principles of grammar and even sought to impose a high degree of order on the vagaries of human thought itself through the development of logic.

Another philosophical standpoint adopted in the Hellenistic period was that of the Cynics. Diogenes, founder of this school, was reportedly interviewed by Alexander himself and the great soldier is said to have declared that if he had not been Alexander he would have liked to be Diogenes. The philosopher's choice of habitat was as revealing as the siting of the Stoic and Epicurean schools. He lived in a large pot and there practised an extreme asceticism. Cynic

30 Epicurus (341–270 BC). Roman copy of a Hellenistic original.

means 'dog-like' and Diogenes believed that there was little that separated man from the beasts. Dogs, for example, could be shown to possess all human qualities including the ability to apply logic. Accordingly, man was only wasting his time in trying to differentiate himself from the animals. The Cynics were linked with another school of renegade philosophers, the Sceptics, who doubted whether any knowledge could be established because of the unreliability of the senses. Colours change, for instance, for the person with bloodshot eyes and the shape of perceived reality can be shown, by analogy with the distortions produced by curved mirrors, to vary according to the shape and position of the eye in relation to the head. The ideas of these last two schools were disseminated by clever, but often ragged, philosophers who wandered at will through the Hellenistic world. The further they travelled the more support for their hostility to system and dogma they found in the diversity of forms and behaviour of man and beast.

All these different philosophies were designed to produce *ataraxia* or 'lack of disturbance', an ancestor of the modern notion of mental stability. What most disturbed the ancient Greeks was the problem of choice. Ionian philosophy had developed out of a need to choose between the oriental cosmologies. Socratic and Platonic philosophy served to guide the choice of the youth of Athens in the face of all the skills and pleasures at their disposal. The conquest of the East by Alexander meant that the complex environment of fifth-century Athens was reproduced on a much larger scale throughout the eastern Mediterranean. The earlier choices still had to be made. Were the heavens ruled by law or chance? Should man follow principles or his appetites? But now there were many more alternatives to choose from. To the possibilities known in Greece were added those to be found in Africa and Asia. Alexander, first of many, had to choose between playing god or man, between wearing Greek or Persian dress, and between devotion to a Hellenic or oriental beauty. Alexander's ambiguity in all these regards could not serve as a model for others who needed, for both social and psychological reasons, to align with conventional positions. The philosophies described above provided the necessary answers on many issues ranging from physics to dress, from politics to sex.

Fortune and Virtue: Chance and Art

The most interesting study of Alexander to survive from antiquity is that by Plutarch already referred to. Its title is particularly suggestive: *On the Fortune or Virtue of Alexander*. Plutarch's work deals with the question of how far Alexander's achievement may have been due to luck or to his own good qualities. These two factors had already been opposed by Alexander's contemporary Menander in the *Arbitrants*, where Onesimus discusses the relative importance of character and chance in human events, but Plutarch uses them specifically to illustrate the special character of the Macedonian ruler's success. According to Plutarch, Alexander could never have set out to do what he did; his achievement cannot have been the result of calculated intention alone. He must, indeed, have taken advantage of every opportunity offered to him by chance. In this he contrasted with earlier figures in Greek history who usually stopped after reaching a desired goal. Thus, to Plutarch, Alexander's success seemed to depend not only

31 Crouching Aphrodite. Roman copy of an original usually attributed to Doidalsas of Bithynia (*fl.* mid-third century BC).

32 Hellenistic terracotta group of two knucklebone players.

on a Stoic capacity to impose himself on his surroundings but also on a response to the random element in events which was given importance by the Epicureans. Curiously, according to Pliny the same combination was found in Alexander's contemporary, the painter Protogenes, who was renowned for his careful execution but who also discovered the best way of reproducing the foam in a horse's mouth when he happened to throw a sponge at a painting in a fit of disgust: 'and so chance created the effect of nature in the picture' (*Natural History* xxxv, 103).

The importance of chance as a factor in artistic creation had first been indicated by Agathon, the fifth-century tragedian, who said: 'Art loves chance and chance art.' However, a more typical Greek opinion was that of the Sophist Polus who had said that experience produces art and inexperience chance. Aristotle gave a limited role to chance but essentially excluded it by his definition of art: 'Art is produced when from many notions of experience a single universal judgment is formed regarding like objects.' Yet *tychē*, chance, was already becoming a benevolent deity, bringer of good fortune, and man felt able to interfere with her random operation. Thus Cephisodotus sculpted her as a goddess holding the infant Ploutos (Wealth) in her arms, and his son Praxiteles made a statue which was probably called Agathe Tyche (Good Fortune); while Lysippus made the related figure of Kairos (Opportunity). Soon *tychē* was linked directly with the success of a Hellenistic state when Eutychides made a statue of the Tyche of Antioch 101 to preside over the newly founded Seleucid capital. Perhaps too, the Greeks became aware that *tychē* came from the same root as the words for art, *technē*, and to create, *tiktein*. At another level, chance as a purely random factor had been taken

as the basis of nature by Epicurus and his followers. Certainly in the Hellenistic period there are a number of works of art which are clearly intended to give the impression of more or less random composition, such as the mosaics from the second century showing fish swimming in the sea or, even more vividly, the food scattered on a floor after a banquet. But these are extreme cases. More common from the late fourth century onwards is a tendency simply to show traditional subjects less carefully posed, as if revealed by a chance glimpse in the middle of movement: for example, the Apoxyomenos of Lysippus and the Crouching Aphrodite of Doidalsas in large sculpture, the Battle of Darius and Alexander in painting, and the many small informal figurines in clay and bronze. In all these cases the artists seem to have introduced an appearance of chance in order to avoid an excessively artificial impression. They seem to

have responded to the warning found in Aristotle about art concealing art for the sake of a more spontaneous and natural effect. The same consideration probably provoked the choice of a boldly asymmetrical placing of the prow on which the Nike of Samothrace alights. At Cnidos a door was made at the back of the shrine containing Praxiteles' naked Aphrodite so that the goddess could be seen as if caught unawares.

All these examples show that Hellenistic artists could either actually abandon careful planning in making a work of art, or could at least attempt to give that impression. This suggests that there was the growth of a spontaneous or even romantic approach to artistic creation in the late fourth century and such an inference is borne out by other stories, for example that told about Silanion the sculptor which claimed that he frequently smashed his completed works in a fit of dissatisfaction. Artists seem to have been more

137
135

39
31

52
32

147
157

24–
25

spontaneous in their personal lives too. While Zeuxis at the beginning of the century could contemplate his naked models unmoved, both Praxiteles and Apelles are supposed to have fallen in love with theirs. Once again there is a close parallel in behaviour with Alexander himself who was known for his readiness to indulge his passions.

Although it was the tragic writer Agathon who had first linked chance and art, it is in the late fourth-century comedies of Menander that chance coincidences and sudden romantic involvements take on a new importance in Greek drama. Menander and comedy were also linked with Epicureanism. Epicurus was one of the poet's closest friends, and Diogenes the Epicurean gave a crown of virtue and a purple cloak to a comic actress who played male roles. There is thus evidence at least of sympathy between Epicureanism, comedy and artistic chance towards the end of the fourth century. There is a similar contemporary sympathy between Stoicism, tragedy and the more careful and considered approach to both life and art. Aristotle had said that tragedy was about better and comedy about worse people; and the Stoics certainly came to be known for their belief that in spite of man's common divinity some men lived up to their heritage while others were little better than animals, and that the former were usually of higher class and more intelligent. The Aristotelian distinction between comedy and tragedy also lies behind a story about two of Alexander's successors, Lysimachus and Demetrius. They are supposed to have ridiculed each other, the one saying of the other that all his courtiers had short two-syllable names, as in comedy, and the other drawing attention to one of his enemy's weak spots by remarking that he had never seen a tragedy with a prostitute in it. Tragedy had indeed always treated of high-born men and the manifestation of divine justice, while comedy took as its subject the ordinary man and his capacity to survive his own stupidity. Tragedy thus revealed a divine plan such as was believed in by the Stoics, just as comedy corresponded to the Epicurean interest in chance. One proof that this distinction was recognized at least by the Romans is the opposition found in Latin writers between the weeping Heraclitus and the laughing Democritus, major precursors respectively of Stoicism and Epicureanism. Hellenistic images of

Zeno and Epicurus point in the same direction with their emphatic contrast between severe concentration and relaxed sensitivity. 29
30

Artistic Naturalism and its Limitations

Another distinction between tragedy and comedy was that tragedy usually took its subject from the heroic age of Greece while comedy usually described contemporary life. This distinction takes on a particular significance when it is related to Aristotle's observation, also in the *Poetics*, that man takes a great pleasure in looking at imitations and even if he has never seen the original model for the imitation he will still take pleasure in the technique and colour employed in it. This suggests that the audience of a comedy, being familiar with its model, could indeed take pleasure in the imitation itself, whereas the audience of a tragedy, never having witnessed the heroic age, would only be able to concentrate on the internal artistry of the play set before them. Success in the imitation would thus be much more important for the writer of comedies. Comedy on these terms should be more naturalistic than tragedy and this seems to have been true, particularly of the post-Aristotelian New Comedy when compared with the tragedies written in Alexandria only slightly later. The contrast was clear not only in literary aspects such as language but also in visual terms, since the comic masks of the period are much closer to the normal human face than the tragic masks. The Romans paid tribute to the naturalism of Menander, the most celebrated writer of the New Comedy, calling his works 'mirrors of life', and there is a direct link between Menander and Aristotle through Aristotle's pupil Theophrastus. The latter's interest in comedy is proved not only by his having adopted its techniques when lecturing, by miming the actions of cooks when talking about them, but also by his having written a book about it, of which his *Characters* may be a surviving section. His careful delineation of the outer and inner manifestations of various forms of vice and stupidity in the *Characters* constitutes an admirable study of Aristotle's 'worse' men, and the characters in Menander's plays represent the fruits of a similar study. The association of comedy and naturalistic imitation was probably reinforced by the existence of a form of Dorian comedy called the *mimos* or 'imitation'. In a

33 Drunken Old Woman. Roman copy of an original, perhaps by Myron of Pergamum, of *c.* 200 BC.

34 Boy servant tending fire. Roman adaptation of a Hellenistic original, possibly a painting.

vulgar form this genre became a staple feature of Hellenistic theatre, replacing tragedy and comedy as the truly popular drama. It was also taken up in another guise by sophisticated writers such as Theocritus and Herondas whose 'mimes' present us with our most vivid glimpses of Hellenistic ordinary life. The development of literary naturalism is thus emphatically linked with the imitation of the everyday world in comedy and mime.

The remark by Aristotle which prompted this discussion referred not to writing but to paintings; so it is reasonable to look for a parallel situation in the visual arts. If Aristotle's theory found any echo in practice we should expect to find the most clearly imitative style, that is the most naturalistic one, applied to the representation of the familiar world of ordinary life. The evidence for painting is, as always, insubstantial, but in the field of sculpture the most memorable examples of Hellenistic naturalism are provided by figures such as the Drunken Old
33 Woman, the bronze Jockey from Athens or the
27 many figurines of cripples and other servants
34 engaged in their daily tasks. By contrast, the great sculptures of remote figures and events, whether heroic or divine, are remarkable for other artistic qualities. So too in the mosaics and paintings of the Late Hellenistic and Roman periods the most naturalistic treatment is reserved for household
rubbish, flowers and leaves, and the many still- 134–
lifes of fruit, birds and small animals. It is true 137
that we might expect artistic conventions to inhibit a naturalistic tendency in high art anyway, but a formulation such as Aristotle's may acutally have discouraged artists from wanting to push high art in that direction.

Art as Deception and the Deceiving Eye

So far the expression 'naturalistic imitation' has been used loosely to refer to relatively accurate representation. It is, however, possible to interpret it more precisely in two different ways. By one interpretation a good imitation would be one that gave the illusion that it was itself the object imitated. By another a good imitation would be one that conveyed the essential information about the object without emphasizing all the accidental detail. Aristotle makes it clear which interpretation he favours. The pleasure we take in imitations derives from our learning from them. For, as he says in the same passage of the *Poetics* 1448b, 'to learn things is not only a great pleasure for philosophers but for all men too'. As he also says that our pleasure in seeing an imitation is greatest when the imitation is of something we already know, he rather surprisingly expects us to enjoy learning even from the familiar.

Aristotle's emphasis on the pleasure of learning from imitations would not seem specially significant were it not for the fact that a number of texts suggest that there was indeed a shift towards what can be called informative imitation at the very time that he was writing. At the beginning of the fourth century artists measured themselves by their capacity to create an illusion of reality. Zeuxis and Parrhasius were supposed to have deceived men and animals, for example with their paintings of curtains and grapes which were taken for the real thing. Few such stories of deception are told of Apelles and his contemporaries later on. The horse which neighed at the painted horse of Apelles was apparently only giving a sign of approval. Generally, that artist's works were famed for the correctness of the information which they conveyed. Overhearing a cobbler's criticisms, Apelles altered a painting by putting the right number of thong holes in a shoe. His portraits were not called speaking likenesses but they did provide enough information for *metōposkopoi*, or face readers, to divine how long the sitter had lived or when he would die. An unfinished charcoal sketch of one of his enemies contained enough information to allow the man to be identified; it could never have given the illusion of reality. All these stories, which are probably contemporary with the artists concerned, show that there had been a definite change in values. It would be wrong to infer that Apelles' works were consequently less successful as illusionistic imitations. All the evidence suggests that the interest in imitation by itself ensured that there was a continuous increase in the capacity for naturalistic representation right into the Hellenistic period. But it ceased to be pursued as an essential goal of art and, perhaps as a result, Greek artists stopped short of the naturalistic illusion achieved by European painters and sculptors since the Renaissance, although previously there had been a consistent movement in that direction. There were two main areas where naturalism continued to be especially developed. One was that of the low and trivial subject mentioned above. The other was that of portraiture, especially dynastic portraiture where the traits of the ruling family might be publicized, especially on coins, in order to make manifest the the continuity and perpetual rejuvenation of a line of monarchs.

In sculpture, then, the movement towards naturalism faltered at the time of its greatest triumphs. The application of technology to art brought new opportunities for accurate imitation of surfaces. Plutarch tells how Silanion mixed silver with the bronze of his Dying Iocasta in order to capture the pallor that precedes death. Pliny records the technique originated by Lysistratus, brother of Lysippus, of taking plaster casts from the surface of the human body in order to work from them. Using this method he was supposed to have reached a new peak of realism. But apart from some portraits which may be based on casts, and an improved understanding of surface anatomy, there is little evidence that his achievement was followed up in the Hellenistic period. Lysippus himself seems to have led the reaction against attention to detail. His portraits of Alexander were the best, according to Plutarch, because others tried too hard to imitate 'the

35–37 Coin portraits of three kings of Pontus. *From top to bottom*: Mithridates III (*c.* 220–185/3 BC), Pharnaces I (185/3–170 BC) and Mithridates IV (170–150 BC).

35–37

38 Alexander the Great (356–323 BC). Roman copy of a Hellenistic original.

way his neck turned and the expressive, moist glance of his eyes, while only he captured his manly and leonine quality'. Lysippus may well have felt that if the spectator were to take pleasure in learning from his imitation he had better learn of Alexander's general character than of the details of his physiognomy. Hellenistic portraiture continued to excel chiefly in the communication of character.

Ancient accounts of Lysippus' life give the impression that he himself had begun as an enthusiast for naturalistic representation and had then moved away from it. Pliny tells how he was first inspired to become an artist by the remark of the painter Eupompus that one should imitate nature and not other artists. But he concludes by quoting the sculptor's own observation that other sculptors represented men as they really were, while he showed them as they appeared. This paradoxical comment probably refers to the need to alter the natural proportions of a statue in order to allow for optical distortions arising from its position and size relative to the spectator. Lysippus, who made both colossal and miniature sculptures, would have been presented with such problems more forcibly than earlier artists. Pliny also tells us that Lysippus altered the standard proportions of the human figure, making his statues nine heads tall instead of eight so that they looked taller. His statues, for example his Agias or his Apoxyomenos, do indeed look taller than earlier works such as Polyclitus' Doryphoros. Like the modern spectator, Lysippus may well have felt that Polyclitus' proportions, however correct, made statues of marble and bronze look embarrassingly heavy; again, his own statues have a much more convincing lightness and liveliness. His realization that by copying something exactly we do not necessarily reproduce its effect on our senses reflects an awareness that naturalistic imitation is often not only an irrelevant goal but also an unattainable one.

39 Apoxyomenos, after Lysippus. Roman copy of an original of c. 330 BC.

41 Thetis in the workshop of Hephaestus. Wall-painting from Pompeii. Roman copy of a Hellenistic original perhaps by Theon of Samos.

The interest in optics from which this awareness sprang was widespread at the time. Both Aristotelians and Epicureans were particularly concerned with problems of perception and their work led up to the *Optics* of Euclid in the early third century. In the absence of the transparent lens one of the main means of optical inquiry was through the study of reflections (catoptrics), the subject of a book by Euclid. The occurrence of several mirror-images in paintings of the period shows how painters too studied optical phenomena. One of the best examples is the fallen Persian staring at his own face reflected in his polished shield in the Battle of Darius and Alexander mosaic, which may derive from an original of about 300. A work which probably dates from the same period was the original of a Pompeian wall-painting of Thetis in the workshop of Hephaestus where the nymph also contemplates her own image in a large shield. The connection of these examples with the science of catoptrics is particularly that in both cases the reflected image is roughly half the size of the real person, thus following the law that reflected images are always smaller than the object represented, except when the mirror is concave, and that the diminution is intensified in a convex surface. The same understanding of the capacity of a mirror to modify appearances is apparent in the strikingly reversed image of Thetis. Contemporary architects also seem to have been deeply conscious of the deforming powers of vision. Vitruvius, relying chiefly on fourth-century and Hellenistic sources, mentions several so-called optical refinements, such as the enlargement of the corner column of a temple to prevent it from being apparently eaten away by the surrounding light. It is true that this feature is found in earlier buildings, but it may well have been introduced originally just to give added strength to a weak design point and only have acquired an optical explanation later.

Artists, then, seem to have been as interested in the mendacity as in the honesty of our eyes and in

40 Fallen Persian and his reflection. Detail of the Battle of Darius and Alexander mosaic (see Pl. 52).

this they reflect the same ambiguity of attitude as is found among the philosophers. While the Aristotelians and others were concerned to show how useful our eyes could be as a means of extending man's knowledge, Epicureans and Sceptics endeavoured to demonstrate, by a study of the distortions involved in sensual perception, the impossibility either of using the senses to acquire secure knowledge or of using such knowledge to establish natural principles. This marks a crucial difference between art around 300 BC and art during the Renaissance. During the Renaissance optics and the visual arts were also closely connected, but they were joined rather in a faith of their common truth than in a consciousness of their common tendencies to distortion. It is characteristic of the almost institutionalized dualism of Greek culture that the period of the greatest development of Greek science and technology, and of the enthusiastic application of both to art, should also be the period during which people came to see the essential fruitlessness of such application.

Beauty and the Beast

Lysippus' distinction between the way people seem and the way they are can be applied not only to the optical problems of representation but also to the problem of the human personality. For centuries the Greeks had noted the correspondence between people's physical appearance and their character. Homer's heroes are beautiful and aristocratic, with noble thoughts. Thersites who takes the part of the common people and who advocates retreat from Troy is ill-favoured in both face and figure. The nobles easily crush him, just as the handsome and intelligent Odysseus easily outwits the stupid, cruel and ugly Cyclops, Polyphemus. *Aischros* (ugly) also came to mean 'bad' as *kalos* (beautiful) 42 also came to mean 'good'. Perhaps Pericles could never have ruled the Athenians if he had not had a divine beauty, nor Alcibiades have inspired the ill-fated attack on Syracuse. By the late fifth century, however, the Greeks started to be conscious of the deceptiveness of such criteria. A group which included Alcibiades came to see in 43 the snub-nosed satyr, Socrates, the most truly 'beautiful' personality. Later still the Athenians rallied to the leadership of the frail Demosthenes who had to strengthen his feeble voice by

42 Pericles (495–429 BC). Roman copy perhaps of an original by Cresilas of the fifth century BC.

shouting against the sea. The statue of the orator by Polyeuctus, erected by the Athenians in 280, 44 analyses his physical weakness as minutely as his strength of mind. The inscription on the base of the statue summed it up: 'If your strength had equalled your resolution, Demosthenes, the Macedonian Ares would never have ruled the Greeks.' The beauty of Socrates and the strength of Demosthenes may have seemed as much an optical illusion as the column eaten away by the surrounding light, but the Greeks came to live with such inconsistencies and to regard them as the basis of the only true reality. Menander's success, and particularly the later acceptance of his plays as 'mirrors of life', was in large part due to his readiness to mix good with evil and evil with good in the alchemy of his characters. A realization that such inconsistencies were more normal than exceptional would have helped the early Hellenistic queen, Stratonice, to tolerate the artist Ctesicles when he painted her romping with a sailor. It would also have made it easier for the Hellenistic monarchs who, while they still

43 Socrates (469–399 BC). Roman copy perhaps of an original of the fourth century BC.

44 Demosthenes (384–322 BC). Roman copy of an original, probably by Polyeuctus, set up in the Athenian Agora *c.* 280 BC.

45 Polyphemus receiving the letter of Galatea. Wall-painting from Pompeii. Roman copy of a Hellenistic original.

claimed divinity, often permitted their features on coins and statues to be shown as much more human than those of the god-like Alexander. The Hellenistic period is thus marked by a new realism in an awareness of the limitations of earlier assumptions about the human personality, just as there was a new realism in the approach to the problem of perception.

One of the most beautiful examples of the new sensitivity to the ambiguities of human character is found in the eleventh idyll of Theocritus, written in the mid-third century, where Polyphemus sings tenderly of his love for Galatea but fears that his shaggy hair and strange face make it impossible that the fair and smooth-skinned nymph should ever requite him. Homer's cannibal giant here reveals himself to be as tender and eloquent as a cultured Greek citizen. The separation between the inner and outer man is so extreme as to be irreconcilable, yet the new sense of the potential complexity of human character is a major step forward in the understanding of

35–
38

45

pyschology. The mask of the lover described in
an epigram of Callimachus suggests yet another
dualism of character. It was brown like a dried fig
on one side and light as a lamp on the other. The
similes from agriculture and interior furnishings
may well suggest that the wearer of the mask led a
double life, one outside, in the country, and the
other inside, in the town. In the same way the
rustic Polyphemus contrasted in colour with
Galatea who led a sheltered life in her father's
palace under the sea. The Greeks had continued
an earlier artistic convention by which men were
painted with brown skins and women with white
but they now came to realize that this depended
on the difference in normal environment between
the two sexes. Thus when Achilles is seen in a
Pompeian painting, probably dependent on a
Hellenistic model, being discovered in the
womens' quarters of the palace of Lycomedes
where he has spent some time, he is shown as
white as the girls in contrast to his tanned
discoverers. Achilles' situation is the reverse of
Polyphemus'. The aggressive inner man is belied
by the tender outer appearance. The inconsistencies of both figures are seen combined in the
representations of Hercules tamed by Omphale
also found in Roman versions of Hellenistic
compositions. The mighty hero is led by his inner
weakness for the opposite sex to put on his
mistress's flimsy dress, while she takes his club
and lion-skin as if as emblems of her power. Yet
another version of sexual inconsistency is the
figure of Hermaphrodite known in various
Hellenistic statues.

46 Achilles recognized by Odysseus at the court of
Lycomedes. Wall-painting from Pompeii. Roman copy of a
Hellenistic original perhaps by Theon of Samos.

47 Hermaphrodite. Roman copy of a Hellenistic original.

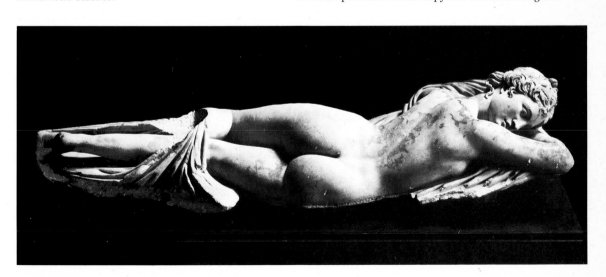

The opposition between the male and the female, the outdoor and the indoor, the rustic and the urban obviously intrigued Hellenistic artists, especially when the opposition was embodied in a single individual. Although they are not directly dependent on philosophical traditions, it is not unreasonable to see the different approaches to this conflict as reflecting different streams in contemporary thought. Certainly the basic assumption that terms such as male and female, rural and urban are associated with consistent and opposed sets of qualities would be acceptable to the more dogmatic schools, the Pythagoreans, the early followers of Plato, and the Stoics, while the observation that these opposites could co-exist in one person was one that might be made by a critic of such systemization, for example a Sceptic, or Carneades, a later leader of Plato's Academy. It should not surprise us that these and other approaches are often manifested together in the work of Hellenistic artists as it is characteristic of popular culture that it does not divide itself up into schools, like philosophy, but rather absorbs a mixture of current and fashionable notions.

Town and Country

It would, of course, be quite wrong to see popular culture simply as a derivative of philosophy, especially at a time in the Late Classical and Early Hellenistic period when the citizen body of a state such as Athens created its own cultural life in the different Mysteries, local cults and Dionysiac festivals. Indeed, these activities were themselves a major influence on the great philosophical developments. Both Plato and Zeno seem to have found inspiration in the current vogue for the Mysteries. The *Symposium* describes a philosophical Dionysiac rite. The gymnasia where Plato and Aristotle taught, the Academy and the Lyceum, were associated with local cults, those of the hero Academus and the god Apollo Lyceius, outside the walls of Athens. Epicurus in his garden was like a cult figure himself and was later called by Lucretius 'Epicurus the Saviour'.

One of the most important links between the new popular religions and the new philosophical schools can be seen in their common association with the countryside rather than the city. Each had a different interest in the rural environment. The philosophers naturally gravitated to the gymnasia where idle young men gathered for physical and intellectual exercise and where they could seek a calm rationality away from the pleasures and pressures of the city. By contrast, it was an interest in the irrational that brought the Athenians to worship the nature deity Dionysus, god of wine, and led them into the Attic countryside to visit the sacred places of their ancestors, such as the hall of the Mysteries at Eleusis and the shrines of Pan in the hinterland. Different again was the pursuit of health which led to the sudden growth of the cult of Asclepius at rural Epidaurus in the northern Peloponnese. Whether philosophical or religious, all these movements are associated with the late fifth and the fourth centuries and there can be little doubt that they are symptoms of a general change of mood, reflected particularly in a disenchantment with the city of Athens after the sieges and the plague that accompanied the Peloponnesian War and after the initial excitement at rapid urban economic growth had worn off. In the Hellenistic period the urban neurosis was exported with many other features of Athenian life. The frightening growth of urban concentrations in places such as Alexandria must have exaggerated a fear in a large section of the population that they were losing contact with the country, from which most Greeks had only recently moved.

The expansion of interest in the new cults and the associated interest in the countryside is documented in literature and art from the late fifth century onwards. Euripides described the Dionysiac orgies in the *Bacchae* and contemporary vase-painters illustrated many Dionysiac scenes. In the fourth century Praxiteles made a famous statue of the infant Dionysus himself, and Scopas a statue of a maenad devotee. 126 From then on Dionysus appears frequently in Hellenistic art, often in the domestic environment, on minor objects and in floor mosaics. Pan appears in a whole series of votive reliefs, and 48 satyrs become a regular subject particularly in scenes of erotic assaults. Hellenistic writers and 61 artists frequently raise our sympathy and not our fear or derision when treating of the wild inhabitants of the country. Theocritus sings engagingly of goats and sheep and their herdsmen. Unheroic animals begin to take on a major role in sculpture and painting, as in Boethus' statue of a boy with a goose, Praxiteles' statue of Apollo about to kill a lizard, and a whole series of

134 later mosaics showing birds and fishes. There is
137 no evidence of a separate genre of landscape
painting, but landscape elements naturally take
on an unprecedented importance in scenes
associated with the new cults. Fifth-century vase-
paintings show that painters such as Polygnotus
introduced landscape features when they were
called for by the narrative, and landscapes may
have appeared in the new scene-paintings. But in
both cases their function would be as an indicator
of locale, not as an object of interest in their own
right. This approach continued in the funerary
paintings and reliefs of the fourth century
which often show figures beside tombs in the
open. On the other hand, the importance of the
new cults for the development of a more genuine
landscape art is illustrated by monuments such as
the frieze of the Choragic Monument of Lysicrates
49 of 334. There, in scenes from the life of Dionysus,
we find land, sea and trees introduced not just
as stage props but in order to demonstrate
the god's association with and control of natural
forces. Deities such as Pan, Hermes, Artemis
and Asclepius bore the same rural associations
and consequently, as their cults grew in importance, artists were ever more frequently called to
represent natural environments. Thus there are
the Attic marble reliefs showing Hermes and the
nymphs in a cave with Pan and shepherds above
them, moulded terracotta figures of Dionysus also
standing in a cave, flatter reliefs such as the
bronze plaque from Delos showing an open-air
sacrifice to Artemis and deeper ones illustrating,
50 for instance, the worship of Asclepius, all of the
late fourth and third centuries.

One major feature of several of these works is
that the height of the figures no longer limits the

48 Relief showing grotto with Pan, Apollo and nymphs,
from the sacred cave at Vari in Attica, c.340 BC.

height of the relief as was usual in earlier
sculptures. Whether or not these backgrounds
were filled with painted detail, it is apparent that
the artists' interests extend beyond the figures
and a few essential trees to the representation of
the space in which the figures move as something
important in its own right. A further impression
of empty space is given in some reliefs by an
increasing depth. In these cases the depth of the
relief is greater than the depth of an individual

49 Dionysus and the Tyrrhenian pirates. Detail of frieze (cast) from the Choragic Monument of Lysicrates,
Athens, c. 330 BC.

50 Votive relief showing Asclepius, Hygieia and worshippers, fourth century BC.

figure, although the figures too approach closer to three-dimensional reality. It is perhaps not a coincidence that this development is associated with the representation of country scenes. A characteristic of towns is that both the individual buildings and the whole area within the walls are no larger than is necessary for the people within it. Etymologizing was a popular activity at the time and the Greek word for city, *polis*, may already have been linked with *pimplēmi* (I fill), as it has been (though wrongly) by more recent philologists. Aristotle specifically warned against having empty space in a city, urging instead that neither cities nor houses should be larger than was necessary to accommodate their occupants. If cities can be said to reflect the same limitation of space as was normal in earlier reliefs, then a connection also seems possible between the new

spacious reliefs and the new rural cults. For just as the flight from the city which had fostered the growth of these cults was partly stimulated by an awareness of constriction in the city and by a need for open space, so one of the new reliefs' most important characteristics is a rejection of the limits of human scale. The connection between the two ideas of 'country' and 'space' is further confirmed by linguistic usage. It is precisely at this period, in the works of Athenian writers such as Xenophon and Demosthenes, that an opposition between 'town' and 'country' becomes a verbal cliché. Moreover, although the word used by these writers for town is *astu*, not *polis*, the term used for country is *chōra*, whose basic meaning was an empty space where one could put something. The country and space had thus become almost synonymous.

Chapter Two

Art: its Classification and Criticism

'Art is produced when from many notions of experience a single universal judgment is formed with regard to like objects' (*Metaphysics* 981a). An art, for Aristotle, was any systematized human activity which relied on a set of techniques or principles. According to him necessary arts, such as shoemaking, came first in time, arts for pleasure, such as painting, came next, and the last to develop were the arts, such as arithmetic, which had no use at all. Aristotle was the first to see quite so clearly what such different activities have in common, but the importance of systems of rules as backgrounds to many human skills had been increasingly acknowledged by the Greeks from the late sixth century onwards. For some skills systematic understanding had progressed so far that a new genre of literature, the *technē* or 'Art', had emerged, giving an exhaustive treatment of individual subjects. Aristotle's own *Rhetoric* and *Poetics* are both related to this genre, though their aim is less comprehensive and more critical. The stages by which painting and sculpture were elevated to the level of art in the Aristotelian sense are seen in Polyclitus' book, the *Kanōn* or *Rule*, which tried to establish normative mathematical proportions for the human body, and in the educational method of the fourth-century painter Pamphilus, which was based on arithmetic and geometry. Polyclitus' statue of the Doryphoros which embodied the *kanōn*, and the perspective foreshortenings relying on geometrical knowledge for which Pausias, one of Pamphilus' pupils, was famous, show how the developments in theory were reflected in practice. In architecture commentaries had been written on individual build-

ings from the mid-sixth century when Rhoecus and Theodorus had written on their temple of Hera at Samos. Pythius around 350 left writings on two of his works, the Mausoleum at Halicarnassus and the temple of Athena at Priene, 17 buildings whose designs were characterized by 117 an unprecedented degree of regularity.

Ethos *and* Pathos

Aristotle comes nearest to separating the arts as we know them when he talks of a group of arts, intermediate between the useful arts and those without use, whose specific purpose is to provide pleasure. This rather strange category, which would include painting, sculpture and poetry, is clearly created to satisfy his feeling that there were some arts that did not fit into the other two rather obvious classifications. From the many strands of his experience Aristotle arrived at the universal judgment that what these arts shared was the power to provide pleasure. The most important consequence of his definition is that he defines the function of these arts psychologically. Their origin in religious ritual is forgotten. The problems, discussed by Plato, of their morality or correspondence to a higher level of reality are disregarded. The idea of the divine inspiration of music and poetry, traditional among the Greeks, becomes irrelevant. The usefulness of these arts to man, their effect on his understanding, is of incidental importance. What interests Aristotle is their effect on man's feelings. Although Aristotle's judgment is unusually decisive, earlier writers had been moving in the same direction. The psychological effects of music had been studied for some time, as we can see from Plato's observations on the dangerously emotive effects of certain musical modes. Gorgias and Isocrates among others had been interested in the power of rhetoric. Artists contemporary with Aristotle showed their concern for the way art affects us in different ways. Lysippus' boast about his ability to represent men as they appear to our senses is one example. Apelles' concern for the effect of his works on the spectator was even more explicit, as is shown by his supposed claim that the quality which the art of other painters lacked and in which he excelled was that of *charis* (charm or physical attractiveness). The sensual and emotive

51 Pothos, after Scopas. Roman copy of an original of the mid-fourth century BC.

response to art was thus of major importance for the leading painter and sculptor of the late fourth century.

The most detailed account of the response to art at the period is Aristotle's study of the particular pleasures of tragedy and comedy. The pleasure peculiar to tragedy is that which the audience derives from its feeling of fear and pity. The importance of devices such as 'discoveries' and 'reversals' is that they help to bring these feelings into existence. They have their greatest effect when they happen to good people of noble birth. By contrast, the pleasure of comedy derives from the ludicrous, or laughable, nature of its subject. The laughable, Aristotle continues, is a 'part of the bad or ugly'. The Greek word used here, *aischros*, had always carried both associations. Aristotle thus defines the essential quality of the two forms of drama in terms of their effect upon the emotions: fear, pity and laughter. This means that the essential response to drama is now thought of in terms of *pathos* (emotion) rather than *ēthos* (character). For it had been in terms of character that Plato had discussed the response to drama previously, when he had said that older men like tragedy, younger men comedy and children mimes – older men being traditionally wise and stable and younger ones more foolish and irresponsible. The distinction between *ēthos* and *pathos* was indeed a critical one. *Ēthos* was the more or less constant personality of the individual. It could be good or bad, but its presence was regarded as a positive quality, as with our word character. It was the source of an individual's active relation with the world. *Pathos* was the basis for the individual's passive relation with the world, the inconstant reaction brought about by outside influences. For Socrates and Plato it was as likely to be bad as *ēthos* was likely to be good. For them the arts were suspect largely because they could break down *ēthos* through *pathos*. Aristotle's opposed point of view reflects his comparatively mechanistic view of human psychology and his relative lack of interest in the personal soul. His changed valuation of *ēthos* and *pathos* is closely paralleled in his approach to the problem of vision. Plato thought of sight as depending on an active emanation from the eyes. Aristotle realized that emanations from the object were as, or more, important and that the eye has to some extent a passive function.

52 Battle of Darius and Alexander. Mosaic from the House of the Faun, Pompeii. Work of the second century BC probably based on an original painting, perhaps by Philoxenus of Eretria, of *c.* 300 BC.

It was inevitable that the increasing awareness of man's passive responses to stimuli meant that emotion became of increasing importance. But character was not neglected either. We have already quoted Xenophon's record of a conversation between Socrates and Parrhasius around 400 in which the painter agrees that he can paint not only the forms of bodies but also the expression of character in the face. The expression of emotion is mentioned only incidentally. Fourth-century philosophers and artists continued to study character, as we saw in the last chapter. Theophrastus wrote his *Characters* which parallels Menander's interests and Aristotle worked on physiognomics, the new science which purported to enable one to know someone's character by noticing a correspondence between his face and that of some animal with known propensities. Lysippus revealed a similar interest in character when he claimed that, while others copied Alexander's individual features, only he captured his true 'manliness' and 'lion-like quality'. Nevertheless it is significant that character itself was often thought of as little more than the disposition to exhibit a particular emotion constantly. Hence

Scopas in the middle of the fourth century made his expressive statue of Pothos (Desire), while Apelles' painting of Calumny consisted of a whole compendium of emotions, such as Jealousy and Suspicion, each portrayed as a separate character. Clearly the study of character and emotion went hand in hand, and it is not surprising that it is of a contemporary of Apelles, Aristides, that Pliny says that he was the first to have painted both characters and emotions.

Aristotle himself had shown how character and emotion were linked in his analysis of tragedy and comedy. Not only do the two forms differ in the emotions which they arouse, but they also differ in the nature of their subjects: tragedy deals with better men and comedy with worse. The misfortunes of the good awake in us fear and pity, while the doings of the bad make us laugh. All this takes on added significance since Aristotle illustrates his point about the two different types of character by reference to two fifth-century painters, Polygnotus who made people look better and Pauson who made them look worse than they were. The comparison is probably forced, but it does encourage us to look further at works of art in the fourth century for

51
99

53 Aphrodite Kallipygos. Roman copy of a Hellenistic original.

54 Satyr admiring his hindquarters. Roman copy of a Hellenistic original.

correspondences with the Aristotelian distinction between the two forms of drama, especially in their appeal to the emotions. An excellent example is provided by the work of Aristides. One of his most striking works was of a mother who, although dying from a wound in her breast, showed only her fear that her infant might suck her blood together with her milk. Such a painting would be well calculated to awake feelings of fear and pity in the spectator. Other works by Aristides, such as his Suppliant, his Woman dying for Love of her Brother and his Invalid

must have appealed just as directly to the emotions, and it may not be an accident that all have close parallels in tragedy, for example in the *Suppliant Women* of Aeschylus, and in the loyal Antigone and the sick Philoctetes of Sophocles. Similarly, there could hardly be a better example of a 'reversal' of fortune overwhelming a great man than the defeat of Darius shown in the Battle of Darius and Alexander mosaic, which probably 52 derives from an original of about 300. Many would have recalled the similar defeat of Darius' ancestor Xerxes which inspired Aeschylus' *Per-*

sae. The task of identifying paintings of a humorous character is made easier by Pliny's listing of a whole series which were funny in different ways, and which were apparently also made in the years around 300. Calates specialized in 'comic' pictures. This may mean works whose subjects were taken directly from comedy; two mosaics from Pompeii have been identified as deriving from early third-century illustrations of Menander. Antiphilus painted a figure in an absurd costume with the joking name of Gryllos, a name that came to be applied to all works of a similar type. Ctesilochus, a pupil of Apelles, made a burlesque painting of Zeus, dressed as a woman, in labour with Dionysus and attended by goddess midwives, a portrayal which continues the mocking of the gods found earlier in Aristophanes. Perhaps another example of an artistic caricature of a great theme is Praxiteles' Apollo Sauroktonos, a work in which the mighty god is shown as an idle young man about to squash a lizard rather than as a hero killing a terrible serpent. The Aphrodite Kallipygos (of the beautiful buttocks) where the goddess gazes at her well-formed posterior with as much fascination as the visitor to her shrine at Cnidos was perhaps created in a similar spirit somewhat later. The statue of a satyr in a similar pose would then represent the accretion of a further level of satire

55 Hellenistic head.

56 Comic scene, perhaps from Menander's *Synaristōsai*. Detail of mosaic from the Villa of Cicero, Pompeii, signed by Dioscorides of Samos (*fl.* 100 BC) and probably based on an original of the third century BC.

on the same theme. Satire of another sort, and one that also can be found in Aristophanes, appeared in Ctesicles' cheeky painting of Queen Stratonice romping with a fisherman whom she was supposed to fancy. These works all have parallels in comic practice but it is rather to the Aristotelian theory of the *geloion*, the principle of laughter itself on which comedy is founded, that we should turn for an explanation for the many portrayals of ugliness and deformity which are found from the late fourth century onwards. Aristotle illustrates the connection between ugliness and laughter by pointing to the ugly comic mask which we find funny rather than distressing. That he should describe the essence of the comic in this way may seem odd to us, but it does help us to appreciate how the Hellenistic Greeks would have considered the portrayals of deformity of which they were fond. Apparently such works were considered as jokes. In all these cases it is only by analogy that we can argue for an influence from the theory of tragedy and comedy on art, but in one pair of sculptures the opposition between the two dramatic forms seems quite explicit. Praxiteles, according to Pliny, made two statues of a Weeping Matron and a Smiling Courtesan, figures which, by the opposition both of their emotions and of their characters, seem designed almost as emblems of the tragic and the comic.

If all these last works demonstrate the double interest in *ēthos* and *pathos* at this period, the story of Praxiteles' two famous statues of Aphrodite well documents the shift from the former to the latter as the main popular criterion of excellence. The people of Cos were offered a choice between two images of the goddess, both at the same price, the one clothed, as had been normal up until then, and the other naked, a recent innovation. They chose the clothed statue, that being, as Pliny puts it, 'the sober and proper thing to do'. The people of Cnidos then acquired the naked Aphrodite. Within a few years, however, the statue which had been considered as second best became perhaps the most famous in the world and was set in a shrine where it could better satisfy the interest which it aroused. The modest Aphrodite of Cos was hardly noticed.

At a popular level it is possible to talk of a shift in values, but in loftier regions *ēthos* and *pathos* remained competing alternatives. Aristotle in the *Rhetoric* describes two different methods of

persuasion, one *ēthikē*, based on presenting one's moral point of view, and the other *pathētikē*, involving an appeal to the audience's emotions. Shortly afterwards the Stoics and Epicureans formulated their disagreement in terms of the same opposition. Zeno, according to Stobaeus, said that '*ethos* is the fountain of life'. Epicurus, on the other hand, affirmed in a letter to Menoeceus, that 'pleasure is primarily and naturally good for us. It is the origin of every choice and aversion, and we always return to it as we judge everything by the standard of *pathos*.' The old-fashioned contrast between the sober Stoic moralist and the Epicurean hedonist is nowadays seen as a great exaggeration. Nevertheless, it remains true that the Stoics were told to disregard emotions as emphatically as the Epicureans were encouraged to study them. In fact, the members of neither school were interested in art, but in so far as they were, the Stoics were more interested in the approach called by Aristotle *ēthikē*, which naturally produced a concentration on moral content. They approved of writers, such as Homer, who communicated elements of wisdom or goodness and paid little attention to style. The Epicureans, although they might on principle have been able to accept many stylistic devices that the Stoics would not, took no interest in either style or content because they were suspicious of all rules and formulations, including those applied to the arts. Only at the end of the Hellenistic period did Stoicism modify its exclusive approach to the human personality and, by allowing the existence of an emotional element in the soul, begin to permit and even encourage the use of stylistic devices which would make some use of *pathos*. This development will be discussed at the end of the chapter.

Chronological Classification and Criticism

From what has just been said it seems that artists in the late fourth century were increasingly influenced by current attitudes to literature. This suggests that artists were certainly becoming more literate. It also shows that Aristotle's recognition of the essential unity of the pleasure-giving arts was reflected in his environment. All this makes it worth following Aristotle further. At the beginning of the *Poetics* he discusses the problem of the imitative arts.

'Imitations' may differ from each other in three ways: in using completely different means of imitation, in imitating different things and in imitating in a different manner. The first type of difference is one of *genos* (genus); thus imitations in colour and form are generically different from those employing the human voice. Within the latter group, which is Aristotle's specific concern at this point, there are different *eidē* (species); thus epic, tragedy and flute-playing all use rhythm, language and tune in different combinations. The principle of classification used here derives from the field of biology and it is biology too which provides the key to Aristotle's approach to chronological development. One species develops out of another. Homer's *Margites*, a mock epic, is as much a prototype for comedy as the *Iliad* and *Odyssey* are for tragedy. Aristotle goes on in the *Poetics* to introduce a very important notion. Tragedy, he states, evolved out of satyric drama through a number of stages. These involved the placing of a greater emphasis on dialogue and less on dance, and a corresponding introduction of the more appropriate iambic metre. 'It then stopped when it had its natural form.' Aristotle here transfers his theory about the natural world, that things are formed as they are as the optimum way of achieving a particular goal, to the world of art. The idea of development until the achievement of perfection thus emerges in the infancy of art theory. Together with the Platonic notion of an original god-given perfection from which man had lapsed, it was to become deeply embedded in Western culture. It is perhaps worth pointing out that neither Plato's nor Aristotle's remarks on art were based on an objective analysis of the history of the arts themselves. Both men had evolved their philosophical systems to deal with other problems, that of human morality and the relation of man to the divine in the case of Plato and, in the case of Aristotle, that of the order of the natural world. Applied to the arts their approaches were only metaphors. However, in this field as in others the metaphors of the Greeks have become the realities of later generations.

Aristotle's belief that everything was generated for a particular end and that it would go on developing until it reached this end was not unrelated to the Platonic notion of ideas, the set of norms from which everything in the earthly world is copied. Plato, for example, thought that the 'ideal' shoe would most perfectly fulfil the function which a shoe had to perform. Aristotle employed the same standard. He measured whether tragedy had realized its final nature by whether it fulfilled the function of tragedy, that is the provision of pleasure through the use of pity and fear. It is evident that if he had not defined what he thought was the goal of the genre he would not have been able to talk about it as a fixed form, nor could he have arrived at a formulation of the perfect type. He would only have been able to see each individual tragedy as an incident in the history of human creativity. He would certainly not have been able to do what he does at the end of the *Poetics*, which is to compare the relative merits of epic and tragedy, assuming they both have the same purpose, and then show that tragedy is best at fulfilling that purpose. Aristotle thus makes it clear that the criticism and classification of works of art is an essential part of their study. It was impossible even to begin the work of classification without first establishing a norm for each class.

The classification into genres, then, necessitated the formation of normative judgments, but there were two other basic means of organizing material for which this was not so automatically true. The use of chronological and geographical groupings would seem inherently more objective. How then did Aristotle use chronology? As we saw, the *Poetics* begins with a historical account of the treatment of serious and inferior subjects in literature. It had become regular practice in Greece when studying a particular subject to go first into its origins. The *historiai* or 'inquiries' of Herodotus and Thucydides were inquiries into the origins of relatively short wars. Both writers felt that it was impossible to understand either the Persian or the Peloponnesian Wars without tracing their antecedents. This approach to history produces a narrative in which parallels from the past are slowly accumulated until the final event which is the heart of the *historia* becomes apparently inevitable. Herodotus records earlier conflicts between Europe and Asia and selected events from the histories of the participating countries until the Persian Wars emerge as the climax. Aristotle's study in the *Poetics* of the opposition between the serious and trivial streams in literature culminates as inevitably in the confrontation between perfect embodiments of each. Such a pattern was doubly appealing to Aristotle with his belief that the origins of all things in the world were already influenced by their final purposes. So, with a house, from the time the first brick is brought to the site the final structure is already in view, and, with man, the process of growing up is seen as the gradual accumulation of faculties and skills in order that the complete man should appear at the end. This is the pattern behind Aristotle's history of philosophy in the first book of the *Metaphysics* where philosopher succeeds philosopher up to Plato until Aristotle himself finally brings the threads together. The same pattern too is revealed in the numerous references to the history of painting and sculpture in later writers, which are thought to derive from two main accounts of the arts composed after 300. Douris' work is difficult to reconstruct, although he seems to have transmitted to us many anecdotes. It is from Xenocrates that the accounts of the two arts which were most influential in antiquity seem to descend. Both culminate in artists of the Sicyonian school, Lysippus in sculpture and Apelles in painting, and such a bias would be natural in a member of that school, as Xenocrates was. Apparently the accounts of both arts were based on a series of artists, each of whom added something new to the art, such as 'symmetry' or 'shading', until the 'greatest contribution' was made by the two Sicyonians. The pattern of growth to culmination, which Aristotle had applied to literature, was thus also imposed on the history of painting and sculpture.

Much the strongest evidence for the reconstruction of Xenocrates' work is found in the *Natural History* of Pliny, who himself clearly accepted Aristotle's biological metaphor. Pliny's observation that painting in Italy *absoluta erat*, 'achieved its full development', very rapidly closely parallels Aristotle's language. Even more revealing is Pliny's statement about sculpture in the 290s that *cessavit deinde ars*, 'art then stopped'. The stopping here referred to is the stopping of death rather than of the process of growth to maturity as is shown by Pliny's next statement that art *revixit*, 'came alive again', in the fifty-sixth Olympiad (156–153). This further extension of the metaphor naturally arose from a need to continue the history of cultural developments after the stage described by Aristotle and his school in the late fourth century. Once the notion of growth to maturity had become

established it was almost necessary that decline and even death should follow. History on the larger scale thus becomes an alternating cycle of life and death. On the smaller scale Pliny, or rather his source, applies the metaphor to the lives of individual artists. When he gives their dates he says when they *floruerunt*, 'flourished', almost certainly giving the sense of the Greek 'were at their *akmē*' (peak). The Greek word for the physical prime of life is transferred to the period of greatest artistic achievement.

The principles of chronological organization both of Aristotle and of later writers concerned specifically with art were thus dominated by the idea of a mature achievement, led up to by growth and followed by decline or at best stagnation. The standard for mature achievement in art which first became established in the ancient world was that which was embodied in the works of the later fourth-century artists and their pupils and which was returned to again in the mid-second century. Pliny says that the last sculptors to reveal the fullness of art were the pupils of Lysippus and Praxiteles, and the artists whom he mentions as being responsible for the revival of this fullness were Polycles and his descendants. We know that the latter group looked back to earlier standards because Pliny says that the sons of Polycles copied the reliefs on the shield of Phidias' Athena Parthenos, while a statue found in Delos and 57 signed by two members of the group is related to the work of Praxiteles. The family was Attic and it seems likely that they were leading members of the school, called by modern scholars Neo-Attic, which was responsible for a whole mass of work 153 more or less closely derived from Athenian fifth- 158 and fourth-century originals. 162

This concentration on Athenian art and also on the fifth century marks a new departure and shows that we are dealing with more than just a restatement of the values of Xenocrates and Douris. Several factors contributed to it, some of which will be discussed later, but one which must have had an indirect effect was the new emphasis placed on Athenian fifth-century writers in the classification of literature undertaken during the third and early second centuries by scholars who called themselves *kritikoi*, that is those 'capable of discerning difference'. These scholars, who worked chiefly at Alexandria, became increasingly skilled in differentiating genuine and spurious works by established authors and in

57 'Strangford' shield. Roman adaptation of the shield of Phidias' Athena Parthenos.

grouping works by genus and species. First fruits of their efforts were the *Pinakes*, or *Tables*, of Callimachus which classified the bulk of earlier Greek literature by author, medium and subject. Later scholars became more selective and Quintilian tells us that Apollonius, the great epic writer of Alexandria, was not brought into the classification because critics such as Aristophanes and Aristarchus, both librarians in the early second century, specifically excluded their contemporaries. Latin writers confirm that by this time the best writers were grouped in *ordines* (ranks) with, for example, five epic writers, three each of tragedy and comedy, and nine lyric poets. These writers were said to be *enkrithentes*, that is accepted for inclusion in the highest class. The word was regularly used previously to refer to social and political acceptability and became translated by the Romans as *classici*, that is belonging to the highest tax class. It is thus at this time that a literary aristocracy of the classics, many of them Attic in origin, was established.

The impact of this recognition of a set of preferred examples is immediately manifest in the characteristic imitativeness and archaism of Hellenistic writers and it is a similar growth of

58 Electra and Orestes at the tomb of Agamemnon.
Work of the first century BC signed by Menelaus.

chosen as models were those created in fifth-century Athens. From certain passages, particularly in Cicero and Quintilian, it appears that the quality most valued in the earlier Attic artists, especially in Phidias, was that of *phantasia*. This word may be translated 'imagination', but it also refers specifically to the imaginative vision of divine beauty. It was this quality which had enabled Phidias in the Zeus at Olympia to 'add something to traditional religion'. Quintilian shows that work displaying *phantasia* was regarded as a high-point and that the realism of Praxiteles and Lysippus was already thought of as a decline leading to the excesses of Demetrius, who was 'more interested in similitude than beauty'. Aristotelian realism is thus apparently replaced by a more Platonic idealism as a standard. The best preserved creation of the Neo-Attic movement to survive illustrates what such a standard meant in practice. A calm beauty of face and expression marks the first-century group usually identified as Electra with her Brother Orestes and signed by Menelaus pupil of Stephanus who was in turn a pupil of Pasiteles. Naturalism is deliberately avoided in the geometrical regularity of hair and drapery. The subject, the love of a brother and sister and their joint devotion to their father, reflects a moral enthusiasm, a *pietas*, such as that which animates the *Aeneid* of the same period. The contrast with the earlier Hellenistic tradition is evident. The theory of *phantasia* seems to have both Platonic and Stoic overtones and was probably developed as part of the revival in those schools in the second and first centuries. This revival was fostered by the same Roman patronage which encouraged the Neo-Attic sculptors, and Pasiteles may well have formed an essential link between the intellectual and artistic worlds of his day.

Expenditure on art followed the pattern of art criticism. The patronage of living artists waned in the Hellenistic period and the new monarchs turned to collecting older works. At first in the third century it was the Sicyonian works most admired by Xenocrates that were most in favour. Ptolemy III had Sicyonian paintings and drawings bought for him by one Aratus, 'for', as Plutarch says, 'the fame of that school was still at its height'. This last remark suggests that the Sicyonian school was to become less fashionable and it is true that the Attalids of Pergamum definitely seem to have shifted their attention to

imitativeness in the visual arts around 200 which suggests that painters and sculptors were also becoming increasingly selective in their use of models. The eventual formulation of an actual written canon of works of art is associated with Pasiteles, who wrote five volumes on 'wonderful' or 'noble' works in the early first century, and who, as a sculptor, was linked to the so-called Neo-Attic school. Classic art thus came into being as an equivalent to classic literature, and in sculpture, as for example in tragedy, the works spokesman of the new trend, wrote on works of art and not on artistic biography as had Xenocrates and Douris. The latter had been interested in the role of individuals in the historical development of art as masters of particular techniques of representing aspects of reality such as light and shade, depth and emotion. One result of the fact that the favourite artists of Xenocrates and Douris were admired for their personal skills was that even their unfinished works came to be highly valued – a situation which we know also occurred in the case of several fourth-century artists. Pliny is expressing similar critical values when he remarks that the sketchy lines of unfinished works seem to embody the artist's actual thoughts. Pasiteles and the Neo-Attic artists, however, looked for quite different qualities. Many of the earlier works which they copied, for example the balustrade of the temple of Athena Nike at Athens, were anonymous. Artists such as Phidias and Polygnotus were important individuals, but it was not so much their skill as their vision that was admired. Their works could be copied because their importance was not as *tours de force* but as ideals. Since they were not copies of reality, but objects of a higher level, copying them helped to disseminate the higher vision. Even if the practice of copying was soon extended to all types of art, it is important that at its introduction it was applied to a restricted type of 'classic' works.

One curious consequence of the difference between the Early and Late Hellenistic approaches to the history of art has been of great significance for the later study of the visual arts. This is that, although our image of what is truly 'classic' in a work of art is associated with the largely anonymous sculptures of the Acropolis, our image of the 'classic' artist is based on the later fourth-century artists with their sexual passions, assertive opinions and arrogant social behaviour. The Neo-Attic revival succeeded in establishing a new set of standards for judging works of art, but in its neglect of the role of the individual artist it allowed the survival in that area of the values of Xenocrates and Douris.

Geographical Classification and Criticism

In geographical classification even more than in chronological classification Hellenistic scholars

59 Athena, from the library at Pergamum, early second century BC.

fifth-century Athenian works, acquiring, for example, an adaptation of Phidias' Athena Parthenos. By the first century large numbers of copies of earlier works were being made. One reason for this change from the buying of originals to the buying of copies was certainly the greatly increased pressure on the market when the competition was not just between a few wealthy Hellenistic kings but between all wealthy Romans. But the change may also reflect the shift in values of art criticism. For Pasiteles, and artists appear to have defined their positions in terms of earlier cultures. As was seen in the prologue, the norms of geographical classification and an associated value system had long existed in Greece. Areas were classed as occupied by Dorian, Ionian and other racial groups. Within the races individual states were indentified, such as Corinth and Athens, and within these a sharp separation could be made between the country communities and the urban centres around which they were grouped. Greece as a whole was contrasted with other areas. Plato had described the decoration of the temple of Poseidon at Atlantis as 'barbaric', implying that its opulence was characteristic of the non-Greek world. Aristotle, who told Alexander to treat the barbarians as slaves, also used the term 'barbarism' to brand an excessive use of unusual words and made the first element of good style the employment of language that was truly Greek. In music Dorian, Ionian, Aeolian, Lydian and Phrygian were all used from the sixth and fifth centuries as accepted terms for classifying the modes or arrangements of notes which served the Greeks rather as we are served by keys. As we saw, Plato in the *Republic* subsequently rejected all but the Dorian and Phrygian modes, and in the *Laches* Phrygian too is excluded by him as being associated with a non-Greek tribe. The exclusion of all modes of non-Greek origin was taken up again by Plato's pupil Aristides Ponticus. This vehement partisan discussion of musical forms on regional lines in the fourth century provides a prototype for the polemical criticisms of rhetorical schools in the later Hellenistic period. While it lacked the same clear basis for differentiation as music with its various modes, painting was probably also organized into a complicated system of local schools at this time. For Pliny (*Natural History* xxxv, 75) tells us that until the time of Eupompus of Sicyon in the early fourth century painters were divided into two schools, Helladic and Asiatic; but that after him the Helladic was subdivided into Sicyonian and Attic. Ptolemy III's systematic collections of Sicyonian masters confirms the establishment of this classification.

By generating one international Greek culture and replacing the small geographically coherent city states with large amorphous kingdoms, Alexander's conquests rendered the old groupings out of date. In these circumstances the distinction between rural and urban life, which was now more accentuated than ever, provided a much more relevant key to classification. This distinction also acquired greater interest from its association with the parallel dualism of male and female. Already Aristophanes had contrasted the 60 effeminate speech of the city with the rude country dialect. Yet another dualism which seemed to parallel that of town and country was that of man and beast. Examples from Hellenistic literature and art confirm that these three pairs in different combinations offered considerable help in the classification of experience. It has been suggested that the first two idylls of Theocritus form a diptych of rural and urban life; certainly the speakers of the first idyll are male and the single voice of the second idyll female. Another idyll which is even more urban in character records the behaviour of women at a festival of Adonis in crowded Alexandria. The main actors in the rural idylls, which constitute the majority, are all men. Theocritus' study of the contrast between the rustic Cyclops, Polyphemus, and the indoor-dwelling Galatea has already been referred to in the previous chapter. Galatea is milk-white and delicate, and Polyphemus is conscious that she shuns him because of his shaggy brows, enormous eye and broad nose. But it is in *Idyll* xx, which must be later than Theocritus, that such a contrast is most clearly expressed. There a herdsman laments his rejection by one Eunica, who insists that she does not know how to kiss in the country fashion because she is used to pressing the lips of city gentlemen. Drawing attention to his rustic character, she had ridiculed his beard, his diseased lips, his black hands and unpleasant smell. Another idyll which can hardly be by Theocritus describes the seduction of a shepherdess by a goatherd who is called by her a satyr. In these poems the male protagonists are bearded, hairy, dark and generally satyr-like. The female characters are soft, fair and delicate. The same opposition is found along with the tension of attraction and rejection in a whole series of sculptures that derive from Hellenistic originals, with subjects such as Satyr and Nymph, 61 Satyr and Hermaphrodite, and Pan and Aphro- 62 dite. In each group the male element is aggressive and the female resistant. Although there is often nothing to connect the female figures with the town, they would have lived indoors like Galatea in contrast to the satyr and Pan

60 Glass goblet from Begram, Afghanistan, with painted decoration illustrating the parallel abductions of Ganymede (*left*) and Europa (*right*), Roman period.

61 Satyr and Nymph. Roman copy of an original probably of the second century BC.

62 Aphrodite, Eros and Pan, from the Establishment of the Posidoniasts on Delos, *c.* 100 BC.

65

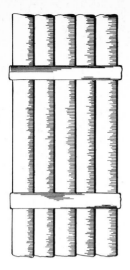

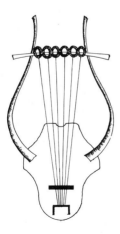

63 Greek musical instruments. *From top to bottom*: Pan pipes, double flute, and lyre.

figures who are embodiments of rustic vitality.

The reference to Pan draws attention to the developing tendency in the Hellenistic period to endow particular geographical areas with particular cultural associations, and also to see music as one of the most evocative means of cultural expression. Pan was associated with Arcadia and 63 it was in the Hellenistic period that the notion became established that that area of the Peloponnese was the true homeland of all herdsmen and the place where a rustic way of life had survived from the Golden Age. One of the earliest poets of the countryside was Anyte who herself lived in Arcadia in the later fourth century: 'Why, rural Pan, thus seated in the dark and lonely wood do you sound this sweet-voiced reed pipe? So that these heifers may graze over these dewy mountains, cropping the luxuriant blades of grass' (*Palatine Anthology,* xvi,231). The pipes were firmly associated with Pan and with herdsmen. With the Greek flute they also occupy a significant place in several myths which shed light on Greek musical aesthetics in a way that is relevant here. One such myth tells how the flute was invented by Athena but was rejected by her when she saw her own face reflected in a pool, distorted and discoloured by the puffing involved in playing. The flute was then picked up and played by the Phrygian satyr, Marsyas, to such good effect that he became involved in a competition with Apollo and his lyre. Apollo won the competition because he could sing at the same time as he played, which Marsyas could not. A similar story tells how Apollo with his lyre also defeated Pan and his pipes. These tales identify two generic weaknesses of wind instruments. They deform the face of the player and make it impossible for him to sing and play at the same time. The fact that the Arcadian Pan and the Phrygian satyr both neglected these weaknesses reveals their bestial affinities, just as the behaviour of Athena and Apollo expresses the godlike Greek's respect for articulate speech and the beauty of the human face.

The essential core of these myths must have grown up shortly after the original invasion of both the Peloponnese and Asia Minor by Greek-speaking peoples. Already in Homer the courtly bards who entertain the Greek heroes play a sort of lyre, while it is pipe music which is heard to come from Asiatic Troy. Later the Greek contempt for the Asiatics, from the time of the

64 Contest between Apollo and Marsyas. One of three reliefs from the base of a statuary group, attributed by Pausanias to Praxiteles, from the shrine of Leto at Mantinea, *c.* 330 BC.

Persian Wars to Alexander's conquests, must have given added point to the illustration of different aspects of the Marsyas story by Myron, Zeuxis and Praxiteles. The aristocratic and conservative associations of the lyre within Greek culture are emphasized by many classical writers. Pindar talks of his 'Dorian lyre'. Pratinas says that 'the flute must dance behind, being a servant'. Plato in the *Laws* complains how popular taste is having the effect of making lyre players try to imitate the wavering noise of the flute. This complaint should be related to Plato's repeated preference for the Dorian mode. For the late fifth-century Telestes, according to Athenaeus, said that it was 'the Phrygian king of the hole flute who first tuned a wavering Lydian strain, rival to the Dorian muse'. Apparently around 400 a 'firm' Dorian manner of music, relying on the rigid tunings of a lyre, was tending to be replaced in popular taste by a Phrygian manner which

exploited the uncertain warblings of the flute. Plato's criticisms were evidently based on the opinion, also preserved by Athenaeus, that lyre music tended to assuage emotions but flute music to excite them. Theoretically the wavering notes of the flute corresponded to the inconstant state of emotion. Historically the flute was the instrument most played by women, especially those of the looser sort. If more evidence were needed of a musical decline from a manly Dorian music played on the lyre it could be found in the increasing tendency for a chromatic scale with its many sensual colours (*chrōmata*) to replace simpler series of notes. Also harmonic theory could represent the increasingly popular Phrygian tunings as being higher in the scale than the Dorian tunings and thus relatively more suited to the feminine register.

The development of musical theory and practice in the years preceding the Hellenistic period is particularly important because music, with its precise mathematical basis, was much the most widely discussed and highly valued art form at the time. It was, consequently, in relation to music that the Greeks established many of their aesthetic norms. It is equally important to realize that these norms were established by philosophers who, in looking for patterns of order in the world, readily simplified and distorted historical truth. We may contrast the generalization of Aristotle, the philosopher, in the *Politics* that Dorian is a manly mode with the pragmatic observation of his pupil Aristoxenus, a musical theorist, that Dorian was often used for maidens' songs. Naturally it was the formulations of the philosophers which governed general conceptions. It would be interesting to know whether Apollonius the *eidographos*, the librarian at Alexandria in the early second century who classified Greek lyric poems as Dorian, Phrygian, Lydian, Mixo-Lydian and Ionian, based his classification on philosophical generalizations about the suitability of mode to subject or on technical differences in the musical accompaniments. It is, indeed, improbable that much original music could have survived, considering 116 that notation was only systematized in the early Hellenistic period. Also the record says that Apollonius put poems in the classes where they 'seemed' to belong, implying that he did not have absolute technical differences on which to base his classification.

It would, however, be wrong to think that specifically Platonic norms were widely accepted in the Hellenistic world. As we have already seen, Aristotle had established the emotions as essential elements in human psychology. It was thus impossible, with the ever increasing popularity of wind instruments, that Plato's preference for Dorian music played on the lyre should carry much weight. Indeed, Theocritus, who carefully chose an archaic Doric dialect for his idylls and gave them a predominantly masculine character, refers almost solely to wind instruments. Yet among these he does clearly favour the shepherd's pipes over the flute, thus demonstrating that it is the primitive character of the wind instrument rather than its weak femininity which attracts him. It is the instrument of the Greek Pan rather than of the Phrygian Marsyas that he adopts, one which by its multiple pipes of fixed tunings shares some characteristics with the lyre,

and one which is not blown directly like the ancient flute and so does not deform the face as much. Although Theocritus agrees with Plato on the manly associations of Dorian culture and also on its healthy pre-urban characteristics, his primitive Dorians are not lyre-loving intellectuals embodying the ideals of a conservative aristocracy but hireling shepherds expressing their emotions with the aid of rudimentary pipes. We are told by Probus that Theocritus chose the Doric dialect because by that time it had specifically rustic connotations. Certainly although a Dorian by birth he would never have used such language in conversation. The same was true of his near contemporary Herondas who also worked on Dorian Cos and may have been Dorian by origin, but who consistently used an Ionic dialect for his *mimiambi*. These poems represent scenes of urban life in which the dominant personalities are almost entirely women. It seems quite likely that Herondas is deliberately exposing the essence of an Ionian, urban, feminine world as the opposite side of the picture to Theocritus', which is Doric, rustic and masculine. He suggests as much in the *mimiambus* called *The Dream* in which he describes allegorically his defeat of a group of goatherds in a musical competition at Cos and declares his intention to go on singing for the Ionians.

It might be thought that the two poets chose the two different dialects just because the one was imitating the mimes of Sophron, which were Dorian, and the other the choliambics of Hipponax, which were Ionic; but the unique contrast in their favoured subjects, a contrast which is not found in their models, demands a more coherent explanation. The same is not true of Callimachus who wrote, like Theocritus and Herondas, in the first half of the third century. When Callimachus shifts from Homeric hexameters in the early *Hymns*, to Doric elegiacs in *Hymns* v and vi, to Ionic iambics in the *Iambi* and so on, he is simply imitating the metre, dialect and literary form of different earlier models. Such pure stylistic exercises were appropriate to his position as a scholar working in Ptolemy's library. Nevertheless, it is interesting that he still felt it necessary to defend himself in *Iambus* xiii against those who criticized him for his variety of metre, dialect and vocabulary: by varying his poems as he did he claimed to follow the rules not of nature, but of art. As a Dorian born in the late fourth century,

Callimachus should naturally have used the language of his contemporaries and compatriots. However, by disengaging himself from his environment in space and time he was able to choose how to express himself. His choice between different combinations of dialect and metre amounted to a choice of style for each work. There can be little doubt that for Callimachus his disengagement from his natural environment was made possible firstly by his transplantation to a new community, Alexandria, which had no clear 'natural' character, secondly by his comparative isolation even within that community in an academic institution concerned largely with the organization of knowledge in the form of written documents, and finally by the fact that all his verbal creations emerged also in the form of writing deprived of any necessary relation to the spoken language of his own life. These factors applied much less to Theocritus and Herondas, operating outside the Museum in the older communities of Syracuse and Cos with their established characters. Both these poets could claim that their language was related to their local environment. Theocritus' Syracusan woman in *Idyll* xv justifies her broad Doric accent by a claim that Syracuse is a Dorian city. Herondas says at the end of *The Dream* that he is writing for an audience of Ionians.

It is difficult to describe the loss of a sense of local identity suffered by the Greeks with the birth of the Hellenistic world. But its effects are clear. Amidst all the creativity and scholarship which marked the centuries after Alexander's conquests we find hardly a hint that a local school was identified in literature or philosophy, music or painting, sculpture or architecture. We find no references to an Alexandrian school of literature, to Pergamene philosophy, to Syrian music or to Rhodian sculpture. The fact that neither cities, kingdoms nor races were seen to have constant characteristics, even for brief periods, at a time when the traits of earlier cultural and political groupings, a Dorian or Ionian, Spartan, Athenian or Corinthian character, all were becoming more accepted as realities, is revealing of the new psychological situation. The Hellenistic Greek constantly sought to define himself in terms of the pre-Hellenistic world. Pericles could elicit supreme achievements from the Athenians by appealing to their sense of political identity because the Athenians did have their own

goddess, their own language and their own art. The Attalids of Pergamum, with their borrowed gods and derivative institutions, their bought artists and their seduced scholars, certainly endeavoured to be more Attic than the Alexandrians; but it is doubtful how far they aspired to a specifically Pergamene achievement. That is why no mention will be found in this book of the different local schools of Hellenistic art, especially of Hellenistic sculpture, which earlier scholars have tried to isolate.

Stylistic Choice at Alexandria and Syracuse

It would obviously be interesting to establish how the different patrons and artists of the Hellenistic world reacted to the wide range of choice available to them and to see how they chose to express themselves through the selection of both styles and subjects. Unfortunately, this area of investigation is a hazardous one. It is, for example, tempting to compare the silver cups of Alexandria with the grand marble sculpture of Pergamum, since we know something of both. But it is difficult to know how far we may be either really perceiving some essential difference between the art of the two communities or only being misled by the accidents of survival. For this reason it is important to compare like with like, and we are thus lucky to have two Hellenistic descriptions of large boats made for rival rulers which enable us to do just this.

Both accounts are preserved by chance in the late Roman writer Athenaeus. One boat was a sea-going vessel made for Hiero II of Syracuse, the other was intended by Ptolemy IV for use on the Nile. Not only were the two boats nearly contemporary in the later third century, they were also comparable in being floating palaces with considerable architectural character. Hiero's boat was surrounded on the outside by *atlantes*, that is giant male figures like those on the Olympieum at Acragas, bearing an entablature decorated with triglyphs. The forms were thus identifiably Doric and directly recalled the greatest monuments of pre-Hellenistic Sicily. A poem inscribed on the boat said that the giants had made it sail the paths of heaven, while large letters on the prow acclaimed its builder as Hiero the Dorian. These features make it almost certain that the architecture of the boat was intended to be read along with the inscriptions as expressive of Hiero's Dorian character. The inclusion of a gymnasium in the interior arrangements along with the male giants on the outside would fit with virile Dorian interests, as also would the mosaic floors showing scenes from the *Iliad*. Certainly there is no mention of similar features in Ptolemy's boat. There the only order that is identified is Corinthian, if, as seems likely, that is what is meant by the term *Korinthiourgēs* (of Corinthian workmanship) used to describe the capitals of the largest room (*oikos*). With its decoration of acanthus leaves Corinthian was the most elaborate capital type known to the Greeks, contrasting strongly with the simple Doric form. As the Corinthians were best known for their luxury and lasciviousness the mere presence of Corinthian capitals would perhaps suggest a very different set of values from that represented by Hiero's boat. Not surprisingly, there is no gymnasium in Ptolemy's boat; instead there is a symposium or drinking-room. In place of the illustrations from the *Iliad* there is a shrine of Dionysus containing portraits of members of the royal family. Our overall impression of Hiero's boat is that it was characterized by an aesthetic austerity. Its arrangement is described as *symmetron* (proportionate). Ptolemy's boat, on the other hand, satisfied the senses rather than the mind with its scented cedar woodwork, its gold and its varied marbles. The impression of contrast between the two boats is not weakened by the presence in both of shrines to Aphrodite. This is only a proof of the universal dominance of sexual love in the Hellenistic world. The fact that this shrine on the Sicilian boat was an island of sensuality with its many-coloured marbles, paintings, sculptures and drinking-cups only serves to sharpen the contrast with the rest of the boat.

It would be wrong to suggest that Ptolemy wanted to appear as Corinthian as Hiero did Dorian. Each ruler did, however, express himself in terms of architectural forms which, by their nomenclature and associations, were totally diverse. We know that Hiero sent his ship as a gift to Ptolemy and on arrival in Alexandria with the inscription on its prow it must have been as self-

65 Temple of Isis, Philae, Egypt, third century BC and later.

consciously Dorian as Theocritus' Syracusan woman. Perhaps too, Ptolemy's boat was commissioned with a sense of rivalry with the Dorians akin to that felt by Herondas.

Another distinctive feature of Ptolemy's boat was a dining-room, built, according to the text, entirely 'in the Egyptian manner', that is with black and white banded columns whose capitals were shaped like rose blossoms and decorated with lotus flowers and palm blooms. The forms thus corresponded quite closely to column types based on vegetable forms with which we are familiar from early times in Egypt. As this room together with the Corinthian *oikos* seems to have been the most magnificent on the boat, Ptolemy appears to have shown a considerable respect for Egyptian forms, especially since the setting here is not some ancient temple precinct where it would be necessary to continue the tradition of pharaonic art, but a private environment where few concessions to public demands would be necessary. Probably the existence of the two rooms on the boat is a demonstration of how far the Macedonian royal family in Egypt felt its loyalties divided between two cultures. The need to acknowledge the traditional needs of both Greek and Egyptian subjects had already induced Ptolemy I to inaugurate the worship of a new deity, Serapis, embodying features of Osiris and Apis as well as of Dionysus and Pluto. The shrine of Serapis at Memphis with its mixture of Greek and Egyptian architectural and sculptural styles reveals the same artistic eclecticism as Ptolemy's boat. A whole series of statuettes and heads from Alexandria and elsewhere shows a combination of distinct features, such as an Egyptian head-dress and a Greek robe, or of stylistic elements, such as a face with nose, eyes and mouth of Greek accuracy set against forehead, cheeks and chin endowed with the geometrical simplicity and coherence familiar in Egyptian art. The product of this fusion is really a new style and is thus different in kind from the juxtaposition of existing modes which we find in the Egyptian architecture of the period.

This last point serves to emphasize an essential difference between the arts in antiquity. In architecture as in music the modes were absolutely differentiated on a mathematical basis. The proportions and details of Doric, Ionic and Corinthian were all fixed by written texts, and those of Egyptian architecture could be measured

65

66

67

66 Green basalt bust of Serapis. Roman adaptation of an original by Bryaxis of *c.* 300 BC.

67 Head of an Egyptian princess, Ptolemaic period.

71

and recorded too. In sculpture and painting, in spite of the efforts of individuals such as Polyclitus or Pamphilus, it had proved impossible to formulate rules of representation either mathematically or verbally. The most that had been achieved was a general characterization of different artists and schools. Painters and sculptors were thus hardly capable of making the same articulate stylistic references that were easy for the musician or architect. The same distinction existed, though less sharply, between poetry and prose. The rigid character of poetic metres and their close association with definite musical forms ensured that poetic styles were much more easily defined and consciously imitated than those of prose. Typically, rhetoricians and theorists such as Gorgias, Aristotle and Hegesias, who tried to establish norms and principles of style for spoken prose, tended to introduce more and more rigid metrical devices. Moreover, the elaborately rhythmical language of Hegesias was the first and only rhetorical style that acquired a name, Asiatic. It was, admittedly, opposed to an Attic style by the late Hellenistic students of the subject who invented the classification, but the Attic style always remained a much more generalized term. The qualities of natural simplicity and clarity which were attributed to the best Attic orators of the fourth century were much less definable than the elaborate artistic devices employed by Hegesias in third-century Asia Minor.

It is thus apparent that in some arts the establishment of different styles, or rather 'characters' or 'modes' as they were called in antiquity, was easier than in others and, correspondingly, the use of these styles to make particular references occurred more naturally in these arts, as in architecture and poetry. It is also clear that in an art such as rhetoric it was possible to choose between a more, or less, consciously stylistic approach. It is worth noting that the two main alternatives that then emerge are a more artificial style, Asiatic, and a more natural one, Attic. This helps us to understand further the contrast between the two boats of Ptolemy and Hiero. For the Egyptian boat with its sequence of elaborately stylized environments clearly reflects a more artificial, that is highly-wrought and calculated, approach, while the Sicilian boat has fewer 'stylistic' characteristics and, in so far as it has, reveals a consistent respect both for nature as

in its gymnasium and deck-garden and for simplicity as in its use of the Doric order.

Stylistic Choice in Architecture

In no art are the modes so clearly identifiable as in architecture. Almost any Greek building containing a column or entablature can be clearly identified as Doric, Ionic or Corinthian. Hence it is in the different architectures of the two boats of Ptolemy and Hiero that their different characters emerge most decisively. Hence too a study of the way such modes or orders are used throughout the Hellenistic world can be extremely instructive. In the preceding paragraph Doric has been characterized as simple and so natural, and Corinthian as elaborate and so artificial. Earlier in the book in a discussion of Prodicus' 'Choice of Hercules' it was suggested that Ionic could already be contrasted with Doric in the same way. If the three orders are considered together, Doric and Corinthian appear as the two extremes and Ionic as intermediate. The three capital forms together well illustrate one of the paradoxes of artistic criticism, that the representation of natural forms is associated with what is unnatural while the absence of such representations is considered an expression of the essence of nature herself. Their embodiment of this paradox as well as the fact that they constitute a range of minimum, moderate and maximum degrees of ornamentation probably explains why these three orders have held their place in European architecture for so long. Recognition of the potential significance of the three forms first occurred in the Hellenistic period and reflected the fascination of people at that time with such underlying oppositions as that between the rival values of the purity of nature and the refinement of the human artefact. The process by which this recognition came about can be documented in a whole series of monuments.

Reference has already been made to the breaking-down of the barriers which originally separated the Doric tradition of mainland Greece from the Ionic tradition of Asia Minor. The introduction of Ionic elements into Athenian architecture of the later fifth century seems to have been a gesture of racial solidarity, as is clear in the case of the Erechtheum. However the use of Ionic on the inner passage of the Propylaea and probably in the rear chamber of the Parthenon,

12
13

buildings which were essentially Doric, suggests that it was thought particularly appropriate in interiors. It is usually argued that this is because of its relatively greater height, which made it more suitable to support interior ceilings whose level was higher than the external architrave, but the use of superimposed Doric colonnades in the main chamber of the Parthenon shows that the height factor was not an overriding one. If Ionic columns were used in the rear chamber of the Parthenon racial reasons may also have played a part, since that is where the treasure of Athena, including the resources of the essentially Ionian Delian confederacy, was to be kept. This still leaves the Ionic inner columns of the Propylaea and also those on the interior of the temple of Apollo at Bassae which was erected under Athenian influence at some time between 430 and 410. In both cases the height factor may have been of some influence, but there may also have been a similar, though less specific, desire to introduce Ionic features without putting them in too obtrusive a place in order to create a 'biracial' architecture. Pericles called Athens a school for all Greece and the Athenians under him certainly wished their city and its shrines to be a centre for Dorians as well as Ionians. The construction of the temple at Bassae, perhaps after the plague of 430, may have been a deliberate attempt by the Athenians to bring the message of non-exclusiveness to the heart of the Peloponnese itself.

It is at the temple of Apollo at Bassae too that we find the Corinthian capital for the first time. It seems to have been applied to one and possibly to three columns at the innermost end of the cella. Its greater richness would seem to mark the greater holiness of the area close to the cult statue. The idea for this new and richer form of capital seems to have come from the field of furnishing and interior decoration. Callimachus, who is credited with the invention of the Corinthian capital by Vitruvius, also made a bronze chimney for the Erechtheum in the form of a palm-tree, and not only are palmettes found together with acanthus on the earliest Corinthian capitals from Bassae and Delphi, but the open forms of the capital strongly suggest metalwork. The similarity of Corinthian to the capital of the column supporting the Nike on Phidias' Athena Parthenos also suggests an origin in the decorative arts. Whatever its origins, Corinthian remains

68 Reconstruction of interior of the temple of Apollo, Bassae, later fifth century BC.

firmly associated with interiors and when it does appear perhaps for the first time on an exterior on the Choragic Monument of Lysicrates (after 334), it is being applied not to a true building but to a large reproduction of a bronze offering-table. The strongest argument for an origin in bronze working is the term *Korinthiourgēs* (of Corinthian workmanship) which was applied to the capitals in Hellenistic texts and which was normally used to refer to a type of highly-prized bronze which seems to have originated in that city.

Corinthian thus seems to have carried a primary association with the world of interior decoration. It is found inside many fourth-century buildings. It is combined both with a Doric exterior, as in the *tholoi* or round structures of Delphi and Epidaurus, in the temple of Artemis and other buildings at the latter site and in the temple of Athena Alea at Tegea, and with Ionic, as in the Philippeion at Olympia and in the temple of Apollo at Didyma; although in the last building it is applied not to the cella which was open to the sky, but to the even more important oracular area which was near the entrance. From all these examples it appears that Corinthian had become associated decisively with the holier inner parts of temples in contrast to both Ionic and Doric. The Greeks were reluctant to use Corinthian on

69 Tholos, Epidaurus, mid-fourth century BC.

70 Plan of Tholos, Epidaurus, showing arrangement of orders.

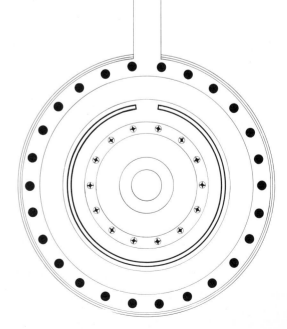

DORIC   ●

IONIC   ⊗

CORINTHIAN   ⊕

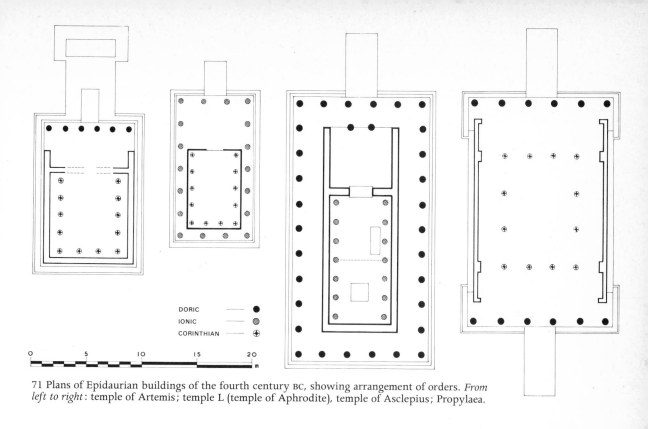

DORIC ────── ●

IONIC ────── ◍

CORINTHIAN ─── ⊕

71 Plans of Epidaurian buildings of the fourth century BC, showing arrangement of orders. *From left to right*: temple of Artemis; temple L (temple of Aphrodite), temple of Asclepius; Propylaea.

72 Temple of Olympian Zeus, Athens, begun in 174 BC in partial fulfilment of a plan by the sons of Pisistratus in the late sixth century BC.

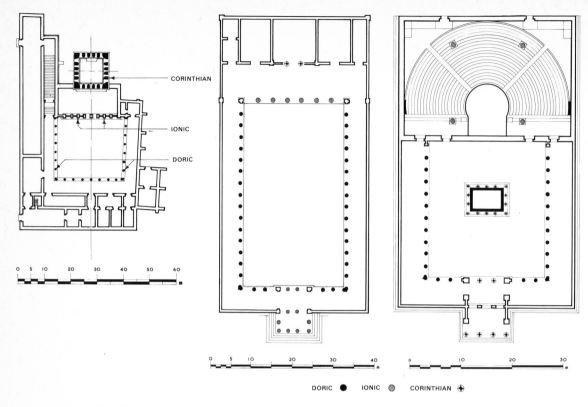

o 5 10 20 30 40 50 60

CORINTHIAN

IONIC

DORIC

o 5 10 20 30 40

o 10 20 30

DORIC ●   IONIC ◉   CORINTHIAN ✛

73 Plans of buildings of the second century BC, showing arrangement of orders. *From left to right*: the Heroön, Pergamum; the Hellenistic gymnasium, Miletus; the Bouleuterion, Miletus.

exteriors but after being applied to the outside of some minor and remote structures it received final recognition in the greatest temple of 72 mainland Greece, the Olympieum at Athens, built after 174.

We should expect this acknowledgment of the importance of Corinthian to be paralleled by a downgrading of the status of Doric and by a consequent acceptance of Ionic as intermediate. This is exactly what happens, though not all at once. Doric is still occasionally used for temples in the Hellenistic period, but progressively more rarely, while Ionic holds its ground better and is still used for temples of major importance, such as those of Hemogenes, in the second century. However, the clearest evidence for the relative status of the orders is provided by a whole series 73 of Hellenistic buildings where they are used together. Typical are the second-century gymnasia at Priene and Miletus. At Priene the Lower gymnasium has a court surrounded with Doric

columns, beyond which on the north side is an interior row of Ionic columns leading into the lecture room or *ephēbeion* which has windows 74 framed in the Corinthian order. At Miletus only three sides of the court are Doric, but the entrance propylon on the south and the whole north side are Ionic; the *ephēbeion*, also on the north side, has even more Corinthian features than at Priene. The Bouleuterion or Council House, also at Miletus, of about 170 has a somewhat simliar 75 arrangement, but here both the entrance propylon and a shrine in the middle of the court are Corinthian; the court itself is Doric, as is the wall decoration both inside and outside the council house itself, but the columns which support its roof are Ionic. In this case the propylon is apparently a prelude to the shrine, a structure which appears to be Roman in its surviving form but which probably replaced a Hellenistic predecessor. Another Corinthian shrine which in its present form is a Roman refurbishing of a

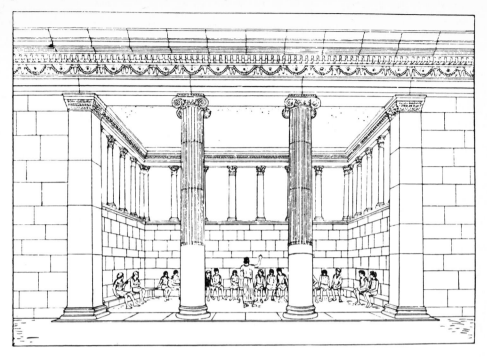

74 Reconstruction of lecture room of the Lower gymnasium, Priene, *c.* 130 BC.

75 Reconstruction of the Bouleuterion, Miletus, *c.* 170 BC.

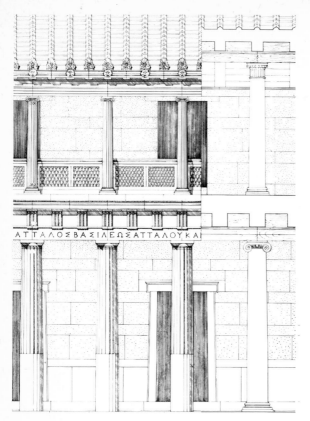

76 Reconstruction of elevation and section of the Stoa of Attalus, Athens, 159–138 BC.

Hellenistic structure is the cult room of the Heroön at Pergamum, a building which otherwise repeats the arrangement of the gymnasia at Priene and Miletus, being entered from an Ionic portico which is itself preceded by a Doric court.

These monuments provide us with enough variety and at the same time enough consistency for us to be able to establish certain principles. The most important rooms, whether shrines or lecture rooms, which often also served as cult places, are Corinthian. The least important areas, the open courts, are Doric. Ionic occupies an intermediate role; this is most obvious when it appears on one side of an otherwise Doric court as an introduction to a Corinthian room and also when, in the Bouleuterion at Miletus, it is used as the main order of the council chamber itself which is less important than the shrine and more important than the minor order of the chamber's wall and preceding court. There seems also to have been an additional principle, or habit, that

the propylon would take the order of the building to which it led most directly: Doric in the Lower gymnasium at Priene where the opposite side of the court is Doric, Ionic in the gymnasium at Miletus where the opposite side of the court is Ionic, and Corinthian in the Bouleuterion at Miletus where there is no opposite portico but only a Corinithian shrine in the middle of the court. The notion that the orders constituted a scale from Doric to Corinthian, which was first hinted at at Bassae in the fifth century, is now quite explicit. The association of Corinthian with interiors and religious furnishings, the traditional association of rich decoration with high status, and the simple fact that the more elaborate orders would cost more to carve must all have contributed to the establishment of this sequence of the orders.

If in any sense it is possible to talk of three classes of capital there may be a parallel to the idea of three social classes which had been clearly formulated for the first time in Aristotle's *Politics*. Here Aristotle had talked of the *euporoi* (people with rich resources), the *mesoi* (middle people) and the *aporoi* (people lacking in resources) – a division which became thereafter an established feature of Western social theories. Aristotle had noted that such a triple system of classes is a feature of large states especially and it is clear that with the greatly increased materialism of the Hellenistic world, and the associated growth of royal courts, powerful commercial interests and a mass of urban poor, such distinctions of wealth became more important than ever. Moreover, class distinctions would automatically have been expressed architecturally by the rights of particular groups to be admitted to particular institutions, whether council houses, law-courts, gymnasia or commercial premises. The new and perhaps increasingly stratified structure of society may thus have encouraged an interest in the orders as expressive of distinctions of status in architectural environments. This does not mean that there was any equivalence made between the orders and the classes. It may however mean that we are justified in seeing the crescendo of orders in, for example, the Lower gymnasium at Priene as expressing the fact that by the second century the physical activities which took place in the Doric court or palaestra would be considered lower in status than the intellectual activities of the Corinthian lecture room. Certainly the physical sports which had once been the favoured pastimes of the aristocracy were increasingly becoming the preserve of paid professionals from the lower classes, while intellectual pursuits were becoming more normally the preserve of those who could afford education.

In all the buildings we have looked at richness and refinement are associated more with interiors and simplicity more with exteriors, and this is a correlation which should not be taken for granted. The same distinction is found neither in Egyptian temples earlier nor in Gothic cathedrals later, just as it was absent from the majority of sixth- and fifth-century Greek temples. The development of such a correlation suggests that the Greeks had slowly come to acknowledge that interiors with their 'exclusive' and possibly also intellectual associations were superior to exteriors with their 'common' and often more physical associations. The more private and the less public an environment was, the higher was its status as marked off by the orders. Certainly such an attitude would provide an explanation for the treatment of stoas. The fact that many stoas have Doric columns on the outside and Ionic on the inside has often been explained as a consequence of the need to have higher columns to support the central ridge, but this argument is weakened by the presence of the same arrangement even when there is no distinction in height and also by the use of Doric columns of different heights in buildings such as the hypostyle hall at Delos. It would thus seem likely that there was a deliberate intention in stoas to distinguish the exterior from the interior. In the same way it has been argued that the use of Ionic above Doric in two-storey stoas is due to its greater lightness, although the many examples of Doric above Doric show that considerations of weight were not primary ones. Again the choice seems more deliberate, and the only consistent way to explain a building such as the Stoa of Attalus at Athens with its four different orders is in terms of a strict correlation between greater relative privacy and greater richness. There the front colonnade below is fluted with Doric; behind it is unfluted Ionic; the latter in turn is clearly simpler than the fluted Ionic in front on the floor above; while in the most remote situation at the rear of the upper floor is the most elaborate capital type of all with a rich leaf decoration. Taking the series of capitals and considering also the increase in richness between the two Ionic column types, the pro-

77 Reconstruction of capital from the inner colonnade of the upper storey of the Stoa of Attalus, Athens, 159–138 BC.

78 Reconstruction of capital from a temple at Neandria, early sixth century BC.

gression is emphatic. The further an order is from the public space of the agora, both horizontally and vertically, the more ornate it is. We will see later how the tendency of people at the end of the Hellenistic period to be conscious of movement through a building as a linear experience made such a modulation of capital and column seem especially expressive.

Stylistic Choice at Pergamum

The capitals of the upper and inner row of columns in the Stoa of Attalus were not Corinthian, as might have been expected, but were decorated instead only with a double row of fleshy leaves. The deliberate rejection of Corinthian may well have been a calculated gesture, since this new capital form seems to have been associated with other Attalid building commissions. Its closest prototypes are the so-called Aeolic capitals which were popular in nearby Aeolis close to the site of Pergamum, as at 78 Neandria and Larisa, in the years around 600, but which later died out. The revival of the form may thus have been an attempt to establish a specifically Pergamene capital based on local tradition. If this is so, then the rulers of Pergamum were as interested in expressing themselves through architectural forms as we suggested earlier were the rulers of Syracuse and Alexandria. It is not surprising that the Attalids chose as their emblem a form closer to the Corinthian of the Ptolemies than to the Doric of Hiero since, by the second century, they revealed both in their creation of the famous library at Pergamum and in their patronage of scholars a preference for intellectual refinement and indoor pastimes.

This revived capital form, however, and the values it represents are only one side of the Pergamene personality and one that probably only emerged around 200. Philetaerus, founder of the Attalid dynasty, had established his independence from Macedon and from the Seleucids and had inflicted a major defeat on the Gauls in the first half of the third century. He also began rebuilding his hilltop fortress on a magnificent 79 scale. Perhaps his first major work was the great 80 Doric temple to Athena. The choice of Doric instead of Ionic, which would have been more natural in the area and which had been used for the temple of Athena at Priene shortly before, together with other features connects this temple directly with the Parthenon which crowned a similar precipitous site on the other side of the Aegean. The intention may have been only a

79 Model of the upper city, Pergamum.

formal correspondence with the temple of Athena on the Acropolis, but it is possible that there was further justification for the choice of Doric. For Callimachus also deviated from the normal Ionic language of his hymns when singing of Athena and introduced instead a Doric dialect. This could be seen as an arbitrary step, but as the poet also stresses that Athena did not use perfume but only an athlete's olive oil and denies that she had enough womanly vanity to look in a mirror, it is likely that he intended the Dorian vocabulary to bring out Athena's anti-aesthetic and manly characteristics. Theocritus had specifically identified the athlete's oil-flask as Dorian. While it seems probable that Callimachus chose the Dorian dialect as expressive of Athena's character, the same argument need not apply to the temple, because the desire to imitate the Parthenon might alone have been sufficient justification for the Doric order. The important point is that the rejection of the local tradition implies a conscious choice and one that is revealing of the aspirations of the city, or rather its rulers.

Whether or not this last argument would have reinforced the choice of Doric for the temple of Athena at Pergamum, it seems likely that in the design of the temple, as in the later introduction of the Pergamene capital, we are witnessing the use of an architectural style to make specific references to the historic past. If we turn to Pergamene sculpture the same approach is found there. In the later third century Attalus I dedicated a series of statues on the Athenian Acropolis which thematically made a clear connection between the two cities on either side of the Aegean. Different groups showed the battle between the gods and the giants, the conflict between the Athenians and the Amazons, the war between the Greeks and the Persians, and finally the defeat of the Gauls by Attalus himself. Just as the Amazonomachy and Gigantomachy had been illustrated on the Parthenon metopes when the Athenians had wanted to glorify their achievement in the Persian Wars, so now the Pergamenes used all those three conflicts to put their own victory over the Gauls into context. The Gallic invasions had made the Pergamenes feel that they had succeeded to the role of Athens as saviours of Greek civilization from barbarian chaos. The pride in physical heroism that this implied accorded well with the character of Athena as they had expressed it in her temple.

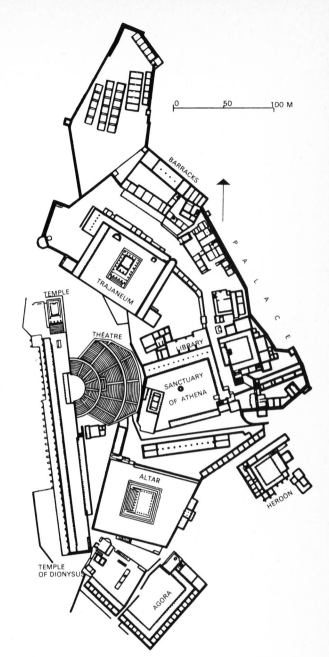

80 Plan of the upper city, Pergamum.

The Pergamenes seem in this way to have had a heightened sense of their place in a historical sequence, a point which is further demonstrated in a set of copies of Pergamene sculptures in Naples. The originals of the group may have been put up either at Athens or at Pergamum itself.

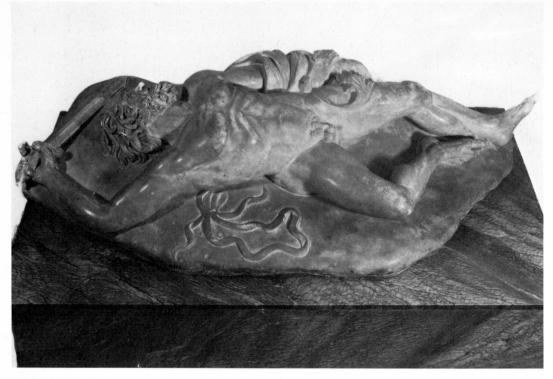

81 Dead Giant. Roman copy of an original of *c.* 200 BC.

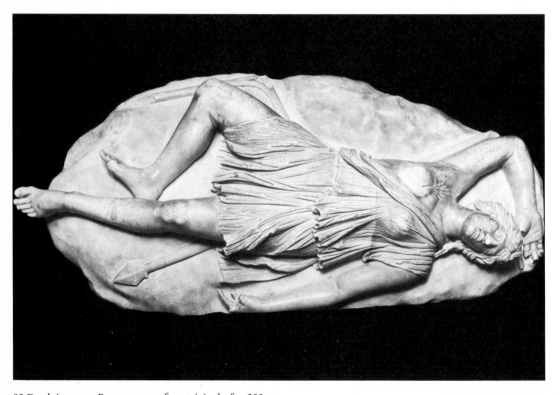

82 Dead Amazon. Roman copy of an original of *c.* 200 BC.

83 Dying Persian. Roman copy of an original of *c.* 200 BC.

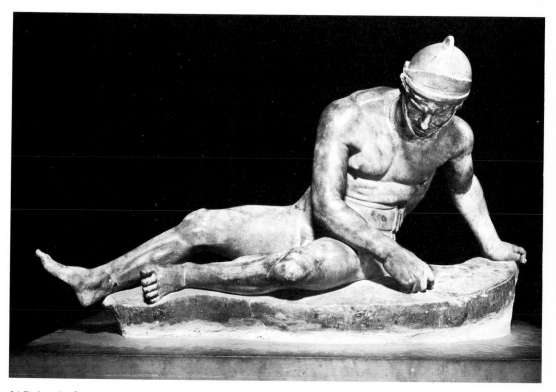

84 Dying Gaul. Roman copy of an original of *c.* 200 BC.

85 Poseidon and Athena competing for Attica, from the west pediment of the Parthenon, Athens, *c.* 440–435 BC. Drawing by Jacques Carrey, *c.* 1674.

What is remarkable in these sculptures is that the degree of life or death in each figure seems intended to provide a measure of the length of time separating the conflict referred to in the figure from that with the Gauls. The Giant lies flat 81 on his back quite dead; the Amazon seems almost 82 equally defunct. The Persian however, lying half 83 on his side, still shows signs of life and the Gaul, 84 although down, is able to rest on one hand. Thus the closer the figure is to the present the more of a living threat it seems. There is probably also an intentional contrast between the two 'dead' figures from the remote world of myth and the two 'dying' ones from the period of recorded history. Each pair employs the same basic pose, showing that they were grouped that way too, with the Giant and the Amazon being viewed from one side and the Persian and the Gaul from

the other. The Naples group thus illustrates once again how the Pergamenes defined their achievement in terms of historical precedents.

It has been suggested that it was the precedent of fifth-century Athens which provided the Attalids with their greatest inspiration. They built a great temple to Athena to match the Parthenon, and dedicated war memorials in both cities, in the goddess's enclosure. Eumenes II reinforced the connection with Athens when he adorned his library at Pergamum with a statue of Athena 59 based on that by Phidias in the Parthenon. Again, 4 when he had his Great Altar of Zeus at Pergamum decorated with a large frieze, not only did the theme of the Gigantomachy, the battle between the gods and the giants, reappear, but the pose and treatment of the major figures on the frieze were carefully derived from the Parthenon's

86 Zeus and Athena in combat with giants, from the large frieze of the Altar of Zeus, Pergamum, *c.* 170 BC.

pediment sculpture. It may seem strange that the turbulent and violent Gigantomachy frieze at Pergamum could have been directly inspired by the sculptures of Classical Athens, which have become a standard for calmness and restraint. Such a characterization of Attic sculpture is, however, based on a misunderstanding of the Attic achievement. The most impressive sculptures of the Periclean Acropolis, after the images of Athena inside and outside her temple, were the Parthenon pediments. The Athena Parthenos conformed in pose to earlier cult images, but in the pediments the Parthenon artists achieved a new standard of large-scale drama. Huge figures up to eleven feet high, and fully detached from the wall behind, were shown in scenes of the utmost violence and movement. We can reconstruct the Birth of Athena at the east and the Competition between Athena and Poseidon for Attica at the west on the basis of a relief from Madrid and seventeenth-century drawings. Comparing these with the reliefs of the Zeus altar at Pergamum, it is clear that they have exercised a profound effect on the sculpture of the Pergamene Gigantomachy. The scale of the Pergamene figures and their three-dimensional quality are closely comparable to the Athenian figures, and the tapering of the field of the frieze where it joins the altar steps has been exploited as elegantly as in the angles of the Parthenon pediments. The way the figure of Earth is cut off at the waist in the frieze also has analogies in the pediments.

In more detailed terms, not only is the Pergamene and Athenian treatment of naked bodies and draperies frequently very similar but whole groups in the Pergamene frieze, such as that of Athena being crowned by Nike, and individuals, such as Zeus who closely resembles the Poseidon of the Parthenon pediment, all imply a close study of the Athenian prototype. Perhaps most revealing is the way the compositional device of two figures striding outwards with strikingly opposed diagonal poses, which is the key to the dynamic unity of the Parthenon pediments, occurs repeatedly in the Pergamene frieze. Such symmetry is found first in the crucial group of Zeus and Athena which immediately confronts the visitor to the altar, and also in the group of Artemis and Apollo which occupies an identical position at the other end of the north frieze; it reappears in the figures of Amphitrite

87 Battle between Lapith and centaur. Metope from the Parthenon, Athens, 447–432 BC.

88 Battle between Apollo and giant, from the large frieze of the Altar of Zeus, Pergamum, c. 170 BC.

and Dionysus who dominate the west frieze either side of the staircase. The Parthenon metopes, which, though smaller, have a depth of relief even more similar to the great frieze, and which in part dealt with the same theme, are also echoed at Pergamum, as can be seen by comparing the Lapith and Apollo illustrated here. A more detailed study of the Parthenon metopes reveals that the Classical Athenians could be as interested

90 Head of a giant, from the large frieze of the Altar of Zeus, Pergamum, *c.* 170 BC.

in emotion as in movement. The few centaurs' heads which survive from the Parthenon metopes show as much pain and anger in their bulging eyes and twisted mouths as do the giants of Pergamum. In both cases the expression of emotion is seen as an animal trait appropriate to beings who are half-bestial in their forms. Likewise both at Athens and at Pergamum Lapiths and divine cohorts are relatively restrained even under extreme provocation.

So the Pergamene Gigantomachy is truly a reincarnation of the art of Classical Athens to match the Attic wisdom of the Pergamene library and the Attic heroism of the Pergamene armies. Our vision of the spirit of ancient Athens as one of Olympian calm is too much based on a later notion which developed in the first century and which received confirmation in modern times both from the headless, and so emotionless, conflicts of the Parthenon metopes and from the Parthenon

89 Head of a centaur. Detail of metope from the Parthenon, Athens, 447–432 BC.

91 Marsyas. Roman copy of a Hellenistic original forming part of a group with Apollo and the Scythian slave (see Pl. 92).

pediments, where only the passive spectators in the corners and not the dramatic actors of the centre have survived. A curious conclusion follows. The change in style that is always remarked between the physically realistic but quiet Gallic victory monuments of the late third century to the violence and expressiveness of the Zeus altar now emerges as a reflection of a new scholarly conservatism and as the fruit of the careful study of earlier art.

A Stoic Style?

The library at Pergamum was, as we saw, adorned with a statue of Athena and from this it seems that 59 the institution was an Athenaeum, in contrast to the Museum at Alexandria. Certainly there is evidence that the scholars of Pergamum concentrated rather heavily on pure scholarship, while at Alexandria there was at least as much emphasis on the actual writing of poetry. Athena had always been associated with practical knowledge and wisdom, the Muses more with inspiration and what we would call creative writing. The apparent neglect of poetry at Pergamum may be connected with Stoic ideas, for the Stoics seem to have had a strong influence in the city. The Stoic grammarian Crates of Mallos was one of the most famous scholars working in Pergamum at the time of Eumenes II. He was the teacher of Panaetius of Rhodes who was responsible for reshaping many Stoic ideas, especially on ethics, about 150. Apollodorus of Athens, who was taught by the Stoic Diogenes of Babylon, dedicated his verse *Chronicle* to Attalus II, though admittedly only after a long stay at Alexandria. The Stoics were certainly generally sceptical about the value of poetry with its emotional associations and were more concerned with discovering the divine order in the world. The suggestion has also been made that the decoration of the Gigantomachy frieze of the Zeus altar at Pergamum reveals the direct influence of Stoic thought. According to this interpretation, Zeus who leads the gods to victory on the frieze is the Stoic Zeus described in a hymn by Cleanthes: the prince of rational order. Both in the hymn and on the altar Zeus is represented as punishing lawlessness and overwhelming the chaotic impulses of the giants with his thunderbolt. The allegorical interpretation of myths was first popularized by the Stoics, especially Cleanthes, and was taken up again by Crates. Also the large number of personifications of elemental and psychological forces, who are identified by inscription, gives the battle represented on the frieze the character of a grand symbolic drama, which would be acceptable to Stoic didactic theory. That the frieze had a didactic function and not simply a ritual one like the usual temple frieze is suggested by its scale and accessibility and also by the plentiful use of inscriptions. The same was certainly true of another lost Pergamene monument, the temple erected at Cyzicus by Eumenes II and Attalus II in honour of their mother Apollonis. Here nineteen reliefs illustrated examples of filial respect and piety which were expounded in the accompanying epigrams preserved for us in the *Palatine Anthology*. The sense of duty celebrated in these reliefs was typical of Stoic ethics and especially of those theories developed by Panaetius, whose most famous work was *On Duties*.

There is indeed a whole series of works of later Hellenistic art which either reflect a general interest in moral themes, as did the Cyzicene reliefs, or else specifically point out how punishment falls on those who break the laws of the gods, as in the Pergamene Gigantomachy. One of these, which has been associated with Pergamum because a fragmentary version was excavated there, is the group of Apollo, Marsyas and the 91 Scythian slave. Apollo sits and watches the slave 92 sharpen his knife in preparation for the flaying of Marsyas who is shown tied to a tree. The face of the satyr is already disfigured with pain and fear. A group by Myron in the fifth century had shown an earlier moment when Marsyas enthusiastically

92 Scythian slave. Roman copy of a Hellenistic original forming part of a group with Apollo and Marsyas (see Pl. 91).

93 Farnese Bull (the punishment of Dirce). Roman adaptation of an original by Apollonius and Tauriscus of Tralles of *c.* 150 BC.

experimented with the pipes thrown down by Athena. A fourth-century relief associated with 64 the workshop of Praxiteles illustrates the subsequent competition between Marsyas and Apollo, with the Scythian slave waiting in the background. These earlier scenes thus concentrate on describing the difference of taste between deity and satyr. It is only in the Hellenistic group that the awful lesson behind the myth is brought before our eyes. The two most 94 famous late Hellenistic groups, the Laocoön and 93 the so-called Farnese Bull, each illustrates a famous divine punishment. The latter is connected with Pergamum by the fact that its authors, Apollonius and Tauriscus of Tralles, sons of Artemidorus, were adopted by Menecrates of Rhodes who was probably one of the most important sculptors of the Zeus altar. Moreover its subject, the loyalty of Zethus and Amphion to

their mother Antiope as demonstrated by their punishment of the wicked Dirce who had supplanted her, had already been commemorated in the shrine of Apollonis at Cyzicus. The Laocoön by Agesander, Polydorus and Athenodorus of Rhodes showed not just the preparations for vengeance, as did the Farnese Bull and the Marsyas group, but the actual punishment itself. Though a dating in the Roman Empire has recently been proposed for the present Laocoön group the stylistic correspondence with the Zeus altar at Pergamum makes it virtually certain that either it or its original dates from the second century BC. It is usually assumed that Laocoön is being made the victim of divine wrath for his attempt to warn the Trojans about the wooden horse; but even in a Roman context it is hard to see why such a scene should merit such artistic attention, while to show a good man suffering in

94 The punishment of Laocoön and his two sons. Hellenistic original by
Agesander, Polydorus and Athenodorus of Rhodes of *c*. 150 BC, or Roman adaptation.

this way because of the petty jealousies of the
gods is quite unparalleled. Instead, the serpents
should probably be thought of as being sent by
Apollo to punish his priest for his sacrilege in
marrying and begetting children, as is described
in another version of the story. This interpretation would explain both the prominence
given to Laocoön's offspring and the sensuality of
96 his face which he shares with the giants of the
Pergamum frieze. These last two groups are
associated with Rhodes rather than Pergamum,
but Menecrates is an example of an artistic link
between the two capitals, and in philosophy
Panaetius was a pupil of Crates at the Attalid
capital. Another group which may reflect this
interest in punishment is that showing the
95 destruction of the children of Niobe by Apollo
and Diana in revenge for the arrogance of their
mother. Pliny claims that the original group was a

95 Son of Niobe. Roman copy of a probably Late Hellenistic original group.

96 Face of Laocoön (detail of Pl. 94).

fourth-century work, but it is better placed in the second century. Although the Niobid group is not directly connected with Pergamum similar scenes of Apollo and Diana administering punishment had again been illustrated in the shrine of Apollonis at Cyzicus.

It would be possible to argue that the common element in all these works is not punishment but pain. However, were this so we should also expect to find similar heroic treatments of undeserved pain, where the psychological interest would be even greater. As it is, in the examples quoted all the sufferers deserve their pain, for some moral failing. The connection of pain with evil had been long established in Stoicism. The Stoic wise man was supposed not to have the basic feelings of pain, fear, desire and pleasure. These were the mark of the bad man. If a man was susceptible to any of these feelings he was susceptible to the others. One could not feel pleasure and avoid pain, have desires and not be afflicted with fear. The pain and fear on the faces and in the gestures of Marsyas, Dirce and Laocoön identified their fatal weaknesses as their enslavement to passions. In fact, the Stoics saw desire as the pursuit of what seemed, wrongly, to be good and pain as the subsequent experience of its badness.

The notion that desire is always mistaken and leads us to pain seems to be the basis of another group of Late Hellenistic works. In the group of a
61 Satyr attacking a Nymph in Rome and a similar

attack on a Hermaphrodite in Dresden the emphasis is not on the playful rejection by the object of desire but quite specifically on the pain caused by the hair-pulling in the former and on the hand thrust in the face in the latter example. In a statue of about 100 erected by a Syrian merchant in Delos it is the threat of pain rather than its realization that is important. Here the Pan 62 who is too importunate with Aphrodite is about to receive a blow from her sandal. In a less narrative and more symbolic representation of a similar theme an Old Centaur known in several 97 versions is tortured by a small figure of Eros. It is 127 notable that in all these cases the irrational surrender to emotions is associated with half-human creatures. The Greeks had traditionally identified such tendencies with animals. Marsyas was a satyr and on the Zeus altar at Pergamum the giants were given an unprecedented array of bestial attributes in order to emphasize their irrationality.

The Stoics illustrated the notion of man dominated by his feelings with the image of someone being carried away by an uncontrollable horse. Posidonius, the most important pupil of Panaetius and also long a resident of Rhodes, claimed the authority of Cleanthes for his view that there were two elements in the human psyche: *logismos* (rationality) and *thymos* (the seat of desire). The one he called noble and 'godlike' and the other inferior and 'animal-like'. This does not mean that these ideas were uniquely Stoic, or

97 Face of Old Centaur (detail of Pl. 127). Roman copy probably deriving from one of a pair of statues made in the mid-second century BC.

uniquely Late Hellenistic. They were common-places of Greek culture and had long been enshrined in myth. But it is certain that the later Stoics, with their adoption of a less theological and more pragmatic approach, mirrored contemporary interest and attitudes more closely than at any previous time, especially in their concentration on ethical problems. The historian Polybius, born in the Peloponnese about 200, admirably illustrates this last point. He claims his great universal history as a 'pragmatic' account without the rhetorical distortions of his predecessors. Nor is his intention to entertain, but rather to instruct. His main theme is the expansion of Roman power which he sees as resulting from the superior quality of Roman institutions and from the noble austerity of Roman life. Polybius' respect for Rome links him closely with Pergamene attitudes, while his compatibility with the Stoics and especially those associated with Rhodes is proved by his friendship with Panaetius when with him in Rome in 144 and also by the fact that his history was continued by Posidonius. This parallelism between Polybius and both the Pergamenes and the Stoics leads us back once again to the question of the internal relations between Pergamum and the Stoa.

Any argument that Pergamene art of the second century is influenced by Stoic thought has to take account of the fact that earlier Stoics had little interest in art in general and could have had little sympathy with the Pergamene style in particular. These objections can, however, be at least partly dealt with by understanding the direction in which Stoicism was moving at just this time. To begin with, those philosophers who, while owing a considerable debt to the Stoa, taught as individuals in cities far from Athens all enjoyed a considerable degree of freedom in relation to established dogma. But even apart from this it is possible to identify a definite tendency away from the almost theological and mystical absolutism of figures such as Chrysippus and towards a more realistic acceptance of the weaknesses of human nature. One example of this reaction is Posidonius' assertion of the duality of the human personality as outlined above. This assertion was made in vehement contradiction to Chrysippus' belief that it was possible to rid oneself of everything but the rational principle. Panaetius, whose thought is largely revealed to us in Cicero's De Officiis (On Duties), shows the same

awareness of reality. In a careful analysis of a number of precise situations he established not only what was good but what was expedient. Crates, admittedly more independent of the Stoa, even went so far in his grammatical theories as to elevate irrationality as a principle of language. He argued for the importance of 'anomaly' or irregularity and against the principle of 'analogy' or consistent regularity, which was associated particularly with the Alexandrians. The strange reversal of roles between the objective Aristotelians and the systematic Stoics arose because the Aristotelians believed that the disorderly origins of language in convention and chance needed to be subjected to civilizing principles, while the Stoics, who thought that language had originally possessed a true and logical relationship with the natural world, felt that it had been corrupted and distorted by erratic human nature, and consequently insisted that a system of grammar should take account of this. Crates' collection of linguistic abnormalities may thus be thought of as parallel to the collection of psychic and physical deviations presented by the giants of the Zeus altar at Pergamum, in which case the violent and contorted forms of the altar would not necessarily be incompatible with Stoic ideas.

It is also possible to see in contemporary Stoicism evidence that the acceptance of the weakness of human nature had produced a new interest in artistic elaboration. In Stoic writings there is certainly a shift away from dry prose. Apollodorus chose the comic iambic metre for both his historical and his geographical works, because it was more easily memorable. Panaetius too rejected the crabbed style of his predecessors and sought instead an eloquence that would be more appetizing. Such men would not automatically have looked with disfavour on the highly-wrought rhythms of the Pergamene altar frieze. Another point to be kept in mind, and one discussed in the next chapter, is the fondness for the use of verbal images which is recurrent in Stoicism and which provided its followers with a ready-made subject-matter when they turned to the use of visual art. The verbal images already mentioned, that of Zeus punishing the wicked with his thunderbolt, that of man carried away by an uncontrollable horse and that of the conflict between the god-like and the animal-like in man, all seem to have echoes in the great Gigantomachy frieze at Pergamum.

Chapter Three

Allegory, Images and Signs

Allegory

At the end of the last chapter it was noted that the Stoics used verbal images, such as that of a man being carried away by a horse, and that the Gigantomachy frieze from Pergamum may have been a real example of such a Stoic didactic image in art. Earlier, in the story of the 'Choice of Hercules', we found Prodicus using the image of two different types of women to stand for two

ways of life. A painting by one Aëtion, probably of the late fourth century, used a somewhat different imagery to turn a scene from the life of Alexander into a similar allegory of choice. The painting, described by Lucian and represented here by a Renaissance reconstruction, showed the marriage chamber of Alexander and the Persian princess, Roxane. The two figures were shown surrounded by cupids, who not only introduced the bride to her master but also were shown 98

98 Marriage chamber of Alexander and Roxane, by Giovanni Antonio Bazzi ('Il Sodoma'). Early sixteenth-century fresco. Renaissance reconstruction of a painting by Aëtion (*fl. c.* 325 BC).

playing with his armour. Lucian comments that these are not just childish amusements on which Aëtion has wasted his time. The cupids serve to indicate Alexander's passion for military activities, showing that in spite of his love for Roxane he still remembers his armour. Whether this was in fact the reason for introducing the cupids or whether, as is perhaps more likely, the latter are intended to show that love has made the great warrior take off his armour and forget it, it is clear that the painting has an allegorical as well as a descriptive level of meaning. Indeed, all these images, whether verbal or visual, are examples of allegory (*allēgoria* – 'saying something else'); that is their underlying message is saying something 'other' than seems at first sight to be intended. Although the word itself only became current in the first century, it grows out of an important tradition of Greek culture and one which flourished especially in the Hellenistic period.

Myths and the Homeric poems, the foundations of Greek civilization, often explain complex historical or astronomical facts with simple stories of divine or human relationships. These stories satisfied rather than stimulated the questioning mind. The hearer was not originally expected to look behind them and study the phenomena which they explained. Only as their excessive simplicity became apparent to the Greeks, exposed to the wisdom of the East in the seventh and sixth centuries, were attempts made by poets and philosophers to find in them deeper meanings. Already in Hesiod's *Theogony* myths about the Olympians are connected to form a skeleton of universal history. The gods become depersonalized and take on a new grandeur as representations of abstract forces. At the same time abstract forces such as Strife and Forgetfulness themselves become gods. The most frequent way in which philosophers attempted to uncover the mysteries hidden in the old stories was by the interpretation of the names of divinities. Plato has preserved several of these usually erroneous etymologies for us in the *Cratylus*. We learn that Zeus represents the principle of life (*zōē*) while Hera is connected with air (*aēr*). The idea that a word had a true (*etymos*) meaning underlying its pattern of sounds fathered the whole science of etymology. This science was developed particularly by the Stoics, and Chrysippus wrote a book about it. The Stoics used the science to show that Homer's poems supported many of their ideas. The relations which Homer described between the gods were seen by the Stoics as an allegory of the relationships between the physical elements. The principle that both language and literature had two distinct levels, the one understandable by everybody and the other only comprehensible to the wise, had thus become firmly established in the Platonic and Stoic traditions.

Parallel and related to the development of etymology and allegory was the establishment of consistent theories of language and perception. In Aristotle the process of perception is frequently broken down into two stages, first the reception of the stimulus by the sense organ and second its absorption and interpretation by the mind. The awareness of this separation led later philosophers to study in detail the operations of both the senses and the mind. A distinction of similar importance to that between sense and mind is that between noise and significant sound, also found in Aristotle and his successors. Another is the idea that the significant sound, that is language, could be analysed in terms of that which signifies (the word itself) and that which is signified (its meaning). Noise and significant sound are equal for the ear but only significant sound is of interest to the mind. A word may be received through the senses but only the mind can establish its meaning. There is much the same distinction, though at a deeper level, between the apparent form and the allegorical significance of words and stories.

One result of the discrimination between significant sound and noise was that people concerned themselves with the problem of how sounds became significant, that is with the origin of words. Aristotle and Epicurus believed that words were established by arbitrary determination (*thesis*). But this theory, which deprived words of their mystery, was not held by Plato or the Stoics. In the *Cratylus* Plato tells how words are exact imitations of the things they refer to, just as a painting is an imitation of a thing. Plato's theory encouraged the study of words as physical representations of often non-physical concepts and thus led to the idea that words could themselves represent sources of enlightenment. In the same spirit the Stoics argued that words existed by nature (*physis*) and came from God. Some of them believed too that abstract qualities, such as virtues, were physical

99 Calumny of Apelles, by Botticelli. Late fifteenth-century painting on panel. Renaissance reconstruction of a painting by Apelles of the late fourth century BC.

bodies and even living beings. At the same time as words and concepts were taking on more and more of a literally real existence, the study of the senses led to the acknowledgment of the primacy of the sense of sight. This is implicit in Plato, with his theory of knowledge based on *ideai* or 'visual forms', and explicit in Aristotle, who said that the eye is the first gate of the intellect. As part of his psychological studies, Aristotle also revealed the critical importance of the memory and the dominance there of visual impressions. 'Creatures who can learn', he said, 'are distinguished by their possession of the sense of sight and the faculty of memory.'

These developments prepare us for several of the new features of Hellenistic art. One of these is the introduction of a new sort of visual allegory. Not surprisingly, a good example is found in early Stoicism. Cleanthes used to explain the nature of Epicureanism to his pupils by asking them to imagine a painting of Pleasure dressed in a rich garment and seated on a high throne with the Virtues as her humble servants at her feet. In telling this story he reveals his interest in the visual imagination as the best learning aid as well as his belief in personifications and his fondness for an allusive and allegorical approach. His use of a painting where Plato would normally have used

a myth demonstrates the new interest in visual communication. Such an interest is manifest in almost all the traditionally verbal forms of communication at this time. In the *Rhetoric* Aristotle insisted on the importance of gesture. Theophrastus would mime an accompaniment to his philosophical discussions. In drama new and elaborately characterized masks were developed for the New Comedy.

None of these elements is completely new. The novelty lies in their sudden growth in importance. The same is true of the use of personifications. Figures such as Justice were to be seen on the stage in fifth-century Athens. From there we find them transferred to contemporary vase-paintings when figures such as Madness appear along with the usual maenads in a Dionysiac procession. But here the visual representation still clearly depends on a literary form, drama. Also the personifications are only supporting figures. It is in a very different spirit that Apelles painted his Calumny to defend himself in the eyes of Ptolemy I. There, apart from the king, who was shown with huge ears as in the reconstruction by Botticelli, all the figures are 99 personifications. Calumny, Ignorance, Suspicion and many others are all represented as men and women working on the ruler's mind. They are

100 Eirene and Ploutos, after Cephisodotus. Roman copy of an original of *c.* 370 BC.

identified by their appearance, as, for example, the sallow and ugly Jealousy who looks over his shoulder. The fact that Lucian says that Apelles' work was painted as a defence against slander suggests that it was intended as a true substitute for verbal communication. A similar type of painting must have been in Cleanthes' mind. There are contemporary examples in sculpture too. The Kairos (Opportunity) of Lysippus is known, like the Calumny, from later descriptions. The character of Opportunity was summed up by a number of attributes. The figure had hair in front but was bald behind as an expression of the fact that opportunities can only be taken if you see them coming; once passed they are lost. An earlier example from about 370 was Cephisodotus' statue of Eirene (Peace) holding in her arms the infant Ploutos (Wealth). The relationship made the point that peace produces and encourages the growth of wealth. This is a simple combination of personification and allegory and as such represents a transitional stage between the religious and philosophical uses of these devices. The connection with the religious past is seen in the fact that the statue was probably the cult image for the newly introduced worship of Eirene. It thus fitted into a long tradition of divine images. On the other hand, it was connected with philosophical developments in that it reflected the new interest in concepts and abstractions and in the study of their relationships.

It was suggested earlier that the use of personifications and allegory in literature grew out of the attempts to interpret the ancient myths, especially by the application of etymology to the names of the Olympians. The connection between these streams in Greek culture is demonstrated for the visual arts by a Hellenistic epigram on an archaic statue of Apollo. The poet Callimachus, librarian at Alexandria around 250, provides the visual equivalent of an etymology of the statue. The god, he says, has the bow in his left hand because he is slow to chastise, while the Graces stand in his right hand because he is disposed to distribute pleasant things. Callimachus' interpretation with its Stoic associations is as unwarranted as the association of Hera with *aēr* and it springs from the same spirit. Unwarranted interpretations were not reserved for ancient statues. Perhaps not long after Alexander's death someone wrote an epigram on a statue of him by

Lysippus which gratuitously interpreted the statue's upward looking pose as expressing the thought of Alexander that Zeus should rule the heavens and he the earth.

It is clear from these last two epigrams that an interest in allegory focused attention not on form and technique but on attributes and pose. The development of personification had the same effect. This can be observed in works such as the 101 Tyche (Fortune) of Antioch carved by Eutychides in the early third century. Antioch was the city founded on the river Orontes by Seleucus, one of Alexander's generals, as capital of his kingdom in Asia Minor and the Levant. Accordingly the sculpture represented a woman, the Fortune of the city, seated on a rock past which flowed a watery mass out of which emerged a swimming figure, the river. The woman was identified as the spirit of a city by the crown in the form of a city wall upon her head. She probably held in her hand some emblem of prosperity such as the corn found in Roman copies. The two figures are identified by their attributes as respectively a city and a river. Their poses and relationship explain that the one is situated on the banks of the other. The spectator is expected to go through the same processes as did the writers of the epigrams mentioned above. He is expected to identify the personifications and interpret the allegory of their relationship. In the case of the statue of Eirene and Ploutos the relationship was causal. Here the relationship is primarily spatial. Later there are good examples of temporal relationships.

One such temporal relationship can be observed in a description, preserved by Athenaeus, of a Dionysiac procession organized for Ptolemy II in Alexandria. The procession apparently opened at dawn with a figure of the Morning Star and closed as night fell with a figure of the Evening Star. During the day itself the procession presented to the spectator figures of the Four Seasons bearing their appropriate fruits, of the Year and of the Five Year Cycle, the interval at which the festival occurred (every four years by our reckoning). This contemplation of extending time scales prepared the audience for the most important part of the procession which was devoted to Dionysus. Different scenes from his life were shown. After the nuptial chamber where his parents, Zeus and Semele, slept together came the cave where he was nursed, his triumphal return from India and

101 Tyche of Antioch, after Eutychides. Roman copy of an original of *c.* 295 BC.

102 Roman relief showing Dionysus with Spring, Summer and Autumn. Probably adaptation of an original of *c.* 200 BC.

his flight to the altar of Rhea. Thereafter came Alexander and Ptolemy I wearing gold crowns of ivy leaves. It is possible that the Four Seasons, the Five Year Cycle and the four Dionysiac scenes are all intended as allegories of the cycle of beginning, growth, maturity and decline which was essential to the Dionysiac cult. Dionysus and the Seasons were often shown together. Such an implication that natural, ritual and mythical realities are all embodiments of the same truth could easily be paralleled in Stoic thought. Whether or not this is the case here, it is certain that an assimilation is intended between mythical and historical reality. First Alexander and then Ptolemy had taken on the Dionysiac role of Saviour. Ptolemy II, whose glorification is the real purpose of the festival, would thus be the fourth in line to the god himself. This religious and political meaning is purposely left at an implicit level where it has the most mystery. But at other levels the procession seeks to communicate as explicitly as possible. Great emphasis is laid in the description on the use of visual communication. The Seasons are identified by their fruits and the gods by their associated attributes. Ptolemy Soter's qualities are pointed out by the figure of Virtue standing close beside him. The historical fact that he was first acknowledged as a god by the league of Corinth is indicated by the figure of Corinth who places on his head a golden crown. Many similar personifications of places were developed at this time. Thus on a second-century frieze from Asia Minor the figure of Rome appears alongside those of local cities.

Ptolemy II's procession shows us how far visual communication had come and how art could compete with words. It is interesting that this new development away from the earlier use of statues as icons, or images, of gods and heroes requires that these images have to accept modification, just as a word must be capable of inflection. Gesture and attribute modify the basic form, just as tense or case-ending modify verb or noun. The need to put over a particular meaning stimulated the development of new 'inflections', as with the Kairos of Lysippus who was shown running with his feet barely touching the ground because he was so difficult to catch. Eutychides went to great lengths to make clear that Antioch was seated by a river, so he not only showed the figure under her feet as swimming but also made the surrounding material as water-like as possible. In fact he was famous for making his personifications of river gods really embody the element they represented: 'He made bronze wetter than water.' The use of art as a visual equivalent of verbal language thus stimulates stylistic development. The latter consists partly in an increase in naturalism, but it is important to realize how this type of naturalism, which may be called naturalism for the sake of clarity of expression, differs from the other streams of naturalism in Greek art. The increasing naturalism of the sixth and fifth centuries, for example, was largely motivated by a desire to make gods and heroes more real, their physical potencies more explicit; in these earlier works the development of naturalism is measured mainly by the revelation of the physical complexity of the human body. Another type of naturalism, found

103 Detail of frieze from the temple of Hecate, Lagina, showing the personifications of Rome and various local Carian cities, *c.* 100 BC.

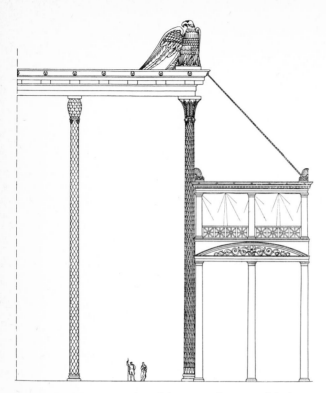

104 Reconstruction of the symposium tent of Ptolemy II, *c.* 275–270 BC.

105 Wall-painting from the House of Obellius Firmus, Pompeii, first century BC.

especially in the art of the fourth century and later, can be related to Aristotle's notion that art is imitation and that man moreover likes imitation for itself whatever the subject. This type of naturalism produces a general correspondence with nature in all aspects of art and particularly an application of skills learned previously in the representation of gods and heroes not only to lower physical types, women, old men and beggars, but also to animals and vegetation. The type of naturalism that concerns us here is much more selective. In search of new poses and attributes artists are forced to study new actions and objects. But this naturalism is inherently less long-lasting than the other types because once the essential character of a pose or attribute has been grasped for identification purposes representations of it can be reduced to a summary, as happened in Roman art which had a high informative content.

The growth of these three main types of naturalism can be studied clearly in the field of architectural sculpture. In the sixth and fifth centuries it is only in figure decorations that a development of naturalism is to be found. Sculpture derived from oriental vegetable forms became, if anything, more abstract, as can be observed by comparing the clear leaf mouldings of sixth-century Ionic with the dry egg and dart pattern this had become by the fifth century. It is only in the late fifth and fourth centuries that brilliantly accurate acanthus leaves and stems start to appear on acroteria, cornices and most prominently on the new Corinthian capital. The extension of naturalism as a result of the use of personification and allegory can be seen somewhat vaguely at first in the Caryatids of Delphi and Athens and more precisely in the Atlas figures supporting the roof of the early fifth-century temple of Olympian Zeus at Acragas. These presumably relate the temple to the mythical home of Zeus in the heavens, traditionally supported by Atlas. Figures of Persians were also introduced to support roofs and, whether this feature appeared first in fifth-century Sparta or in the tent of Alexander, the pose of the figures was intended to express the role of the Persians as slaves rather than as masters of the Greeks. In the Hellenistic period columns were even replaced with vegetable forms for symbolic reasons, as in the symposium tent of 104 Ptolemy II which had corner columns in the form of palm-trees and the rest in the form of *thyrsoi*, or Dionysiac wands, twined with ivy and crowned with pine cones. Here passive architectural forms become actively appropriate to the building's function as the site of feasts in honour of Dionysus. The columns of this tent were of wood, and so temporary, but as in other periods the transition from temporary to permanent materials was not difficult. The branches, flowers and shields, which were all used to provide an appropriate decoration for the tent, appear carved in stone on the altars, friezes and parapets of second-century Pergamum. Other ornaments such as animal hides, tripods and the palm 105 columns all appear in Roman wall-paintings. The tent of Ptolemy II thus represents an essential stage in the development of expressively appropriate architectural environments. Architecture and interior decoration had been greatly enriched by the introduction of symbolic and associative elements.

A form of imagery closely related to that of the Ptolemaic festival is found in a relief from Italy in

106 Homer crowned by Time and the World (detail of Pl. 107).

the British Museum signed by Archelaos of Priene. It is dateable to the late second century. In 107 the lowest of the three main bands of the relief a sacrifice takes place before a statue of a seated man. He is Homer. On either side of his throne are crouching figures identified by inscriptions as *Iliad* and *Odyssey*. The poet is being crowned by two figures labelled Time and the World. This 106 tells us that Homer's achievement is recognized at many periods and in many places. But the fact that these last figures have the facial traits of Ptolemy IV and his wife Arsinoë also refers to the fact that it was that monarch who by founding the Homereion had first established an official cult of the poet. The range of Homer's influence in the history of literature is also revealed by the figures who perform the sacrifice: Myth, History, Poiesis (probably non-dramatic Poetry), Tragedy and Comedy. A group of four other figures who attend more passively probably refer to the qualities of the Homeric poems. Physis (Nature) acknowledges their conformity to nature, Arete (Virtue) their moral tone, Mneme (Memory) their

memorability, Pistis (Trust) their credibility and Sophia (Cleverness) their technical excellence. The artist has thus been able, by the careful deployment of numerous figures, to list Homer's major works and to describe his position in literary history and criticism. Whether this scheme is wholly or partly the invention of Archelaos is unclear. It could derive from some festival tableau or permanent work of art associated with the Homereion. Certainly other works actually in the shrine used visual images in a similar way. In one of these the statue of the poet himself was surrounded by other statues of the different cities that claimed him as their own. A painting by one Galaton attempted to stress Homer's authority by showing him as a river god with water flowing from his mouth only to be collected in jugs by other poets. Yet Archelaos' relief is much more sophisticated in its imagery than these other works. It not only uses gesture and attribute, as we have seen, but also makes clever play with grouping. Myth and History, for example, are separated from the other literary forms by being most actively involved in the sacrifice because they are more essential elements in Homer's work. It is not only the visual language that is developed but the underlying thought. The relief tells us that criticism had established a poetic œuvre, that the question of the influence of epic on other literary forms was being considered and that a number of critical standards had been established for the evaluation of a work of art. Dualistic concepts such as space and time, and myth and history, which remain to this day essential to the classification of experience, can already be seen here providing a firm structure to Hellenistic thought.

The process by which the integration of thought and image revealed in the Archelaos relief was arrived at can best be studied in the Greek treatment of the Muses. In Homer the Muses are goddesses who are responsible for music on Olympus and who also inspire earthly bards. In Hesiod they are nine and have individual names such as Kalliope (beautiful face) and Terpsichore (joy of the dance). When we see them in pre-Hellenistic art they are sometimes three and sometimes nine, sometimes dancing, sometimes playing instruments. Then in the Hellenistic world, as scholars set about classifying the Greek cultural heritage and plumbing the mysteries of mythology, the names of the Muses

were interpreted as carrying associations with different literary and musical forms. Terpsichore became understandably the Muse of dancing, Thalia (festivity) was justifiably associated with comedy, but Melpomene (songstress) was much more arbitrarily linked with tragedy. This process may well have occurred in the early third century. The presence of statues of Tragedy, Comedy, Dithyramb and Nykterinos in a shrine by the theatre at Thasos erected about this time 165 shows that there was certainly a tendency towards the monumental personification of such genres. The earliest near concrete evidence of an association of the Muses with different genres is provided by Pliny who tells us that the Muses were shown identified by their separate attributes on a ring owned by Pyrrhus (319–272). But the earliest certain document of a developed characterization of the Muses is on the Archelaos relief described above. There in the two bands 107 above the scene already discussed the nine Muses are seen sitting, standing, dancing and playing around Apollo. Each has her appropriate attribute, large lyre, small lyre, flute, scroll or globe. It is clear that the personality of each Muse was now firmly established, and the existence of Roman statues related to these types suggests that they had already been portrayed in monumental form. Allusions in the writings of Callimachus and Apollonius Rhodius show that their personalities were at least partially recognized in the literary world of third-century Alexandria. It was certainly in Alexandria that the work of classification was most ardently pursued, the method of etymology most enthusiastically applied and the use of allegorical personifications most fully developed.

Word and Image

One of the most striking features of the Archelaos relief is the use of inscribed names to identify many of the figures depicted on the relief. Although such inscriptions were not unusual on Greek vases there is little evidence that they were used in monumental painting or sculpture. It is possible that they were sometimes painted on reliefs that are now bare, but as the dedicatory inscriptions often associated with such reliefs were usually carved this does not seem very likely. Another notable feature of the Archelaos relief is the fact that it is not every figure that is

107 Relief showing the apotheosis of Homer, signed by Archelaos of Priene, c. 150 BC.

108 Drawing of a relief from a clay cup of *c*. 200 BC illustrating scenes from Euripides' *Iphigenia in Aulis*.

identified, but only those whose identity is not clear from their forms and attributes, that is the personifications in the lowest band of the relief and not the traditional deities represented in the higher bands. The names are thus used to clarify the process of communication, making it more analogous in character to a verbal message. It is hardly surprising that the growing use of the representational arts as a means of communication equivalent to the spoken or written word also encouraged the use of image and word alongside each other. Plato had prepared the way for this development when he claimed that both word and image should convey the essential qualities of the underlying idea.

It has been suggested that the Archelaos relief actually represents pictorially the content of a poem. This is certainly the case with the much smaller pottery cups mostly of second century date and probably based on silver models which show scenes from works such as the *Iliad* or 108 Euripidean dramas. In order to make the often very complicated and not very dramatic scenes clearly identifiable, inscriptions are added which give the names of the figures and often a summary of the plot too. The inscriptions are evidently intended to enable the series of representational images to become a self-sufficient alternative to the poetic narrative. On a larger scale letters are also used to identify figures on the great frieze of the Zeus altar at Pergamum. The overall subject of the frieze, the battle between the gods and giants, would be recognizable without any inscription. The value of the inscriptions is rather that they add greatly to the interest of the composition by surrounding each individual figure with a wealth of associations. Indeed they create an entirely new relationship between the reliefs and the spectator. Whereas earlier temple friezes and metopes would only remind the spectator of a well-known event and enable him to recognize what he already knew, the great frieze at Pergamum could be read, when all the inscriptions were complete, and would communicate previously unknown information. The necessity of legibility implied by this attitude was satisfied on the Zeus altar by adding an unusual concave element under the Ionic cornice that crowned the frieze, on which letters two or three inches high could be set. The spectator whose eye would be roughly on a line bisecting at right angles the chord of the concave arc was thus perfectly placed to read them. From the same period dates the shrine put up at Cyzicus by Eumenes II and his brother, the later Attalus II, to honour their mother. The reliefs illustrating examples of filial loyalty, even including the unfamiliar Italians, Romulus and Remus, would have been largely meaningless to visitors without the epigrams which accompanied each of them. In both these cases the lettering may, as was suggested in the last chapter, form part of a Stoic didactic programme.

An example of how lettering on an even bigger scale could be used at this time is provided by the inscription on the entry porch of the precinct of Athena at Pergamum, also erected by Eumenes II. 109 On the lower architrave of the two-storey gateway large letters declared *BASILEUS EUMENĒS ATHĒNAI NIKĒPHORŌI* (King

Eumenes to Athena Bringer of Victory). This inscription turned what would otherwise have been just a rich entrance to a temple into an articulate communication. The gate became a symbol of thanksgiving for the victory over the Gauls accorded to Eumenes by Athena, protectress of the city. The further decoration of the parapet of the upper portico with reliefs of arms and armour served to emphasize this function. Earlier rulers had put their names on buildings to which they had contributed, as had Croesus with the Artemisium of Ephesus or Alexander with the temple of Athena at Priene. Such inscriptions, however, were small and difficult to find. It had also long been a tradition to dedicate one's own or one's enemy's armour in a temple, but these would never have been thought of as part of the building itself. The prominence of the inscription and the permanence of the attributes on Eumenes' gateway reveal a new attitude in the builder and impose a new response on the spectator. This is not a pre-existing building to which a ruler has contributed and in which he has dedicated his thank-offering. It is itself his offering and his prayer of thanks. For all who approach it, it is a permanent commemoration of a ritual act. The Propylaea in Athens had been erected in a similar spirit 250 years earlier, but in this case the simple need for a new and elaborate gateway to replace one destroyed by the Persians was the predominant influence upon its form. There was no message to be read on its architrave or metopes. To the approaching visitor it was simply the richest gateway in Greece as was appropriate in the richest city. Art had changed much by the second century when a relief could be a piece of literary criticism, a cup a poem, or a building a prayer.

The development of art as a method of communication resulted, as we have seen, in a new acknowledgment of the needs of the spectator. This was apparent not only in the extended use of inscriptions but also in the care taken to place them in a visible position and to make them large enough to be read at the distance from which they would be seen. It is appropriate that there should have been a new emphasis too on the source and on the vehicle of the communication. As a result both artist and patron may emerge into positions of prominence. On the Archelaos relief the name of the artist appears in large letters in the centre under the throne of Zeus. Because of

109 Propylon of the temple of Athena Polias, Pergamum, c. 170 BC.

110 Artist's signature on a mosaic from the palace at Pergamum, c. 200 BC (see also Pl. 136).

Κωτίλας

τῇ τόδ' ἄτριον νέον

πρόφρων δὲ θυμῷ δέξο· δὴ γὰρ ἁγνᾶς

τὸ μὲν θεᾶν ἐριβόας Ἑρμᾶς ἔκιξε κᾱρυξ

ἄνωγε δ' ἐκ μέτρου μονοβάμονος μέγαν πάροιθ' ἀέξειν

θοᾶς δ' ὕπερθεν ὦκα λέχριον φέρων νεῦμα ποδῶν σποράδων πίφαυσκεν

θοαῖς ἴσ' αἰόλαις νεβροῖς κῶλ' ἀλλάσσων ὀρσιπόδων ἐλάφων τέκεσσιν

πᾶσαι κραιπνοῖς ὑπὲρ ἄκρων ἱέμεναι ποσὶ λόφων κατ' ἀρθμίας ἴχνος τιθήνας

καί τις ὠμόθυμος ἀμφίπαλτον αἶψ' αὐδὰν θὴρ ἐν κόλπῳ δεξάμενος θαλαμᾶν μυχοιτάτῳ

κᾆτ' ὦκα βοᾶς ἀκοὰν μεθέπων, ὕγ' ἄφαρ λάσιον νιφοβόλων ἀν' ὀρέων ἔσσυται ἄγκος

ταῖσι δὴ δαίμων κλυτᾶς ἴσα θοοῖς δονέων ποσὶ πολύπλοκα μετίει μέτρα μολπᾶς

ῥίμφα πετρόκοιτον ἐκλιπὼν ὄρουσ' εἰνάν, ματρὸς πλαγκτὸν μαιόμενος βαλίας ἑλεῖν τέκος

βλαχαὶ δ' οἴων πολυβότων ἀν' ὀρέων νομὸν ἔβαν τανυσφύρων ἐς ἀν' ἄντρα Νυμφῶν

ταὶ δ' ἀμβρότῳ πόθῳ φίλας ματρὸς ῥώοντ' αἶψα μεθ' ἱμερόεντα μαζὸν

ἴχνει θένων . . ταν παναίολον Πιερίδων μονόδουπον αὐδὰν

ἀριθμὸν εἰς ἄκραν δεκάδ' ἰχνίων κόσμον νέμοντα ῥυθμῶν

φῦλ' ἐς βροτῶν, ὑπὸ φίλας ἑλὼν πτεροῖσι ματρύς

λίγειά μιν κάμ' ἶφι ματρὸς ὠδίς

Δωρίας ἀηδόνος

ματέρος.

111 *The Egg*, by Simias.

the shape of the relief, this position corresponds almost exactly with that of an architrave under a pediment and is thus closely related to the site of the inscription on the Pergamum gateway, where the name of the patron, Eumenes, features so strikingly. How far this contrasts with the situation in fifth-century Athens is revealed by the fact that both the political career of Pericles and the artistic career of Phidias were supposed to have been severely damaged by Phidias' placing of portraits of Pericles and himself on the shield of the great statue of Athena Parthenos. Such an assertion of personal importance by the two men was quite unacceptable to their fellow-citizens who regarded them simply as politician and craftsman respectively. By the second century, on the other hand, the authority of artist and ruler was firmly established.

Writers and Images

The realization of an essential equivalence between word and image did not only result in an extension of the activity of the artist. Writers too were influenced by the development. One of the most striking examples of this can be seen in the exploitation of the epigram as a commentary on or even as a translation of the work of art. Examples of such epigrams have already been mentioned, gratuitous in the case of the epigram on the Apollo from Delos and valid in the case of the epigram on the Kairos of Lysippus. Sometimes, as probably in the case of the Attalid shrine at Cyzicus, the verbal commentary was contemporary with the representational image.

In all these cases, however, the image is primary and it is thus not surprising that some poets reasserted their independence of the visual artists. They did this by turning the poem itself into an image. Instead of the lines of a poem being all the same length, or varied only according to the demands of the metre, they were made shorter or longer in order to compose, as a whole, a silhouette corresponding to the subject of the poem. The poem thus becomes an epigram on itself. None of the poems of this type is securely dated, either because there is doubt about the ascription, as in the case of the *Pipes of Theocritus*, or because the poets are otherwise virtually unknown, as in the case of works by Simias and Dosiadas. Only one passing reference suggests that Simias, who was the chief writer in the genre, worked early in the third century. One of his poems, which has the shape of the *Wings of Eros*, may have been inscribed on that part of a statue, but in the other two examples of poems by him this seems unlikely. The simpler of these is in the shape of a *Double Axe* and purports to be inscribed on one of the most famous of such weapons, that with which Aegistheus killed Agamemnon. In fact, as in the case of the *Wings of Eros*, the subject is never explicitly given. A series of obscure references serve as clues and the answer to the riddle is only obtained when the

form made by the poem as a whole is seen to be significant. A further obstacle to an immediate understanding of the *Axe* poem was that the lines could not be read consecutively, as was normal, but in the order 1, 20, 2, 19, etc. This is also the case with Simias' most sophisticated work which has the shape of an egg. The egg in question turns 111 out to be that of a nightingale, and as the nightingale is the poet among the birds, the poem is also the egg of the poet. The poem well reveals the Hellenistic poet's love of metaphor, allegory and symbolism.

Another poem rich in complexity and difficult to date is one that claims to be written by Theocritus as an inscription on a set of pipes which he dedicated to Pan. The poem is also of 112 twenty lines, but is arranged as a series of ten pairs, the first, of ten metrical feet, and the last, of one. The form of the poem thus corresponds to that of a set of pipes with a sloping side. This is one of the problems of the poem. For the Greek syrinx was rectangular in outline and only in the 63 Roman world is the sloping form documented. But as the variation in the length of pipes was the same in both (the reeds in the Greek version being made effectively shorter by being filled with wax, while those in the Roman type were actually

112 *The Pipes of Theocritus.*

Οὐδενὸς εὐνάτειρα, Μακροπτολέμοιο δὲ μάτηρ,
μαίας ἀντιπέτροιο θοὸν τέκεν ἰθυντῆρα,
οὐχὶ Κεράσταν, ὅν ποτ' ἐθρέψατο ταυροπάτωρ,
ἀλλ' οὗ πιλιπὲς αἶθε πάρος φρένα τέρμα σάκους,
οὔνομ' ὅλον, δίζων, ὃς τᾶς Μέροπος πόθον
κούρας γηρυγόνας ἔχε τᾶς ἀνεμώδεος·
ὃς Μοίσᾳ λιγὺ πᾶξεν ἰοστεφάνῳ
ἕλκος, ἄγαλμα πόθοιο πυρισμαράγῳ·
ὃς σβέσεν ἀνορέαν ἰσαυδέα
παπποφόνου Τυρίαν τ' . . .,
ᾧ τόδε τυφλοφόρων ἐρατὸν
πᾶμα Πάρις θέτο Σιμιχίδας.
ψυχάν, ἃ βοτοβάμων,
στήτας οἶστρε Σαέττας,
κλωποπάτωρ, ἀπάτωρ,
λαρνακόγυιε, χαρείς
ἁδὺ μελίσδοις
ἔλλοπι κούρᾳ,
Καλλιόπᾳ,
νηλεύστῳ.

cut off) it has been argued that the poem could still be applied to the Greek syrinx. The question of dating must, then, remain open. The interest of the poem for us lies in the further expansion of the range of written poetry. For the poem has properties that are not only pictorial, like others of the genre, but also musical. Just as in the instrument itself the decreasing length of the pipes was the expression of an ascending musical scale, so too in the poem the regularly decreasing length of the lines was probably thought of as giving the poem musical qualities. This may seem far-fetched to us but in the Hellenistic period we know that attempts were made to give musical properties both to drinks and to whole meals by using musical proportions to determine the relationships between ingredients. A drink could be tuned to the octave with a half and half admixture of water to the wine and could be accompanied by dishes of more complex harmony.

The wings, the axe, the egg and the pipes are all small-scale objects on which, because of their character, it would have been just possible to set an inscription of corresponding form. The *Altar*
113 of Dosiadas, which is written in the same enigmatic spirit as the *Pipes of Theocritus*, is an expansion of the genre not only in terms of scale to something of considerable mass, but also in that the object which is the subject of the poem could no longer provide a flat surface or a shape suitable to receive an inscription. For the outline of the *Altar* poem corresponds not only to the block of the altar itself with its flat upper surface but also to the projecting cornice mouldings and base mouldings. The poem can thus no longer claim to be an inscription on an object; it becomes the object itself. In these epigrams poets were striving for a new compression and mystery. Apparently they felt that these two goals could best be achieved by taking a lesson from the visual arts, that is by turning their poems into images. There was, however, an even more direct way in which words could be translated into a visual language.

Images as Words

In no situation did image and word enjoy such equality as on the tombstone. Free-standing sculpture, reliefs, paintings and inscriptions had long been used together in different combinations on graves. Consequently it was natural with the development of the verse epitaph as a literary form that the writer should refer not only to the dead man but also to the figured decoration of his tomb. In the case of poems of this type which survive in the *Greek Anthology* it is often impossible to know whether they really were inscribed on tombs or whether they were just written as literary exercises. One epigram, supposedly by the fifth-century poet Simonides, comments on the lion carved on a tomb that it is a brave beast just as the inhabitant of the tomb was a brave man. The Simonides epitaph may even have been composed for the tomb of Leonidas, defender of Thermopylae, in which case there is an implication that the animal was chosen to allude to his name as well as to his virtue (Gr. *leōn* = lion). This is explicitly the case in an imitation of the Simonides epitaph by Callimachus: 'Never unless Leon had my courage and name would I have set foot on this tomb.' Even if these examples are both epitaphs we should not accept them as providing the reason for the presence of the lion on the tomb. Lions were conventional tomb decorations, probably for apotropaic reasons. But two epigrams of another early Hellenistic writer, Leonidas of Tarentum, refer to less usual ornaments. One of them points out the significance 'evident to all' of the wine cup that crowns the tomb of the aged female drinker Maronis. The other tries to explain the presence on a tombstone of a carving of a particular throw of the dice which was called 'Chian' and which also was the worst throw one could make. After considering and dismissing the possible explanations that the dead man could have been a Chian or that he was just unlucky, Leonidas concludes that the real message is that he died from drinking too much Chian wine. Whether or not there ever was such a tombstone, it is clear that Leonidas at least conceived of the possibility that information could be conveyed in such a context by the use of enigmatic images. From what we have seen so far there were three main ways of reading such an image. One was to translate it simply into the phonetic value of its name (as in Callimachus' *leōn*, animal = Leon). Another was to take its literal meaning (Leonidas' Chian = of Chios). Yet another was to select the major attribute of the object represented (lion = brave) and apply that to the person.

The hints which we find in the third century that a language of images could be formed on this

Εἰμάρσενός με στήτας
πόσις, μέροψ δίσαβος,
τεῦξ', οὐ σποδεύνας, ἶνις ἐμπούσας, μόρος
Τεύκροιο βοῦτα καὶ κυνὸς τεκνώματος,
Χρύσας δ' ἀΐτας, ἆμος ἐψάνδρα
τὸν γυιόχαλκον οὖρον ἔρραισεν,
ὃν ὠπάτωρ δίσευνος
μόρησε ματρόρριπτος.
ἐμὸν δὲ τεῦγμ' ἀθρήσας
Θεοκρίτοιο κτάντας,
Τριεσπέροιο καύτας,
θώϋξεν †ἀνιύξας
χάλεψε γάρ νιν ἰῷ
σύργαστρος ἐκδὺς γῆρας.
τὸν δ' †ἀεὶ λινεῦντ' ἐν ἀμφικλύστῳ
Πανός τε ματρὸς εὐνέτας, φὼρ
δίζωος, ἶνίς τ' ἀνδροβρῶτος ἰλιοραιστᾶν
ἦρ' ἀρδίων ἐς Τευκρίδ' ἄγαγον τρίπορθον.

113 *The Altar*, by Dosiadas.

basis are followed up enthusiastically in the second century, especially by Antipater of Sidon. His dependence on his predecessors' attempts at interpreting single images is revealed by his incorporation of their 'vocabulary' in his own accounts of a whole series of such images. In one epigram, for example, Antipater describes a tombstone which has no inscription but only a series of dice. The last throw represented is again that called Chian, but there are two others called Alexander and Youth respectively. The whole is firmly interpreted as telling that one Alexander from Chios died in his youth. This is not so clearly a real epitaph as are other poems by Antipater. In one of these the dead woman, Bittis, herself explains the five images on her tomb. The jay tells she was talkative, the cup that she liked drinking, the bow that she came from Crete (famous for its bows), the wool that she worked well, and the snood that she wore her hair up because it was grey. In other poems Antipater uses many more images. Reins, a horse's muzzle and a bird from Tanagra are used in one; a whip, an owl, a bow again, a goose and a swift bitch in another. As we might infer from his enthusiastic employment of these devices, Antipater is quite clear that images can actually be used like language. In one poem, for example, he says that the images 'bear a message' and that the designer of the tombstone has told about the dead man through 'voiceless' dice. The word he uses to describe more precisely the relationship between the image and the concept it represents is *symbolon* (tally, token, sign). In one epitaph a lion is called *symbolon halkēs* (token of bravery).

Such images are also called *symbola* by Meleager who wrote two epigrams of the same genre about 100. The first of these is an imaginary epitaph on Antipater and the second is an epitaph on himself. Both are rather enigmatic. The epitaph on Antipater describes a very compressed image, a cock with a sceptre under its wing and a palm branch in its claw. After a futile attempt at trying to interpret the sceptre as a royal attribute and rejecting the idea because the tomb is too simple, Meleager decides that the cock means that the man made himself heard, was an expert in love and an accomplished singer, the sceptre reveals his interest in words (messengers carried them), and the palm shows that he came from Tyre which was celebrated for that tree. Fortunately Antipater's name is inscribed beside the symbols. In Meleager's epitaph on himself, however, which deals with a winged figure carrying a spear and a bear skin, not only Meleager's attributes but also his name have to be extracted from the symbols. The puzzle is solved at the end of the epitaph when the whole is seen to represent the great hunter of old also called Meleager. This discovery of the final solution to the riddle by looking at the image as a whole after studying its details for clues is analogous to the recognition of the significance of the total shape of the picture-poems after accumulating hints in the individual lines.

Another type of enigmatic tomb carving which conceals the name of the dead person is referred to in a poem by Alcaeus of Messene probably from the early second century. The tomb only has two Greek letter *phis* inscribed on it. Alcaeus first tries to add the numerical value of the letters together and gets the unacceptable name Chilias (*phi* = 500; therefore two *phis* = a thousand, Gr. *chilias*). He then tries using phonetic instead of numerical values and gets Phidis (*phi* twice = Gr. *phi dis*). This solution he proudly approves and he praises the tomb-designer for making an enigma which was 'a light to the intelligent and darkness to the unintelligent'. There could hardly be a better example of the Hellenistic fondness for mystery and compression than these two letters.

Fortunately evidence exists that the device used in these poems was not isolated from the world in a narrow literary tradition. Examples of such epitaphs have been found on real tomb-stones. One of a girl called Menophila from Sardis, quite possibly also from the second century, has a relief with a lily, a Greek *alpha*, a scroll, a basket and a wreath. The accompanying verse provides explanations in the spirit of Antipater and Alcaeus. The scroll, for example, tells that the dead girl was wise and the *alpha*, the symbol for the number one, tells that she was an only child.

It would be possible to regard these last poems as being just a typical manifestation of the Hellenistic fondness for allusiveness and obscurity. But we would then be no further toward knowing either why the Hellenistic Greeks were so fond of such qualities or why they evolved this particular manifestation to express them. The essential characteristic of these poems is their reference to a system of written communication relying not on an alphabet but on the use of representations of men, animals, plants and other objects. There had long existed just such a system, the hieroglyphics of Egypt. For three thousand years the Egyptian priests had recorded their wisdom with the aid of ideograms. These

began just as pictures of the objects referred to. But as such they could only be used to transcribe a limited and materialistic vocabulary. In order to give the script the possibility of reproducing more of the complexities of normal speech, two main devices were used. First, the ideogram for an object could be used for more or less abstract words associated with that object; the picture of a sail could thus mean not only sail' but also 'skipper', 'wind' or even 'breath'. The second and much more sophisticated device was that of using the ideograms not for the word presented but for the sound value of that word; for example, the ideogram for 'nfr', our consonantal value for the Egyptian word for 'good', 'beautiful', could also be used for another word, or part of a word, where these consonants recurred. This double system of the Egyptians is not dissimilar to that of the Hellenistic epitaphs. The use of a sail for 'wind' is parallel to the use of a scroll for 'wisdom'. The use of the number two just for the sound 'dis' is like the Egyptian use of 'nfr', 'beautiful', just for that sound pattern. It is, moreover, particularly the late developments in the use of Egyptian hieroglyphics which resemble the pictorial 'script' of the Hellenistic epitaphs. From the sixth century onwards, and especially in the Hellenistic period, hieroglyphs were developed into a new and more enigmatic language, possibly in order to preserve their mystery from the Persian and Greek rulers who successively dominated Egypt after the collapse of the Saite dynasty. This was done in several ways. The name Montuhemat, for example, could be presented not by a series of ancient hieroglyphs but by a hieroglyph-like picture of Montu holding a sail, because in Egyptian 'Montu holding a sail' sounds like Montuhemat. Hieroglyph symbols for objects could also be used almost alphabetically, just for the value of the first sound of the object's name. Further, instead of using the old hieroglyphic transcription of the word for 'swim', the scribes invented a new allegorical picture of a man swimming. In other words they strengthened just those elements of pictorial allegory and ambiguous enigma which were so important in the Hellenistic epitaphs.

The Greeks in Egypt were certainly interested in hieroglyphs. They frequently commissioned inscriptions in the hieroglyphic script and Manetho, an Egyptian priest, had written several books in Greek on Egyptian culture and history

114

for Ptolemy I. We know too from the writings of Diodorus and Plutarch that it was particularly the pictorial, allegorical and enigmatic character of late hieroglyphic texts which fascinated the Greeks. Diodorus tells how a picture of a hawk represents the concept of swiftness because that is the property of that bird. Plutarch says that it was specifically the 'symbolic', 'mysterious' and 'enigmatic' quality of the hieroglyphs that had impressed Pythagoras centuries earlier. He even gives an example of a carved Egyptian picture-text from Sais. This showed a child, an old man, a hawk, a fish and finally a hippopotamus, and should be translated 'O you who are coming into being and you who are fading away, God hates shamelessness'. The translation is explained in detail. We are told that a child symbolizes birth and so on. The whole passage sounds exactly like one of our Hellenistic epitaphs.

But why do the real or imaginary examples of Hellenistic 'hieroglyphics' occur only in sepulchral contexts? The reason presumably lies in their funerary associations. The traditional inventor of hieroglyphics was the Egyptian god Thoth or Theuth, who was also celebrated for his part in bringing the murdered Osiris back to life. This achievement was due to the power of his magic incantations to control nature. In art Theuth frequently appeared in charge of the weighing of souls. For both these reasons he became identified for the Greeks with their Hermes, who not only controlled the traffic between the Upper and Lower worlds but also rescued Dionysus, the Greek equivalent of Osiris, from the flames which threatened to destroy him at birth. Theuth appears repeatedly in Plato where he is attributed with the invention not only of writing but also, among other things, of the dice which also played a part in our epitaphs. Early Greek interest in the Osiris legend is documented by Plutarch who tells that Pythagoras, Plato and Chrysippus all successively regarded Osiris as a demi-god. In the Hellenistic period, with the creation under the Ptolemies of a new divinity, Serapis, by the fusion of aspects of the Greek Dionysus and Pluto with the Egyptian Osiris, Egyptian authority on problems of the after-life achieved a new prestige. The cult of Serapis spread rapidly together with that of Isis all over the Hellenistic world. In no place was Egyptian authority so likely to be readily received as in ancient Phoenicia. It was there that

114 Funeral stele of Menophila, from Sardis, second century BC.

the body of the dead Osiris had been borne by the Mediterranean current and it was from the king of that area that Isis had recovered it. In the late second millennium Egyptian political and artistic influence had been dominant in Phoenicia, especially at Byblos. A new wave of Egyptian influence on Phoenician sepulchral art is seen in the series of Egyptian-style sarcophagi from Sidon dating from the fifth and fourth centuries. Antipater of Sidon and Meleager, the two writers who exploit the notion of a pictorial script, both come from this area. Their epitaphs are no more surprising a reversion to an Egyptian idea than the sarcophagi of a century earlier and confirm a continuing respect for Egyptian practices especially in the field of sepulchral art.

114 The stele of Menophila from Sardis in Asia Minor cannot so easily be related to Egyptian hieroglyphics. Not only is Sardis far from Egyptian influence but also, instead of showing a string of objects which could not belong together in a single scene, it shows a woman standing quite normally with objects portrayed realistically behind her on a shelf. It has been suggested that the carvings on this stele are based on Pythagorean ideas. Both the wisdom referred to by the scroll and the domestic orderliness alluded to by the basket were qualities thought by the Pythagoreans to help men to a happier after-life. Pythagoreanism was strong in Ionia, the home of its founder. Plutarch was quite certain that Pythagoras was fascinated by the mystery of the hieroglyphics and that he tried to use the methods found in their enigmatic symbols for his own purposes. Plutarch may not have been absolutely correct; yet as someone who knew more about Pythagoreanism and the Egyptians than most people he must have been partly right in seeing a connection between them. He was certainly right about the Pythagoreans' interest in visual symbols, as we can see from the carvings on a tomb

115 from Philadelphia, not far inland from Sardis. The inscription shows that it belongs to someone of the same name as the founder of the sect. The lettering dates it to the first century. The man standing at the top in the centre may be either the philosopher or his namesake. The two women accompanied by children standing left and right at the bottom are identified by inscriptions as Asotia (Prodigality) and Arete (Virtue). The activities associated with these qualities are shown above: a man lying on a couch caressing a woman,

on the left, and a man ploughing, on the right. In order to show which way of life he has chosen, the dead man is shown at the Banquet of the Dead above the ploughman. The respect for work is the same as that found on Menophila's stele. Similar too is the patchwork imagery. There is also a symbolic use of a letter of the alphabet. It has been well argued that the raised lines dividing the scenes should be seen as forming the Greek capital Y (upsilon) which was used in Roman times by the Pythagoreans to symbolize the growth of the child and his subsequent confrontation with the two alternative paths of pleasure and toil – rather as in the 'Choice of Hercules' – the first of which led to doom and the second to salvation. The figured scenes certainly refer to these two alternatives. Moreover their placing left and right on the stele, under the bifurcating arms of the Y, also fits with Pythagorean notions. The Pythagoreans believed, as both Aristotle and Plutarch tell us, that the world was composed of opposites of which one extreme was bad and the other good. In the first group came, for instance, left, female, duality and darkness and in the second, right, male, unity and light. On our relief too, bad and good are respectively left and right of the spectator.

In the end it is impossible to establish how far the tombs from Asia Minor may depend on Pythagorean ideas or to what extent the epigrams of the Phoenician writers may be connected with hieroglyphics. Nevertheless it is clear that they share a common interest in symbols, an interest which was ascribed by Plutarch both to the Egyptian priests and to the followers of Pythagoras. Both Egyptians and Pythagoreans were obsessed with the after-life, and our reliefs and epigrams all have sepulchral contexts. Clearly it was the magic power inherent in a symbol, when compared to the normal language and representational art of everyday, that made it particularly attractive in such circumstances. The power of the Egyptian priests was greatly enhanced by their possession of mastery over what they called 'the writing of the house of god'. The power of the initiate into the Pythagorean mystery was based largely on his understanding of the mathematical order of the universe which could be summed up in visual representation of numbers such as ∴∴ ten or ∴ five. In both cases a large element of the power of the symbol derived from its incomprehensibility to all but a

115 Funeral stele of Pythagoras, from Philadelphia, first century BC.

select few, and it is interesting that the same point is stressed in the epitaph of Alcaeus of Messene explaining the two *phis*: 'praiseworthy is the man who made an enigma from the two letters, a light to the intelligent and darkness [literally, underworld] to the unintelligent'. Indeed, the contrast implied here between the light of the sun and the darkness of the underworld fits very well with the Pythagorean belief in an eventual union of the enlightened with the sun. Light is, of course, associated with understanding because it is essential for vision, and, since the special property of all these pictorial texts is that they only operate visually, it is worth examining further the whole subject of sight and its importance at this time.

The Power of Sight

Light and the eyes were for the early Greeks primarily complementary sources of pleasure. Hence someone or something that was beloved or admired could be called 'eye' or 'light'. In fact the early Greeks did not make our distinction between light and the eye. For them the eye seemed to emanate light and sources of light seemed to be large eyes. Thus the sun could be called an eye and one's eye could be called a light. It was only slowly that light became valued as a

vehicle and indeed an embodiment of wisdom and that the eye became highly valued for its power to receive it. This development can be traced in the worship of fire as the ruling principle by groups such as the Pythagoreans in the sixth century, in the discovery of the optic nerve connecting the eye with the brain or *nous* by Alcmaeon in the fifth century, and in Plato's subsequent assertion of the importance of beauty as goodness perceived by the mind through the eye. Euripides' use of the expression the 'light of truth' represents the new attitude. However, much the most explicit acknowledgment of the importance of the eye is found in Aristotle. At the beginning of the *Metaphysics* he remarks how we value the senses, and sight above all: 'The reason is that this, more than any other sense, makes us know and reveals to us, many differences between things.' Not that he had completely broken with Plato who had once observed that we learn better through words than pictures. For in *On Sense and Sensible Objects* 437a Aristotle says that 'sight is the best sense inherently and especially as far as necessities are concerned, but hearing is more important for the intellect, though only accidentally'. He admits that sight reveals more differences, because all bodies have colour, a point on which he contradicts Plato who in the *Cratylus* 423 had said that all objects have sound and form but only a majority colour; yet he insists that hearing, which only reveals difference of sound, is still more important intellectually because it deals with words and they are the cause of learning. It is clear that not only Plato but also Aristotle when they thought of words thought automatically of sounds rather than the written letters, and this certainly prevented both from acknowledging the full importance of vision.

Fortunately, however, both philosophers did possess some insights which prepared for the absolute victory of sight once the conquests of Alexander had made possible the rapid expansion of the use of books. It was the control of Egyptian papyrus production which enabled the Ptolemies to embark on the task of putting all knowledge on paper, and later the development of parchment (originally pergament), associated with Pergamum, is linked to a similar expansion of book production there. Plato, as we have seen, had claimed in the *Cratylus* that a name should embody the essentials of an object as much as a picture of it would. To prove his point he had observed that the letter 'r' (Greek *rhō*) recurred in numerous words expressing roughness or movement because it actually embodied those qualities. If it is unclear here whether he is really thinking primarily of the letter or of the sound, there is little doubt that when he notes that 'o' expresses roundness and refers to its repetition in the Greek word for 'round' (*strongylos*) he is concentrating on the visual properties of the letter. Plato's sad recognition that most objects have lost the appropriately expressive or 'imitative' names which were originally given to them by the lawgiver of language, and his implied acknowledgment that a picture is a much better imitation of an object than most names, are both highly suggestive for later Greek attitudes to hieroglyphics. The first point reminds us of Plato's remark in the *Laws* that Egyptian arts and dances have retained down the ages their god-given purity. The second could well suggest a preference for a written language based, not on an alphabet, but on pictograms. The opinion on hieroglyphics of the Neo-Platonist Plotinus follows this train of thought. Perhaps too we can see Plato's closeness to Pythagoreanism in his concentration on the 'roundness' of the letter 'o'. This is parallel to the Pythagorean concentration on the property of 'bifurcation' underlying the Pythagoreans' use of the Greek capital Y. Plato certainly depended on the Pythagorean tradition in many ways, particularly in his appreciation of geometry as the best example of the visual embodiment of truth, an appreciation which has an obvious application here. With his theory of ideas (derived from *idein*, to see) he became almost the high-priest of vision, but this theory was for him only a suggestive metaphor from vision which was designed precisely to avoid any reference to corporeal function. Once again it was the Neo-Platonists who followed up the metaphor more literally.

Aristotle realized the short-sightedness of Plato's neglect of the senses and the physical body. The studies he embarked on to remedy this did much to increase his respect for the sense of sight, as we have seen from his observations in the *Metaphysics* and in *On Sense and Sensible Objects*. Particularly important too was his work on the operations of perception and on thought, and his most interesting remarks on these are contained in *On the Soul*. There he establishes the existence of the faculty of *phantasia* (imagination) which is the part of the mind where visual impressions are received and which can even show us *phantasmata* (mental images) when our eyes are closed, as in the case of dreams. He correctly associates *phantasia* with *phaos* (light). Later he goes on from perception to thought:

> But since apart from sensible magnitudes there is nothing, as it would seem, independently existent, it is in the sensible forms that the intelligible forms exist, both the abstractions of mathematics, as they are called, and all the qualities and attributes of sensible things. And for this reason, as without sensation a man would not learn or understand anything, so at the very time when he is actually thinking he must have an image [*phantasma*] before him. For mental images are like present sensations except that they are immaterial. (On the Soul 432a)

In *On Memory and Recollection* Aristotle reaffirms the visual nature of thought: 'It is impossible to think without a mental image' (449b). He explains what he means by saying that the use of pictures by the mind is exactly the same as the geometer's use of diagrams of a particular triangle even when the geometer is only concerned with the triangle as an abstraction. He further emphasizes the intellectual importance of these mental images by asserting that they are also the basis of memory: 'all things which are mental images are themselves subjects of memory' (450a). A belief in the visual character of memory had long been current among the Greeks and a whole science of mnemonics had been based on that assumption. Aristotle's achievement was to recognize the visual basis not only of memory but of thought itself, and to explain this by a common dependence on the faculty of *phantasia*, which was in turn itself largely dependent on the sense of sight.

If we relate this point of view to the passage referred to from *On Sense and Sensible Objects* it is easy to understand Aristotle's reluctance to acknowledge the superiority of hearing as the most important sense for learning simply because of the accidental importance of speech. There he emphasized that speech had nothing essentially to do with thought: 'speech is composed of words and words are symbols (*symbola*) of things' (437a). For Plato, on the other hand, words were composed of sounds which were directly imitative of the thing referred to; they had, moreover, been formed by a primitive lawgiver. According to Plato the aural property of words was virtually sanctified. For Aristotle words had only a

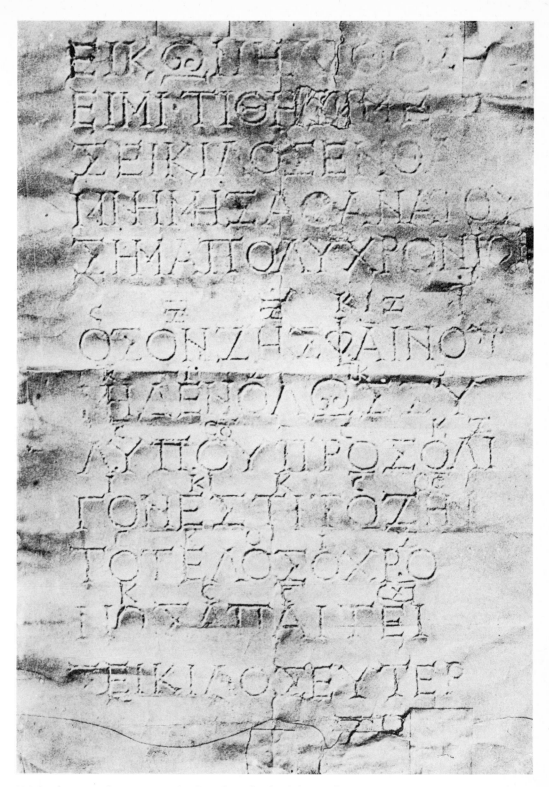

116 Greek song with notation marks, from the stele of Seikilos, Tralles, *c*. 100 BC.

conventional symbolic relation to the things they stood for; he would have had no difficulty in accepting another set of symbols. Indeed, it would obviously fit his theories of psychology better if aural symbols could be replaced by visual symbols, whether in the form of letters or, more literally, images. There is no evidence that Aristotle ever went so far as this, but it is certainly possible to point to an extended use of visual symbols both in his work and in that of later inheritors of his tradition. Aristotle himself probably introduced the use of symbols in logic. The symbols most often used were the Greek capital letters and it was clearly their form rather than their sound that interested him, as when he turned them on their sides.

More interesting is the evolution of other sets of symbols by the scholars who, in the spirit of Aristotle, worked in the Museum of Alexandria from the third century onwards. Their main concern was the establishment of good written texts of earlier works of literature and so as to communicate their critical opinions without writing elaborate commentaries they employed a number of symbols. These were only slowly introduced by Zenodotus and his successors and sometimes they changed their meaning. Perhaps the first of such signs was the *obelos* — used by Zenodotus to indicate a line he would reject. Other signs to express displacement, weakness, doubt about order, and other concepts, were the *asterisk, the sigma,* the *sigma* reversed, and

the *diplē*, > (this latter could be modified by dots). Another task of the critics was to analyse the different poetic metres and for this the ∪ for short, and the – for long syllables were devised. These signs do not represent sounds or even words, but concepts. They communicate at a purely visual level and they were designed to accompany the new written texts which were increasingly to replace spoken lectures and public readings as the sources of learning for Hellenistic and Roman students. Music also needed to be recorded and for this a notation was developed using letters, though it was never 116 carried very far. It can thus be seen how the theoretical exposition of the visual nature of mental operations prepared the way for the practical expansion of visual learning, and how out of a union of the two there developed a new language of signs.

The increasing tendency to learn by reading books must be seen as one of the most important features of the Hellenistic period. The growth of the libraries of Alexandria, Pergamum and Antioch documents the change. It is a necessary background both to the introduction of critical signs and to the use of shaped poems. It must also have served as a stimulus to the other developments mentioned in this chapter. People would have become more susceptible to didactic inscriptions and would also have been more prepared to see carved or painted images as analogous to words.

Chapter Four

Measure and Scale

Measure, Scale and Perception

When Socrates said that even Phoenician pots looked beautiful if they were arranged in a regular order he was stating a point of view that was not only to be systematically explored by Plato but which also underlies much of the artistic achievement of Classical Greece. This can be seen in the development of temple plans where a whole series shows a steady increase in regularity culminating in the temple of Athena Polias at 117 Priene of *c.* 350 with its whole plan laid out as a grid of large and small squares. It is also apparent in the great relief friezes of the temple of Apollo at Bassae and of the Mausoleum at Halicarnassus with their repeated poses. Polyclitus in his 16 Doryphoros established a canon of proportions for the human figure ensuring the commensurability of all its limbs, while Pamphilus, the painter, applied mathematical principles to painting. Sound too was subjected to mathematical rules as theorists analysed metre, rhythm and pitch in rhetoric and music. Town-planning and inscriptions provide examples of the fifth-century interest in regular order on both large and small scales. The type of town plan associated with the mid-fifth-century Hippodamus of Miletus and found throughout the Greek world, for example at Peiraeus and Thurii as well as in Hip-118 podamus' own home town, relied on a simple grid organization by which the urban area was divided up into a regular series of rectangles. The inscriptions of the same period which have the 119 letters arranged *stoichēdon*, or 'in rows', use the same principle with the letters aligned vertically and horizontally, as if laid out on graph paper,

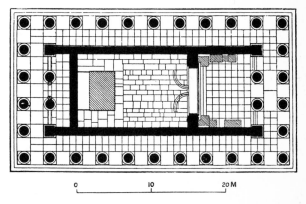

117 Plan of the temple of Athena Polias, Priene, mid-fourth century BC.

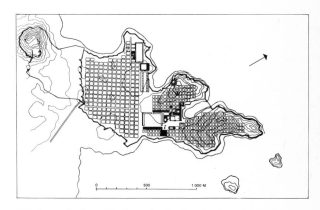

118 Ground-plan of Miletus in the first century BC.

and with words being arbitrarily divided to fill the spaces at the ends of the lines. The discovery of constant mathematical patterns in the natural world by the sixth-century philosophers of Ionia and the West thus led in the fifth century to an enthusiastic imposition of mathematical relationships on human activities, particularly the arts.

Oudeis ageōmetrētos eisitō was written over the door of Plato's Academy. This may well have meant not only that 'no one ignorant of geometry' but also that 'no one ungeometrical' could enter. In either case it is implied that geometry is the basis of the philosophical and largely ethical inquiry that took place there. Plato repeatedly insists on the importance of measure. '*Metriotēs* (measured behaviour, moderation) and *symmetria* (commensurability, symmetry) everywhere produce beauty and goodness' (*Philebus* 64e). Our eyes are frequently deceived as when looking at a stick in water, but the arts of measuring, numbering and weighing come to our rescue (*Republic* 602). 'Is ugliness anything but *ametria* (lack of measure)?' (*Sophist* 228). Plato uses the term *tetragōnos* (square) to describe the perfect man and the same term was used of Polyclitus' statues. In the same way Plato used the term *emmetros* (having measure) both for the moderate person and for metrical language. For him truth, which resided in arithmetic and geometry, was far preferable to pleasure, which came through the senses which frequently gave false information.

Aristotle did not give measure the central importance that Plato had assigned to it. He did study measurement, but for him it was a tool rather than a goal. At *Metaphysics* 1052b he tells how measurement in units can be applied to astronomy, music, colour, line and so on. Colours, he says in *Of Sense and Sensible Objects* 439b, have numerical values, and harmonic colours are those which have simple numerical relationships to each other; even superimposed colours as used by painters can have a ratio between them. Such a notion could obviously be useful to an artist and a similar theory may have been the basis of the careful calculation by Aristotle's younger contemporary Apelles of the darkening effect of varnish and the brilliance of colours, as described by Pliny (*Natural History* xxxv, 97). In general Aristotle's interest in sense experience contrasts with Plato's contempt for all but pure reason. One of Aristotle's basic notions was that even abstract thought relied on material things. It was impossible to have a concept in one's mind without it being an image of something real. All work on general geometrical theorems relied on particular diagrams of a particular magnitude. This made it important for Aristotle to establish the nature of our perception of the real world. For him it was important to note that there were some things which were beyond the powers of our eyes to see or of our ears to hear. While Plato ridiculed the contemporary musicians who tortured the strings of their instruments in a competition to find the smallest audible interval, because, according to him, it was not worth knowing what one's ears heard anyway, Aristotle noted with interest that a quarter tone is virtually impossible to distinguish, that a millet seed is too small to be seen properly and that some sounds are so big and some lights so bright that they maim our senses for some time. The limitation of the powers of the senses noted here even became the basis for artistic criteria in Aristotle's thought. Thus in the *Poetics* Aristotle warns against making works that are either very long or very short on the grounds that a very small object, being perceived almost instantaneously, cannot penetrate our mind, while something very large, such as an animal several thousand miles long, can never be fully understood because we are unable to get a comprehensive view of it. This might be taken to imply that Aristotle favoured a mean between the two extremes, but in the *Nicomachean Ethics* he says that while large people tend to be *kalloi* (beautiful) small ones tend to be *symmetroi* (well-proportioned). As both terms are favourable, and intended to be in some way mutually exclusive, he clearly saw the value of both small and large scales. In all the arts at this period there are many cases of contrasts in scale being exploited, and in the Hellenistic period scale continued to be very important.

Aristotle deals both with the effects of objects of different sizes on our perception and with the effect of the varying distance between an object and the spectator. We have referred earlier to his discussion in the *Rhetoric* of the different styles of oratory which are appropriate to different audiences. There he says: 'the style suitable for public meetings is like *skiagraphia* (painting with shadows). For the larger the audience the more distant the view and in those circumstances a

119 Inscription from Potidaea with lettering arranged *stoichēdon*, late fifth century BC.

detailed style is fussy and weak in both speech and painting. It is in judicial oratory that a sharp and detailed (*akribēs*) style is appropriate.' The meaning of *skiagraphia* is rather unclear but the late fifth-century painter Apollodorus was called *skiagraphos* and was said by Plutarch to have invented the technique of building up and fading out shadows. Presumably then *skiagraphia* refers to the use of broad tonal effects of light and shade to give strong relief to figures, in contrast to the use of fine linear effects. Since it was by developing this technique that Apollodorus 'opened the gates of art' for the great generation of Greek painters, led by Zeuxis, it was probably regarded as being more up to date than the earlier precise style. In fact, though, as Aristotle implies, a precise linear treatment was so essential to Greek painting that the two approaches both remained current. Artists could choose which style to adopt and we know of one Antidotus, a contemporary of Aristotle, who was noted for the precision of his style and the way he kept light and shade in check. As Antidotus was the pupil of Euphranor, who was known for his theoretical interest in *symmetriai*, and the teacher of Nicias, who was famed for his very precise paintings of women, the precise style seems to have been associated with careful calculation, just as it was contrasted with the style that relied on broad effects of shading. The fact that the latter is associated with the style of public oratory and the former with the style appropriate to the law-courts, which were the more intimate scene of private disputes, would suggest that if we knew enough of contemporary paintings we would indeed find some tendency for public paintings to be in the one style and private paintings in the other. More information on how Aristotle felt that linear detail became invisible at a distance is found in the *Problems*, a work which comes from his school. There the phenomenon of vision is described by which squares seen at a distance look polygonal and when seen from even further off actually seem round. The tendency for objects to lose sharp definition, and especially linear angular detail, with distance would clearly make it superfluous to give sharp linear definition to paintings which would be seen from some way away. A technique which suited the portrayal of rounded forms, such as the technique of shading, would be more suitable instead. In this context any effort spent on the careful calculation of mathematical measurements and proportions would also be wasted, as the human eye would not see either correctly.

Large and Small

Although Aristotle says that small people are *symmetroi* and *asteioi* (well-proportioned and elegant), and so does give smallness a positive value, he still sees *kallos* (beauty) as a property reserved for large people. There are indeed a number of other passages which show that he valued size, or greatness, for itself. Earlier, in the *Nicomachean Ethics*, he had discussed *megalo-prepeia* (magnificent expenditure) and had analysed the word into its two parts, *megalo* (great) and *prepeia* (appropriateness), arguing that this

121

120 Themis, by Chaerestratus, from the shrine of Nemesis at Rhamnus in Attica, *c.* 300 BC.

virtue consisted of great expenditure by great people and contrasting it with *mikroprepeia* (small expenditure), which was mean expenditure by mean people. The fact that *megalopsychia* (great-heartedness) was another major virtue reinforced his belief that greater size meant greater excellence. In the *Rhetoric* he discusses physical greatness specifically and says that the quality of great size (*megethos*) is based on superiority of length, depth and breadth, so long as the increase in size does not impede movement. From this it follows that men are 'greater' than women because the largest man is bigger than the largest woman. Later he argues that rhetorical exaggeration should be used to make things seem better because an impression of greatness seems to suggest excellence. Aristotle's interest in the notion of greatness (*megethos*) is significant as an example of the way in which value systems are established. *Megethos* in Homer had referred simply to size of body. Later, in the sixth and fifth centuries, it regularly refers to the quality of power which was found frequently to reside in large bodies. Then, by a further process of abstraction, it came to be applied to 'great' subjects in rhetoric. At this point theorists such as Aristotle, searching for keys to the establishment of styles appropriate to particular subjects looked again at the basic meaning of the word and concentrated on the notions of absolute size and relative largeness. This led them naturally to the principle of exaggeration when treating great themes. The tendency of sophisticated men to take a metaphor so seriously that they begin to read it literally is strange but persistent. Such a tendency led eighteenth-century man, brought up on Longinus' treatise on *hypsos*, metaphorical 'loftiness', to pursue the quality literally by contemplating high mountains, and eventually to believe he had attained it when he had climbed them.

It seems, in fact, that artists came to be influenced by a similar line of thought about greatness. Already in the fifth century Phidias had made enormous statues of Zeus and Athena, but it is in Aristotle's own period, and that immediately following it, that the giant statue came into its own. With Phidias' statues it could be argued that the artist's subjects, the gods, actually were physically enormous because their ordinary movements were supposed to have effects of geological magnitude. When, however,

Euphranor in the fourth century made two colossal statues of Virtue and Greece he must have been pointing to their magnitude as ideas. These
120 works are lost but Chaerestratus' giant Themis (Established Law) of the early third century still survives. The metaphor is here given literal expression. It was with Lysippus and his school that the development of the colossal statue was particularly associated. Lysippus himself made a 70-foot-high Zeus at Tarentum and a huge Hercules in the same city. The most famous colossus of all was, of course, the 105-foot-high Apollo made by his pupil Chares of Lindos for Rhodes around 280:

> This statue was 70 cubits high; after standing 56 years it was thrown down by an earthquake, but even as it lies on the ground it is a marvel. Few people can get their arms around its thumb, and the fingers are larger than most statues. Vast caves yawn within the limbs which have been broken off, and in them are seen great masses of rock, with the weight of which he established it as he was setting it up. (*Natural History* xxxiv, 41)

We know of many contemporary and later statues that were considerably larger than life-size. There are statues of divinities from the whole
148 Hellenistic period, such as the Nike of Samothrace
150 in the Louvre, or the group carved at Lycosura by Damophon of Messene. There are even
121 portraits of rulers, from that of Mausolus of *c*. 350 now in the British Museum to the colossal bronze known to have existed at Delphi representing Antiochus III. It may not be irrelevant that this Antiochus, who lived in the late third century, was called 'the Great'.

Significantly too it was apparently Alexander himself who, first among the Greeks, chose to be identified by this title and thus started its long history in European civilization. As successor to the Persian rulers who had always been called 'great king' by the Greeks he had, in a sense, inherited the title, but there is other evidence for an interest in political 'greatness' slightly earlier, as in the Arcadian foundation of a new capital in 371 called simply Megalopolis, 'The Great City' – an epithet which was never merited. Alexander's interest in greatness certainly parallels that of Aristotle and contemporary artists. Yet we do not know of any colossal figures of Alexander having been made at the time to express his prime attribute, though such could easily have been executed by Lysippus who was his favourite portrait sculptor. Alexander did, however, in-

121 Mausolus, from the Mausoleum, Halicarnassus, *c*. 350 BC.

spire the conception of the most colossal statue of all time. As Vitruvius tells us, an architect, Dinocrates, came to him one day with a project to form Mount Athos into a statue of a man with, in his left hand, a whole city and, in his right hand, a bowl to receive the water of all the rivers of the mountain. The architect said that he had conceived of this scheme as a worthy expression of Alexander's fame. Whether the figure would have represented the personification of Mount Athos or the ruler himself, the city would probably have been called Alexandria like the city in Egypt later laid out by Dinocrates. The size of Alexander's achievement would have been expressed in the whole conception. The scale of Alexander's conquests was certainly a revelation for the Greeks in that it put a new perspective on the relation between tiny man and the great Earth. Seneca was probably recording a traditional proverb when he said: 'Alexander is too great for the world; the world is too small for Alexander.'

Dinocrates dressed up as Hercules to indicate that he was capable of the enormous Mount Athos project and Hercules was, indeed, the supreme example of the mortal who was capable of truly superhuman achievement. We know of several colossal statues of that hero from the late fourth century. Lysippus made at least two. The one from Tarentum has been mentioned, but that most famous today is the version which served as 122 a model for the Hercules Farnese in Naples. This shows the enormous male body leaning on the upturned club, while the figure from Tarentum showed the hero seated on the basket he had used in cleansing the stables of Augeas. Lysippus also made a much smaller seated figure of Hercules, only about a foot long, called Hercules Epi-123 trapezios. This statuette is described in a number of ancient texts which enable us to identify several copies. On a rock covered by his lion-skin Hercules sat drinking a cup of wine, relaxed and oblivious of the degrading tasks he had just completed. The title Epitrapezios (on the table) indicated that the work was a table ornament. Tradition made it adorn the table of Alexander himself and this may well be true. Alexander at table could easily identify himself with the hero who had also enjoyed feasting after his toils. The small size of this statue was clearly an expression of its function in a relatively private setting, a setting which contrasted with the public one of

123 Hercules Epitrapezios, after Lysippus. Roman copy of an original of the later fourth century BC.

the colossal figure. The small size may also have had a particular fascination for Lysippus beyond its obvious desirability in an ornament. The later accounts of the statue constantly draw attention to the skill involved in expressing the greatness of Hercules' strength and deeds in such a small figure: 'he is seen as small but thought of as enormous'; 'a great god compressed into a small bronze'. As this is probably the first truly small work of sculpture to have become famous it is very likely that its small size was remarked on right from the beginning and that Lysippus' intention in executing it was to demonstrate the power of the miniature work of art. There could be no better subject for such a demonstration

122 Hercules Farnese, after Lysippus. Roman copy signed by Glycon of Athens after an original of the later fourth century BC.

124 Hercules and Omphale. Wall-painting from the House of Siricus, Pompeii. Roman copy of a probably Hellenistic original.

than the hero who was elsewhere treated by him on a colossal scale.

One of the most famous anecdotes about contemporary artists suggests that there was a similar interest in miniaturization among painters. Apelles on a visit to Protogenes of Rhodes left as his visiting card a line of incredible fineness drawn across a panel. When Protogenes saw it he identified the hand immediately and divided the line by one even finer. Apelles returned, was ashamed that he had been surpassed, and went to the ultimate by dividing the line once again. The panel was preserved by Protogenes and survived till it was destroyed by fire in Rome. Pliny tells how it made a striking impression among the other works in the imperial collections, being nothing but a large surface decorated with three lines which were hardly visible. The competition between the two artists shows that they too were interested in smallness, though in a different way from Lysippus. Their concern seems to have been more with finding the limits of perception and dexterity. The preservation of the panel shows

that even such 'minimal' art could achieve renown.

There were two main attractions in smallness: first the opportunity to display technical skill in the most refined detail and second the possibility of persuading people that something that was physically tiny, such as a small image of Hercules, could embody all the strength of something huge. This last idea provided artists with a new impetus to study the power of children. Such power might be physical, as in the case of the Infant Hercules strangling the snakes. The subject had already been painted by Zeuxis and several copies of Hellenistic treatments survive. The power of the infant Dionysus, best known from Praxiteles' portrayal, was more mysterious, but it too is eloquently displayed in the sculpted and mosaic images of the tiny god riding lions and leopards, lord among the beasts. A delightful trivialization of a similar theme is found in the group of a boy strangling a goose of which we have several copies and which was described by Herondas in his third-century description of a visit to the temple of Asclepius in Cos. But by far the most fascinating embodiment of infantile power was Eros, or Cupid, god of love. Aëtion's painting of the Marriage of Alexander and Roxane has already been referred to, and there little cupid figures play an important part. Indeed, as Lucian says, the importance of their role is belied by their childish playfulness. Although Lucian gives another explanation of their function, they probably tell us how the great warrior was conquered by the delicate power of love. This is certainly the case in the Pompeian painting of Hercules and Omphale which has also been mentioned earlier. The tiny size of the cupids in both these cases is particularly impressive in view of the proverbial 'greatness' of their victims. There are many Roman copies of Hellenistic statues of the infant Eros and often he appears in groups, as in a pair of statues of centaurs probably deriving from second-century originals. Both centaurs have cupids on their backs, though they react very differently to their riders. One centaur is old and has his hands tied; his upturned face shows how love for him is only a source of pain. The other is young and gallops along free and excited, snapping his fingers. The two statues are vivid images of impotence and exhilaration. Both are in love's sway. It is noteworthy that the increase in the importance of Eros in the late

125 Infant Hercules strangling the snakes.
Roman copy of a probably Hellenistic original.

126 (*right*) Hermes holding the Infant Dionysus,
after Praxiteles. Copy, probably of *c*. 100 BC,
after an original of *c*. 330 BC.

128 Young Centaur (detail). One of a
pair of statues from Hadrian's Villa at
Tivoli. These are signed by Aristeas and
Papias and are Roman copies probably
deriving from an original pair of the
mid-second century BC (see also Pls. 97, 127).

127 (*left*) Old Centaur. Roman copy
probably deriving from one of a pair of
statues made in the mid-second century
BC (see also Pls. 97, 128).

129 Hellenistic gold earrings with figures of Eros.

fourth and early third centuries is contemporary with the tendency for him to be described and represented not as a young man but as a small child. Many copies and a few original works of art survive to show him at work throughout the Hellenistic period. Perhaps the most evocative of these portrayals are the tiny golden earrings evidently popular at the time. The infant Dionysus too is only found from the fourth century onwards and it seems that these two great gods of the Hellenistic world were deliberately made so small in order to show that their power was mysterious, and not physical, as with the other gods, or with mortals such as Hercules and Alexander.

129

Nowhere is the power of the small, and also the power of love, so clearly asserted as in Hellenistic verse. A little poem by Theocritus or an imitator describes how Eros is stung by a bee. It concludes with the thought that Eros himself is like the bee because, in spite of his tiny size, he is capable of inflicting great wounds. In the fourth idyll, which is unanimously accepted as being by Theocritus himself, the same thought is applied to a humble thorn. Here one of two herdsmen, Battus, gets a thorn in his foot which has to be removed by his companion, Corydon. When Battus sees the thorn he remarks with surprise that such a tiny wound can overwhelm such a tall man. Many statues survive from antiquity which show thorns being removed from feet and it is difficult to explain the popularity of the subject except in the same terms. The bee's sting and the thorn are tiny objects which can inflict great pain. In the Hellenistic world there were many small objects such as table silver, glass and jewellery

130

which were valued for their power to give intense pleasure, and the epigram was a parallel and characteristic manifestation of this taste. Small poems of a few lines had been made for two or three centuries, but the genre does not become firmly established until quite suddenly around 300. Its emergence thus reflects the general interest in the small which was current at the time. Not surprisingly, many Hellenistic epigrams also reflect an interest in small subjects. An early third-century poem by Anyte describes a scene of children harnessing a goat to drive it round a temple so that the gods may look on at their infantile pursuits. The notion that the great gods may notice even this childish mimicry not only lends a new importance to the games of children but also reminds us that all human activity is trivial in scale compared to the works of the gods.

This poem is probably, like many, a description of a painting or relief, and there are numerous paintings of the Roman period which must go back to Hellenistic models and which

130 Pan and Satyr. Roman, probably copy of a Hellenistic original.

show children, often winged like cupids, riding animals, driving chariots or hunting in playful mockery of adult activities. These works are usually small in scale, and so have the same relationship in size to the paintings of lofty subjects that epigrams do to the more traditional verse forms. Many epigrams pick up ideas relating to the ephemeral which had already been touched on in earlier lyric poetry, such as the shortness of the night for lovers, or the similar briefness of a flower's blooming and a maiden's prime. Tiny creatures such as ants, cicadas and even mosquitos, which had previously only been brought in incidentally, now become the subjects of whole poems. Meleager, for instance, around 100 prays that the little biting insects will not disturb the sleep of his beloved. Such small creatures also appear in the visual arts, as do other animals only slightly less small. Fishes, birds and reptiles are frequently shown, especially in minor artistic forms such as decorative paintings, mosaics and metalwork. A number of Roman mosaics showing fishes in water clearly derive from some well-known model which is normally thought to have been a Hellenistic work of the second century. Famous mosaics were created in that period at Pergamum, for example a mosaic by Sosus showing pigeons drinking from a bowl, also known from Roman copies. In another part of the same mosaic Sosus apparently went to the extreme in the celebration of the small and worthless with a theme known as the *asarōtos oikos*, or Unswept Room, which showed the fishbones, bruised fruit and other rejected food lying on the dining-room floor after a banquet, as well as a scavenging mouse. The fact that such works were famous enough not only to be copied but even to be discussed by Pliny shows that they should not be dismissed as decorative trivia.

One of the clearest, and also one of the most intriguing, examples of a parallelism between poetry and art as far as interest in the insignificant is concerned can be seen in the Hellenistic treatment of garlands. The first great collection of short poems was that made by Meleager at the end of the second century and in a special poem he likens his collection to a gathering of flowers, the first *anthologia* (flower collection), which are twined into a garland. Poems had been loosely described as flowers before, but here the flowers are the poets and in each of forty-seven cases the flower is made to embody or allude to some

131 Cupids playing with Hera's peacock. Wall-painting from the House of the Bronzes, Pompeii, first half of the first century AD.

132 Cupids with lion. Roman mosaic.

133 Roman silver cup with a design of leaves, birds and insects.

134 Doves at a bowl of water. Roman mosaic deriving from an original composition by Sosus of the second century BC. This design may have formed the centre-piece of Sosus' Unswept Room (see Pl. 135).

135 Unswept Room. Detail of Roman mosaic, after an original by Sosus of the second century BC.

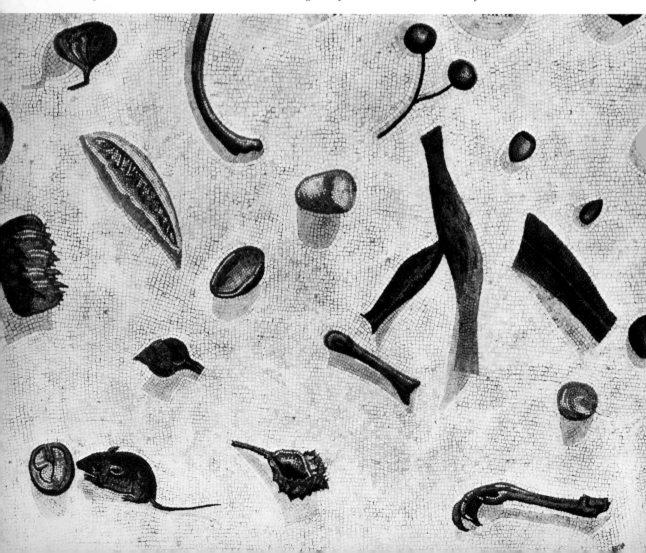

136 Foliate scroll with grasshopper. Detail of mosaic from the palace at Pergamum, *c.* 200 BC (for signature of this mosaic, see Pl. 110).

137 Marine life. Detail of Roman mosaic from Pompeii, after a Hellenistic original of perhaps *c.* 200 BC.

138 Garland with tragic mask, fruit and flowers. Detail of Roman mosaic from Pompeii, after an original of the second century BC.

139 Circular altar with masks and garlands, from the theatre of Dionysus, Athens, *c.* 100 BC.

quality or attribute of the poet in a spirit similar to that of Meleager's enigmatic epitaphs. The comparisons may occasionally seem forced, but the elegance of the idea always carries the reader along. Sometimes both flower and poet come from the same country, as with Antipater and his Syrian bloom. More often an attempt is made to find a flower to fit the poet's character, as with the irritable Archilochus who is likened to a thistle. In the case of Sappho, presumably her femininity, her stylistic richness and her unique excellence are all concealed in the mystery of a rose. Meleager's attempt to compress centuries of literary history into a little over fifty lines admirably expresses how far one strain of Hellenistic thought had freed itself from the grand and the pompous. In the colours, scents and forms of flowers, which are themselves the ultimate embodiment of fragility and transience, we find a code for much of the greatest and most permanent achievement of Greek poetry. It is in the second century too that flowers themselves attain a new permanence in a whole series of sculpted and mosaic garlands. Several of these are 138 associated with Pergamum and others may reflect Pergamene influence abroad, as in the case of the round altar from the theatre of Dionysus in Athens. The contexts of these garlands are very 139 different from the garland of Meleager; they are usually linked by a series of masks which identify them as dedications to Dionysus. Perhaps, however, the difference is not so great as it may seem if we consider that Meleager's poem is an invocation to the Muses and that the garland is described in the last line as belonging to them. The Muses, although more often linked with

Apollo, were frequently associated with Dionysus. So it is not impossible that Meleager may have found the inspiration for his garland of flowers, so sweetly appropriate to the Muses, in the garlands found on Dionysiac altars. At all events both anthology and garlands reveal a sensibility to the individuality of tiny plants.

The Large River and the Small Jug

Given the simultaneous enthusiasm for both the large and the small in the Hellenistic world it is not surprising that an interest in their rival merits could develop into a substantial conflict, and this is exactly what seems to have happened in the Museum at Alexandria. There in the so-called 'birdcage of the Muses', where scholars sought to identify the very essence of literary excellence, a debate of considerable importance for the European tradition was inaugurated. Our most direct contact with this dispute is through the writings of Callimachus where the latter ridicules the poetry of his opponents in a whole series of suggestive images, all of which imply a preference for the small over the large. Probably referring to the recent revivals of the epic form, Callimachus says: 'I hate the cyclic poem; it is a common highroad used by all. I don't drink from the general water supply; I loathe everything public.' Elsewhere, in a similar vein, he advises poets 'not to travel on roads full of chariots, nor follow in the tracks of others', but rather to penetrate 'paths untrodden till now, to discover fresh and pure springs and to pluck new flowers'. Fresh inspiration is contrasted with massive learning, and the fruits of the former are seen as small and refined while the latter only produces heavy effects. As the poet makes Apollo say in *Hymn* ii: 'the Assyrian river's stream is great but it carries most of the filth of the land, while Demeter's bees do not take their water from everywhere, but only from the sacred springs'. The great river full of many sorts of rubbish stands for the works of his rivals which were large and full of many sorts of imitations of earlier writers, while he is the careful bee who distils water from the fountainhead. Again in the same poem he pokes fun at those who sing as the sea, while elsewhere he likens himself to the cicada. The opposition between the light touch of inspiration and the heavy hand of learning is here formulated for the first time.

Callimachus' imagery is allusive but precise. While he himself was mainly interested in smaller verse forms, such as the epigram and the hymn, his rivals had different tastes. Apollonius Rhodius, traditionally his greatest enemy in the war of words, composed a massive epic in four long books, the *Argonautica*. Moreover, Apollonius may well have been as self-conscious a supporter of the large as Callimachus was of the small. He intended his work to follow Aristotle's recommendation that an epic should be based on the traditional dramatic sequence of four plays, and each of the books of the *Argonautica* embodies the Aristotelian qualities of unity and continuity. Since it was also Aristotle who had first extolled the virtues of *megethos*, 'great size', Apollonius' work may have been programmatically Aristotelian in its possession of this quality too. In any case Callimachus could justifiably contrast the roses, springs and footpaths of his own poetry with the highroad, river and sea of his opponents; he could sincerely claim that 'a large book is a big evil' and describe his own muse as *lepton*, 'slight'. What Callimachus means here in terms of a contrast in scale with his rivals is thus fairly clear, but it is less evident what he means by a contrast in terms of originality. To us his work may seem hardly less learned than that of Apollonius Rhodius. However there is little doubt as to the intention behind his general point. A very learned work, especially if it is also large, can be likened to a river at its fullest, swollen by the streams of many tributaries and much else beside, while a small work which is less derivative and imitative in character can be likened more to a spring of fresh water. The image would be a forceful one to the Greeks, who loved clear spring water and were all too conscious of the deficiencies of river water and the municipal supply. Callimachus must have been inspired to develop the image by the traditional association of the Muses, goddesses of song, with the springs of Mount Helicon. The first two great poems in the Greek language, the *Iliad* and the *Odyssey*, both claimed to come directly from 'the Muse' and, in a learned reference which belied his purpose, Callimachus claimed a similar direct inspiration for his greatest work, the *Aetia*. So when he contrasted his own *oligē libas*, or small trickle, with the *megas rhoos*, or great flood, of his rivals Callimachus was developing an image of undoubted potency.

Nevertheless, like many such images, it can easily be turned against its originator. Callimachus intended to show that his own poetry was more essentially natural than the mechanical and artificial verse of his rivals by contrasting his roses, springs and tracks with their chariots, highroads and public fountains; yet the very idea of a bee sucking spring water is fussy and unnatural, while the plucking of the flower kills its vitality completely. The river or the sea, on the other hand, personify perhaps better than anything else the essential power of nature itself. Thus it is not surprising that tradition suggests that it was Apollonius Rhodius who finally won the day and that it was the image of a large and powerful flow of water which served as the touchstone of excellence for the next generation of literary critics around 200. Perhaps the best illustration of this is provided by Galaton's painting which adorned the newly founded Homereion, or shrine to Homer. As we have seen, this lost work showed the poet as a river god spewing out a great stream of water which was collected in little jugs by his imitators. The painting made it clear that Homer's verse was admired for resembling a great river and it exposes to ridicule the controlled artificiality of those who sought to imitate him. Further evidence for the victory of these values is provided by two epigrams by Dioscorides, also from the end of the third century. Talking of the earliest great tragic poet, Aeschylus, Dioscorides in a brilliant metaphor contrasts Aeschylus' natural flow with the artificial elaboration of his successors, comparing his language to an inscription in which the letters are not carved and polished but formed as if by a rushing torrent. Again, in an epitaph on the tragic poet Sositheus who was not long dead, Dioscorides praises him for having 'archaized drama, matching again a masculine rhythm to the Dorian Muse and returning to the use of a large voice'. The qualities of strength, size and violence which Callimachus had criticized in writers such as Apollonius were now regarded as the essence of great poetry.

Not that this implies a complete rejection of Callimachus' critical standpoint. Several of Callimachus' metaphors show that he valued natural movement and that one of his objections to his rivals was precisely the mechanical character of their productions, following in the ruts of other peoples' carriages and drawing on the public

140 Homer. Roman copy after an original of probably *c*. 200 BC.

water supply. He would have approved of the mockery of artificial imitation reflected in Galaton's painting. What seems to have happened is that people realized that Callimachus could not have it both ways, claiming to be at once more refined and more natural than his contemporaries. It must have seemed increasingly clear as the third century advanced that in spite of all their careful study of archaic vocabulary and early poetic metres none of the versifiers of Alexandria could ever regain the essential vitality achieved by earlier writers from Homer to Aeschylus. Callimachus already seems to have been aware of this when he sought to give the impression that his work was not derivative and that, as in the case of the *Aetia*, it was directly inspired by the Muses. This made him, like Homer, almost the passive recipient of some supernatural force and could have been seen to protect him from the charge of learned artificiality.

The loss of the vast bulk of Alexandrian literature prevents us from following more closely this change in taste, but evidence for its

141 Aeschylus. Roman copy of a probably Hellenistic original.

142 Sophocles. Roman copy of a probably Hellenistic original.

diffusion may perhaps be found in some surviving works of sculpture just as it was certainly documented by Galaton's painting. Several versions of a sculpted portrait of Homer do survive 140 which probably derive from the same period and which may even be associated with the Homereion. In at least one version the rich masses of Homer's hair seem moved as by a wind from the bard's right. If this is indeed so then this might be a specific illustration of the breath of the Muse, paralleling Virgil's description of the Cumaean sybil when about to prophesy as being 'blown upon by Apollo', who was the Muses' leader. Even more tentatively, one might suggest that 141 two busts in Florence which have been identified 142 as Aeschylus and Sophocles may illustrate a similar contrast to that made by Dioscorides between the letters of Aeschylus which seem worn by a torrent and the chiselled characters of his successors. There certainly seems to be a clear distinction between the stormy locks of the earlier tragic poet and the still, almost symmetrical hair of the later one.

These last works suggest that the revolution in literary criticism also found expression in paintings and sculptures. It is not impossible, however, that there was a similar revolution in taste within the visual arts themselves. For a number of works produced around and after 200 can be seen to share many of those qualities admired by the critics. The literary evidence suggested that there was a professed reaction against the small and artificial towards largeness, and a strong flowing movement, both to be pursued by the imitation of the spirit of earlier writers. Galaton's Homer-river may have been an effective painted expression of this reaction, and there is a whole tradition of vigorously carved river gods de- 143 scending probably from Ptolemaic representations of the Nile, as versions of the Nile figure now in the Vatican have been found in Alexandria. The pose of the Vatican Nile bears a strong resemblance to river gods in fifth-century temple pediments, especially that on the left of the east pediment of the temple of Zeus at Olympia and that derived from it on the left of the

143 River god. Roman adaptation of a Hellenistic type.

144 River god, from the left corner of the west pediment of the Parthenon, Athens, 447–432 BC.

145 Tazza Farnese (detail). Sardonyx cameo from Alexandria engraved with figures of Nile, Euthenia-Isis, Triptolemus-Horus, Seasons and Winds. Probably Hellenistic.

144 west pediment of the Parthenon. What is new in the Vatican Nile is the way the figure much more directly embodies the property of the great river, with its cascading limbs and flowing beard. 145 Another representation of the Nile can be found on the Tazza Farnese, a large cameo dish which has been dated by the identification of its central striding figure as Ptolemy VI to about 180. This includes not only the river reclining at the side but also flying figures of the winds above. The head of Homer suggested that the new interest in vigorous flow could find expression in the movement of wind as well as of water, and one monument which exploits the power of both elements is the Nike of Samothrace, also of the 148 early second century. Here the great rushing 157 figure of the goddess of Victory, almost twice life size, alights on the prow of a ship with her clothes

pushed back in great masses by the resistance of the wind. In its original situation the prow stood diagonally in a large fountain basin consisting of two levels with water cascading from one to the other and between rocks. Thus in this powerful image of the wind-borne goddess the flow of a mass of water was used perhaps for the first time to create a strong dramatic effect. Once again the statue is not a new invention, but looks back, like the Nile figure, to a fifth-century model, the Nike of Paeonius in Olympia; once again, however, the new element is the increase in grandeur of conception and in vigour of flowing movement. This imitation of fifth-century works requires some explanation, since throughout the third century it was the more delicate works of the fourth century which provided the authoritative models for Hellenistic artists. Could it be that

147 Plan of original setting of the Nike of Samothrace, showing diagonal position of prow in the rock-filled fountain basin (see also Pls. 148, 157).

146 Nike, by Paeonius, after 420 BC. From Olympia.

early second-century sculptors, searching, like the literary critics of the same period, for the most dynamic models with which to renew their inspiration, found them in the works of the mid- to late fifth century?

It may seem strange to us that this period could have provided a sculptural equivalent to the epic violence of Homer and Aeschylus. Yet this is partly due to our seeing its monuments through the eyes of the first century and partly due to a simple historical accident, the destruction in the seventeenth century of the two central groups of the Parthenon pediments. This last event has forced us to console ourselves with the study of the peaceful spectators of these scenes and the relatively minor reliefs of the metopes and frieze. But to anyone around 200 looking back to earlier sculpture, the great free-standing figures of the Parthenon pediments would have been far the most violent and dynamic images available and would have represented the heroic age of Greek

148 Nike of Samothrace, by Pythocritus, early second century BC. From a dedication in the sanctuary of the Cabiri on Samothrace perhaps commemorating the victory of the Rhodians over Antiochus III in 190 BC.

149 Birth of Athena. Drawing from a marble relief in Madrid adapted from the east pediment of the Parthenon, Athens, 447–432 BC.

sculpture just as did Aeschylus for drama and Homer for epic. The west pediment of the Parthenon in particular, with its two great figures of Poseidon and Athena surging apart and flanked by pairs of rearing horses, must have been extremely striking. The authority of this group is demonstrated by its recurrence, noted in chapter three, at the centre of the composition of the main frieze of the Great Altar of Zeus at Pergamum of the 170s. The west pediment of the Parthenon was the one which directly confronted the visitor arriving on the Acropolis, and the group of Zeus and Athena was also the one which most directly confronted the visitor entering the precinct of the Zeus altar at Pergamum. The massive treatment of the diagonal rushing bodies also forms the key to the whole Pergamene frieze with its rhythmic groupings of gods in battle with Titans. *Megas rhoos* or 'great flow', the term used by Callimachus to describe such works as Apollonius' great epic the *Argonautica* with its Homeric cadences, could just as aptly be applied to this battle scene with its echoes of the great age of Athens. It would be tempting, indeed, to see a specifically Rhodian connection linking Apollonius with the aesthetics both of the Pergamene frieze and of the Nike of Samothrace. For the writer was named Rhodius because of his years of exile on the island, while the Nike was a Rhodian dedication carved by a Rhodian sculptor, and Rhodian sculptors had a leading hand in the Zeus altar at Pergamum too.

Another feature of these same years around 180–170 is the revival of the cult of Zeus which is associated with a further diffusion of the same stylistic values. Apart from the Zeus altar at Pergamum we have the restoration of Phidias' chryselephantine statue of Zeus at Olympia by Damophon of Messene, who then went on to carve a gigantic sculptural group at Lycosura using Phidias' work as inspiration but again charging the forms with greater mass and fluidity, as in the head of the Titan Anytus. Again in 174 Antiochus of Syria revived the late sixth-century project for a huge temple of Olympian Zeus in Athens. The main modification to the earlier plan was the introduction of the more opulent forms of the Corinthian order, which was probably invented in fifth-century Athens but which had never been used so prominently before. It may only be a happy chance that the first mention of Corinthian in literature is in a fragment by Apollonius. A final tribute to Zeus is the gigantic head of the god from Aegira, now in Athens and probably dating from the middle of the century, where once again early forms are charged with greater grandeur. The patriarch of Olympus had not been honoured with such attention since the fifth century. No figure so clearly embodied the majesty and physical power which were associated with the heroic age of Greece. Perhaps Poseidon was his nearest rival and he too was honoured with a vigorously turning image at Melos around the middle of the second century, whose beard effectively evokes the fluidity of water. Even the Venus de Milo from the same island can be seen to reflect the same style with her flowing spiral pose, while the fact that she and Poseidon are both made out of two separate blocks united by an asymmetrical

150 Head of the Titan Anytus. From a colossal group at Lycosura, by Damophon of Messene, mid-second century BC.

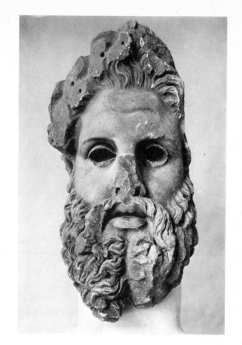

151 Zeus, by Eucleides, *c.* 150 BC. From Aegira.

147 join at the waist reminds one that an asymmetrical diagonal placing was also a feature of the siting of the prow on which the Nike of Samothrace alighted. This feature may well be yet another element in an attempt to avoid an impression of artificiality and control. In view of the coherence of all these works it is hard not to see the new literary taste, the enormous monuments of sculpture and architecture and the revival of the cult of Zeus as all being aspects of the same cultural movement. Each looks to a different period, but all point to an attempt to rediscover something of the simple power which seemed to have been essential to the earlier Greek achievement, but which had become lost in the calculations, refinement and rationalism of the fourth and third centuries.

The Greeks could not long maintain these aspirations. Rome burst rudely in upon the

152 Poseidon, *c.* 150 BC. From Melos.

dreamers. Piece by piece the Hellenistic world was either overwhelmed, as was Macedon in 168, or was given away, like Pergamum in 133. The heroic achievement of Alexander and his successors was rapidly swept aside and absorbed by something much greater. The name of Rome went before her. For the transliteration of *Roma* in Greek was close to *rhōmē*, the Greek word for 'violent strength'. The Greeks soon realized that it was Rome that personified the qualities they remembered as their own. Polybius, one of the last defenders of the liberty of Greece, vividly chronicles this realization in his historical works written in the middle of the second century. Physically defeated, the Greeks found a new source of confidence in their intellectual and artistic achievements. This confidence was fostered by their new masters, as when Paullus, the conqueror of Macedon, summoned the painter-philosopher Metrodorus to Rome. The Romans did not look in their subjects for the qualities of size and strength in which they themselves excelled; rather they admired the Greek capacity for mental ingenuity and subtlety. Consequently both the crisis in their own self-confidence and the enthusiasm of the Romans encouraged the Greeks to shift their admiration from the heroic vigour of their early ancestors, which had found its culmination in the Persian Wars and the following decades, and to concentrate instead on the later fifth and early fourth centuries when Athenian culture had manifested its greatest capacity for refinement and subtlety.

In art this produced the Neo-Attic movement already referred to. Leaders in the movement were the two brothers Timocles and Polycles who founded a whole artistic dynasty around 150. Two members of the family signed a portrait statue with Praxitelean forms, and others made a statue of Athena with a shield decorated with reliefs copied from the shield of Phidias' Athena Parthenos. This suggests that their interests were in the more elegant forms of the late Classical period and that they were particularly interested in Classical low relief. These tastes are indeed reflected in a vast body of works generally grouped together under the heading Neo-Attic and dateable to the later second and first centuries. Characteristic are the reliefs of female figures deriving from the late fifth-century papapet which surrounded the temple of Athena Nike on the Acropolis; though there are many

other examples of low relief both on rectangular panels and applied to the exteriors of vases. The whole Neo-Attic movement represents a return to an interest in the small and detailed. There were, of course, commercial pressures that encouraged miniaturization, particularly the need for the works to be portable for easy export to Rome, but this can only have been one factor behind the remarkable concentration on Late Classical reliefs, which were often reproduced or adapted in figures a few inches high. The exactness of the copying shows that precision of imitation was as important as precision of execution.

Attic and Asiatic in Rhetoric and Sculpture

The centre of production of these works was Athens itself and it is hard not to connect their popularity with the tastes of the group of Romans who went to that city in pursuit of education and the attributes of refinement. Much the most important element in the education of these young Romans, and one for which ancient Athens above all provided the models, was rhetoric. Perhaps the Attic orator most admired at this time was Lysias, a brilliant fourth-century writer of legal speeches whose style, as Quintilian a later Roman writer tells us, was described as more like a 'pure spring' than a 'large river'. This not only shows that the critical vocabulary of earlier Alexandria was still alive but also suggests that once again literary values had swung back in favour of those of Callimachus. A broader picture of the situation in the first century is found in Cicero and other writers. In general there was a strong current against the so-called Asiatic school of oratory, which was characterized by an exuberant florid style, and in favour of the orators of Athens, who were distinguished by their elegance, appropriateness and control. Even within the Attic school the grander style came to be neglected. This leads Cicero in one particular passage (*Orator* ix) to assert that those people who characterize Attic oratory only by elegance and clarity are concentrating too much on the legal speeches of Lysias and disregarding the grander public style found from Pericles to Demosthenes; they are wrong in implying that Attic oratory was exclusively *tenuis* (thin) and *subtilis* (fine), and not at all *amplus* (full) or *grandis* (abundant). Evidently there was a tendency to go too far in the

57

153

14

158

153 Roman relief deriving from the parapet of the temple of Athena Nike, Athens, late fifth century BC (see Pl. 14).

rejection of Asiatic oratory with the result that the whole grand style of oratory, which was so appropriate to the treatment of large public issues at mass meetings, was in danger of dying out.

It is tempting to draw a close parallel between the situations in rhetoric and sculpture. The growth in popularity of the fine and elegant Neo-Attic reliefs coincides with the end of the 'full' and 'abundant' style of second-century Asiatic Pergamum. The Neo-Attic reliefs may have seemed to the Roman collectors to embody more perfectly the Athenian intellectual achievement, but the rejection of the art of Asiatic Pergamum also meant the rejection of the grand Attic style of the Parthenon pediments from which the Pergamene works took their inspiration. Just as in Cicero's opinion the concentration on a style best adapted to the law-courts had meant the neglect of a style suitable for public meetings, so the new low reliefs satisfied a need for private works of art that could be appreciated in a small-scale en-

vironment, while the Pergamene style had been cultivated for great public monuments. This analogy between the development of rhetorical and sculptural taste also receives support from Aristotle's discussion of the difference between legal and public oratory. For Aristotle had related public oratory to a style of painting which used broad effects of light and shade and had implied that a painted equivalent of the rhetoric appropriate to the more private environment of the law-court would be characterized by precision or detail. The first set of traits could be aptly applied to the Pergamene works and the second to the Neo-Attic, and, although sculpture for a private house is not the same as a painted equivalent of legal speech, the critical factor behind Aristotle's choice of style, that is the nearness of the spectator or audience, is just as relevant for both. An admirer of a sculpture in a private house, like the listener in a law-court, would be able to follow all the tiny details that would be lost in the

154 Building of Auge's boat, from the small frieze of the Altar of Zeus, Pergamum, *c.* 170 BC.

remote mass experience of a public speech or monument. Another factor behind the shift in style, in sculpture as in rhetoric, is the difference in the pretensions of the audience. Criticism of the extravagant Asiatic style of oratory explained its grandiose inflation in terms of the comparative naïveté of the audiences of the cities of Asia Minor, while the qualities of the Attic orators were seen as reflecting the intelligence and sharpness of the Athenian citizens as a whole. The distinction made was basically between an appeal to the emotions and an appeal to the intellect. A taste for the fine and detailed Neo-Attic art would thus reflect the same intellectual pretensions as a taste for the purists' Attic oratory. In addition, a rejection of the grander style with its effects of light and shade may have been further encouraged by Plato's branding of *skiagraphia* in general as unclear and deceptive. It is difficult to document such intellectual snobbery, but Vitruvius in the late first century gives a hint of how the grand works of around 174 were thought to

be essentially designed for mass-appeal when he says condescendingly of the gigantic temple of Zeus at Athens, which was restarted by Antiochus, that it was admired not only by the crowd 72 but also by educated people. He seems to imply that its properties of size and richness were such as would normally only impress the unsophisticated, but that it was redeemed by other qualities.

At no stage should it be thought that the opposition between large and small, and their related stylistic traits, meant that the one excluded the other. Sometimes indeed it is possible to see two styles that can be related to this opposition being used effectively on the same monument, as with the Great Altar of Zeus at Pergamum. Here, for instance, the small frieze on the interior of the upper colonnade is very different 154 in character from the large frieze on the exterior of the altar but must have been planned in the context of the same cultural background, even if slightly later in execution. There is a basic

155 Teuthras running to receive Auge, from the small frieze of the Altar of Zeus, Pergamum, *c.* 170 BC.

quite different mode. If we consider again some of the factors that made the style popular we can see that they are present here too. Firstly, the Telephus story can never have been seen from a distance, being concealed high up in the colonnade on top of the altar, and would thus more appropriately use *akribeia* than *skiagraphia*. Secondly, its function is not to make a simple fanfare to celebrate the victory of the Attalids over the Gauls, but rather to persuade by a careful documentation of a series of events that the Attalids can trace their descent from Zeus and Hercules. Its character is thus precisely that of a legal argument, just as the large Gigantomachy frieze is a public oration of praise. This point suggests that the small frieze is aimed not so much at the general public, who in any case might never climb the stairs, as at those in Pergamum and elsewhere who were of a higher social and intellectual class and who might feel they were in competition with the Attalids. The presence of prominent carved inscriptions identifying the

156 Amphitrite, from the large frieze of the Altar of Zeus, Pergamum, *c.* 170 BC.

difference in scale as the figures in the small frieze are about half life-size while those in the large frieze greatly exceed life-size. Also while the large frieze shows one event, the battle of the gods and giants, on all its faces, the small frieze is composed of a whole series of scenes illustrating the story of Telephus, who constituted the link between Zeus and the Attalids. Each scene is filled out with all the landscape details and minor participants who are necessary to make the small frieze a convincing illustration of the scenes selected from the Telephus story. Such features are absent from the large frieze. Moreover, the whole style of the small frieze is much more restrained. The relief is much shallower and effects of light and shade are minimal. Facial expressions and movements are much more controlled, as can be seen in a
155 comparison of the running Teuthras and the
156 aggressive Amphitrite. Drapery lacks mass and frequently hangs in elegant linear patterns. From all this it is clear that the small frieze has much in common with later Neo-Attic art, though still in a

figures in the Gigantomachy and their absence from the Telephus frieze would be consistent with a notion that the one was to be understood by all literate people, but the other only by the few who could follow it. The differences between the two friezes can thus be seen to depend on differences in the distance at which they would have been viewed, on differences in rhetorical function and on differences in the character of the typical spectator, that is on the whole set of related criteria analysed above.

It was claimed earlier that the Pergamene Gigantomachy could be seen as an attempt to create a new grand and heroic work of art in a similar spirit to Apollonius' *Argonautica* and that both works could be seen as a deliberate reaction away from the exaltation of the small and artificial beloved by men such as Callimachus. If this is so, can the smallness and the precision of the Telephus frieze be linked in turn to Callimachus' ideas? Certainly it can in terms of scale, particularly as an undercurrent in Callimachus' admiration for the small is a contempt for the common man and his fondness for vulgar impressiveness. Callimachus, being descended from the Battiadae of Cyrene, considered himself to come from one of the best Greek families, and the Telephus frieze may well have been intended to assert similar pretensions. But even in details of composition the Telephus frieze corresponds with Callimachus' tastes. He had declared himself opposed to the Aristotelian virtues of 'unity' and 'continuity' as represented by Apollonius, and the Telephus frieze just as decisively rejects the unity and continuity of the Gigantomachy, though necessarily in a manner appropriate to the visual arts. Thus, while the Gigantomachy simply shows one group after another as they would have fought side by side in the battle, the Telephus frieze shows a series of scenes which constitute a selection of the most significant events in the lives of different people, events which are often separated from each other by many years or hundreds of miles. The difficulty of following the disjointed whole might well have directly appealed to Callimachus' intellectual snobbery. It is typical of the artistic complexity of the late Hellenistic world that the two sculptural compositions reflecting such different values can happily co-exist on the same monument.

This whole discussion only serves to demonstrate how important the question of scale and allied problems of style were in the Hellenistic world. Aristotle's recommendation of grandeur, based as it is on his understanding of the physiology and psychology of the ordinary man, generated a sharp reaction on the part of those who studied the intriguing paradox of the power of the small. This sophisticated intellectual attitude stimulated a further reaction in a new nostalgia for the simple strength of earlier times. It was, however, almost inevitable that the increasing distance between the wealthy and cultured class and the broad mass of the people in the Roman world should result in the final victory of the qualities of intricacy and refinement.

Active and Passive in Artistic Creation

Perhaps the most fundamental shift represented by these changes of values in the later Hellenistic world is that in the approach to the act of artistic creation itself. When Callimachus contrasted his *oligē libas* with the *megas rhoos* of others he drew attention not only to an opposition of scale but also to different attitudes to the process of literary composition. *Rhoos* derives from *rheō*, I flow, an intransitive verb, while *libas* comes from the basically transitive *leibō*, I pour. Callimachus thus sees his writing as active, that is under his control, and that of his rivals as relatively passive and lacking rational direction. On the other hand, it is precisely this control which is mocked both by Galaton's painting of Homer as a river god with later poets collecting his water in jugs and by Dioscorides' comparison of Aeschylus' letters worn by a rushing torrent with those of his successors which seem carved and polished. Both these latter images reflect a reaction against the tendency, which had been a marked one in the previous two hundred years, to regard the practice of an art as the intellectual application of a systematic discipline. During this period many had claimed that an art could be learned and many artists had indeed written treatises on their *technai* (arts), codifying the procedures involved in them. This position in turn had constituted a significant change, particularly in the literary context, from that of the early poets, such as the writers of the Homeric epics and Hesiod, who regarded their utterances as coming from a divine source, the Muse. Such early poets thought that, as they recited, they were possessed, in a state of *mania* (madness), and could never have viewed themselves as rational craftsmen. The rejection of excessive rationality in the third century was thus in a sense a return to a primitive position.

Callimachus himself illustrates this when he introduces his *Aetia* as if it too was produced under the influence of divine inspiration. But there is still a considerable difference between Callimachus' claim, which is little more than a literary device, and that represented by his rivals' comparison between the act of poetic creation and a great flow of water. The poet may not be self-conscious or intellectual, the god who speaks through him presumably is. The main reason for claiming such inspiration is so that an audience will think they are hearing the thoughts of someone much wiser than the ordinary man. Callimachus despised the idea of the *megas rhoos*, the great stream, because it suggested that the poet was possessed by nothing but an overwhelming natural physical force. His opponents may well have adopted that image because they rejected both the idea of writing as a self-conscious technique and Callimachus' use of the notion of inspiration, which they saw as a device chosen just as self-consciously to enhance the poet's prestige. They dispensed with self-consciousness completely and also with external inspiration, introducing what amounts to a new psychological concept, that of the internal creative force which they could only describe by the metaphor of the river. The image is certainly an important one as it introduces the possibility of a new level of freedom into the highly disciplined world of Greek culture. Water was again to symbolize a liberating force for the Romantic movement when a similar reaction occurred two thousand years later. Sadly, the promise of the image in antiquity was never fulfilled. Callimachus may have contrasted the great uncontrolled flood of Apollonius with his own small and carefully measured libations, but to us the distinction is a narrow one. There is no new artistic reality; there is only a new idea, the idea that artistic activity can be viewed as passive as well as active, and not just passive in the traditional sense that the artist is a vehicle of divine communication.

One of the few works of sculpture which explicitly seems to reflect the new approach to creation is the Nike of Samothrace and one of the ways in which it does this is in its free and 148 157 asymmetrical disposition in its fountain basin, 147 which was moreover filled with freely arranged boulders. Such irregularity well illustrates a reduced amount of apparent control by the artist. Another work that may embody the principle of free flow is the large frieze of the Zeus altar at Pergamum which contains, admittedly, several examples of repeated and echoing poses but which, within that framework of artificial control, reveals a sense of wild liberation. In this it contrasts strongly with friezes such as that of the fourth-century Mausoleum of Halicarnassus where so many of the figures echo and repeat each others' poses that the impression of control is overwhelming. It is perhaps worth looking at the contrast between these two works in the light of Aristotle's comments on how to produce a relatively natural or artificial effect in literature. Aristotle had argued that prose should not have metre because that would make it artificial and detract from its natural character; rhythm, on the other hand, would not disturb a natural effect. Rhythm provided a work with a structure of repeated stresses, while metre prescribed the form and weight of each element. It is thus possible to see the earlier frieze as having the equivalent of both metre and rhythm, while the frieze of the Zeus altar may be considered only to have an equivalent of rhythm. Perhaps *rhythmos* was already associated with *rhoos* and seen as a sort of flow pattern.

Whether or not the control of metre and symmetry could be neglected in a wave of enthusiasm for dynamic free effects around 200, such features soon returned to importance with the Neo-Attic movement. The many marble vases that would have gathered water in the gardens of the Late Republic illustrate beautifully the *oligē* 158 *libas* of Callimachus, in contrast to the *megas rhoos* of the Nike fountain. No sculptural works are so finely metrical as the friezes of figures that adorn them and other works of the period. Many show figures dancing; these figures are uniformly 162 spaced out and their gestures are repeated at intervals. Satyrs and maenads alternate regularly. The sculptor turns choreographer and the human body becomes a vehicle for his notation of patterns. The dance represents the ultimate in ordered movement. Plato had repeatedly made it clear that dancing is an essential instrument of education because it develops a sense of order. It may seem strange that the dancers are frequently

157 Nike of Samothrace, by Pythocritus, early second century BC (see also Pls. 147, 148).

the excited participants in a Dionysiac procession; yet this only emphasizes the need for finding patterns in nature or imposing patterns on her, just as Callimachus' *oligē libas* stressed the controlled use of a natural material. The natural flow discovered in the Hellenistic period is not abandoned in this Classical revival. It is only submitted to more rigorous control. It may be too simplistic a way of describing this style as one in which metre, measure, finds a new importance as a means of ordering rhythm, flow. But it is true that in all the arts new precise techniques were discovered to enable copies to be made of earlier works. Sculptors, and perhaps especially Pasiteles and his school, used devices such as the pointing machine to make copies of Attic monuments which contrast in their accuracy with the free interpretations of such works made at Pergamum. Vitruvius recorded the most detailed procedures for reproducing Greek architectural designs. Poets such as Catullus made highly-wrought translations of Greek poems, forcing Latin into the difficult lyric metres of Sappho and Alcaeus.

158 Sacrifice of Iphigenia, from the 'Medici' vase, first century BC.

159 Roman sundial, after Hellenistic type.

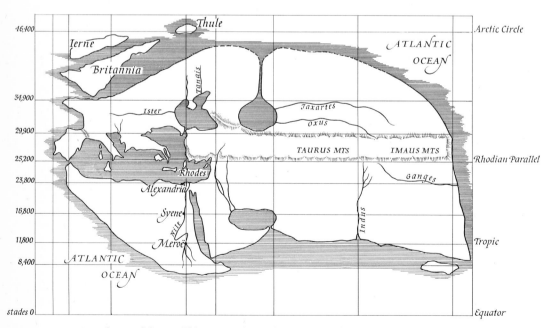

160 Reconstruction of map of the world by Eratosthenes (*c.* 275–194 BC).

Chapter Five

Time and Space

Several of Aristotle's remarks on the perception of large and small objects, which were discussed at the beginning of the previous chapter, imply a correlation of the dimensions of size and time. The perception of a small object is too instantaneous and that of a large one takes too long. In *On the Soul* 430b Aristotle relates the two dimensions in a more general discussion, maintaining that both length and time can be treated either as divisible or as indivisible; both dimensions can be treated as lines. In the *Physics* he says simply that 'time and length are divided into the same and equal divisions'. The problem of the relation of space and time had been pointedly illustrated a century earlier by Zeno of Elea in the story of Achilles and the tortoise. Aristotle's statement describes the relationship less elliptically and in a way which could be more useful in helping man to order his increasingly complex experiences of reality. Man could now clearly isolate himself on the two indices of space and time and establish his precise relationship to other people, places and events. In the third century Eratosthenes, chief librarian at Alexandria, conveniently brought together much information relating to these two indices in his *Chronographiae* and *Geographica*. The lines inscribed on the concave surfaces of Hellenistic sundials show how the same grid of horizontals and verticals was now used to provide a visual measure of time as was used to measure the surface of the earth in new and accurate maps. Also found in this period is the application of a system of proportionate gearing through cog wheels to the development of astronomical calculators for computing the movements of the heavenly bodies and the related passage of time.

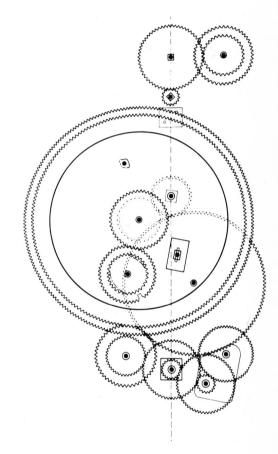

161 Reconstruction of gearing from a Hellenistic astronomical calculator.

159

160

161

One quite special way in which time and space could be correlated was in the operation of the senses. All Greek theories of vision depended on the assumption of movement of some kind between the eye and the object. Some people thought, like Plato, that rays emanated from the eye until they met the object, getting progressively weaker as they travelled. The Atomists, and later the Epicureans, believed that each object gave off small images of itself which were eventually received by the eyes. They too noted that vision became weaker with distance, and they supposed that the images suffered damage as they passed through the atmosphere. Aristotle rightly saw the deficiencies of these theories which put the eye into an excessively active or passive role. In *On the Soul* he says that an object affects the air around it in the same way that a seal affects wax; just as when we put something into water we observe that it affects the water for a long distance around it, though to a diminishing degree, until the process stops entirely, so too the object seen affects not only the air immediately surrounding it but progresssively all the air moving away from it until it reaches the sensitive pupil of our eye, which is also affected, being full of liquid. Aristotle thus comes close to the modern notion that vision is based on the transmission of waves through a medium. In the *Problems*, a later work of the Aristotelian school, vision is described more allusively as a cone which moves outwards in circles. This statement draws attention to a corollary of the earlier theory. Waves from objects which are the same distance from us and are thus arranged on the circumference of a circle of which we are the centre all have the same distance to travel to reach us and consequently reach us at the same time. Waves from objects which are an equal distance beyond the first ring will take correspondingly longer, and so on, From whichever point of view vision is considered it can only be understood by relating divisions of space to divisions of time. The same was true in the case of hearing. The phenomenon of the echo with its time lag had long fascinated the Greeks and with the development of scientific speculation both it and the reflected visual image were recognized as analogous phenomena. Hence it is not surprising that Aristotle and his school thought that sound, like visual information, was transmitted by the progressive disturbance of a medium, air.

Unfortunately Aristotle does not attempt to show how this rather sophisticated theory might affect the work of artists. He does this only in the context of the much more rudimentary notion that it takes a much longer time to look at a large object than a small one because our eye has to travel over it. We saw in the last chapter how he used this notion to argue explicitly in favour of moderate length plays and implicitly in favour of moderate sized works of art. He certainly alerts us to the difference in our visual experience of say a small statuette and a large frieze. He also suggests the possibility that looking at a work of art and experiencing a work of literature are analogous activities. It is thus of interest to consider his remarks on the linear organization of words in the passage of the *Rhetoric* referred to at the end of the last chapter. The orator, he says, should use rhythm, but not metre, in his sentences, as metre gives an impression of artificiality which makes him sound less convincing and also distracts the hearer's attention by making him concentrate on the recurrent element in the sentence. However, one type of metre may be used. This is the paeon which is a reversible unit, $-\cup\cup\cup$ and $\cup\cup\cup-$, and can thus be used symmetrically at the beginning and end of a sentence, $-\cup\cup\cup\ldots\cup\cup\cup-$, allowing a long syllable at the end, which Aristotle says is necessary so that there is more to stop the sentence than a punctuation mark. Aristotle is particularly concerned with beginnings and endings and it is this which makes him favour a 'periodic' rather than a 'continuous' sentence structure. For a period, of which this sentence is an example, being composed of subordinate rather than parallel clauses, starting with a main subject and terminating with a main verb, is, as Aristotle says, a sentence with a clear beginning and end. His recommendation of the period is not surprising since such sentences had largely replaced a simple continuous style by the fifth century. It is nevertheless characteristic that Aristotle defines the principles underlying the period in such as way that they could be readily applied to other art forms. Particularly in the context of his account of the temporal nature of visual experience, and of the problems which this produces in the perception of large objects, it is evident that what is said here about the ordering of literary compositions could also be applied to the organization of large works of art. As the understanding of the 'period' must have been an

162 Dionysiac procession with Silenus, satyrs and maenads. Drawing from a vase of the second century AD, itself a copy of a Neo-Attic original of the first century BC. H indicates position of handles on vase.

essential part of any literate education, the principles recorded by Aristotle must have been widely known.

Time, Length and Distance

In no circle was there such close contact between the literary and artistic worlds as in Late Hellenistic Athens where the Neo-Attic reliefs were produced for Rome's cultural élite. Already in the last chapter an attempt was made loosely to relate Aristotle's notions of rhythm and metre to the friezes of Neo-Attic vases. His remarks on the period form may be related to them more precisely. One of the main characteristics of these friezes is that they cannot be fully appreciated without walking around the vase. This fact may well have influenced artists in their frequent selection of processional dances for the decoration of the vases. The directional movement of the spectator finds a response in the directional movement of the reliefs, as in the example illustrated. The artist's awareness of the relationship in space between the spectator and the vase also implies an awareness of the relationship in time. For it must take the spectator a certain time to walk round the vase. Aristotle had realized that in speech the lapse of time necessitated the use of the reversed paeon metre to mark the beginning and end of a period, and here there is a visual metrical device of a reversed figure used in the same way. The fact that the Greek word period, *periodos*, means originally 'way round' or 'circuit' may indeed have encouraged the application of the literary device to the

sculptural composition. The use of a similar reversed figure under the handle of the vase further subdivides the frieze into two clauses. The flow of movement that unites the whole frieze is thus endowed with the same careful articulation that Aristotle valued in the period. Although the use of symmetrical devices to effect this articulation is reminiscent of the symmetry found in many fifth-century pediments and other compositions, in those works symmetry was used as a traditional method of imposing coherence on one scene. Here, on the other hand, the symmetry is introduced much more selectively into the inherently asymmetrical one-directional flow; and in view of the fact that only a small portion of the frieze could be seen at any one time it can only be understood as a means of giving articulation to a linear temporal experience.

An earlier work which uses this device in a much looser form is the large frieze of the Zeus altar at Pergamum. Here too the relation in space between spectator and monument is carefully considered. The altar was approached from the back through a gate in a wall which was at an oblique angle to the altar. This might have resulted in confusion, but for two facts. The architect has ensured that the spectator first relates to the whole monument, because as he enters he stands where the perpendicular bisector of the rear face of the altar meets the oblique rear enclosure wall. The spectator then notes that the axis of his movement and vision, that is the line of the perpendicular bisector of the gate where he stands, leads him to a point near the north end of the east side of the altar, where the figures of Zeus

153

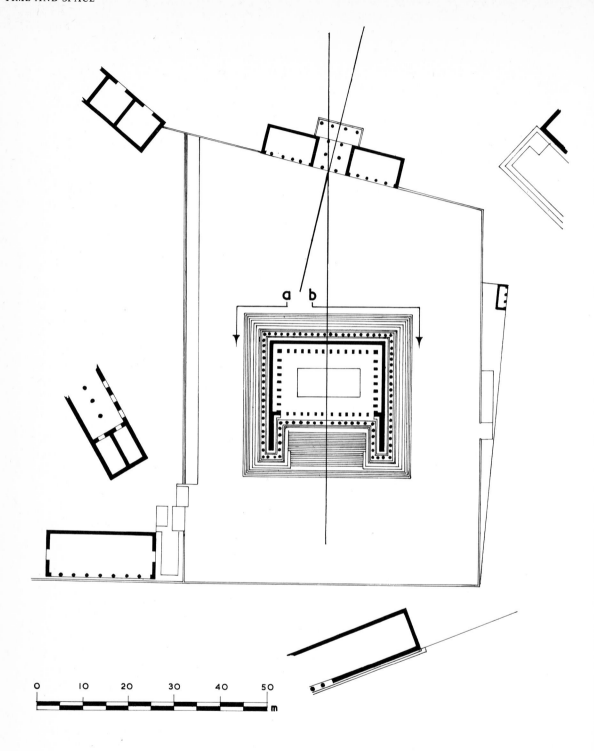

163 Plan of the Altar of Zeus, Pergamum, showing axial lines. (*a*) and (*b*) indicate respective positions of Athena and Zeus on the large frieze.

86 and Athena balance each other symmetrically as they deal with their opponents and by their outward leaning motion start a movement round the altar in two directions. This movement was continued in the majority of the main figures, with Aphrodite, Nyx and the Fates moving westwards on the north frieze and Phoebe, Selene, Helios and Eos moving westwards on the south frieze, only to be stopped by the opposed

156 movement of Dionysus and Amphitrite on the projections at the south and north ends of the west façade. Two odd-shaped sections then

188 balanced each other either side of the steps. There are subsidiary rhythms in the composition, but again the 'metrical' device is used most emphatically to tell the spectator where to begin and where to end. The metrical device both marks off the two halves of the frieze and, by using two male figures to bound one half and two female the other, suggests that each half needs the other in order to achieve biological completeness. Contact between the artistic and intellectual spheres is much less well documented at Pergamum than in first-century Athens, although Antigonus of Carystus seems both to have written extensively and to have been active as a sculptor at the Attalid court. However, it was observed earlier that there was at least a new interest in didactic method and that this led Apollodorus to use metrical language for his writings because of its great memorability. In the same spirit the shrine at Cyzicus was adorned with a combination of reliefs and epigrams. If, then, as was also suggested, the large frieze of the Zeus altar had a didactic purpose, it is less surprising to find it exploiting devices analogous to those metrical ones which Aristotle had specifically recommended as aids to the human faculty of comprehension.

The two friezes just discussed, both Attic and Pergamene, show how the artists' realization of the linear nature of the spectators' perception of such works stimulated the development of particular devices to facilitate this. In an earlier work we can see sculptors responding to the character of the frieze in a way which exploited the spectator's linear movement in time and space in a more direct way. This is the frieze of the Parthenon which illustrates the procession held in honour of the goddess Athena at the Panathenaea. On it there are none of the artificial devices we have just noted. Instead two views of the same procession run continuously round the two sides of the building from the south-west corner to the east front. The south-west corner was chosen as the starting-point because it marks the limit of vision for the spectator approaching from the Propylaea. The procession ends in the centre of the east front because that is the point directly above the visitor's goal, the temple's main entrance. But there is not only this general correlation between the movement of the spectator and that of the procession; the frieze also precisely matches the visitor's movement in time and space. For the procession is not presented as it moves past one particular point. Instead the first scenes show the marshalling of the participants in the Cerameicus, that is, in time, an early event and the one which in space took place furthest from the Acropolis, while the last scene shows the final event on the Acropolis, that is the actual presentation of the offering to the goddess. The intervening slabs, crowded with movement, 164 show the passage of the procession through the day and along the route between these two places and events. The progress of the spectator from the point where he can first see the frieze to the point where he arrives at the door of the temple is thus precisely matched by that of the procession. The lapse of time and movement in space had already been roughly synchronized in oriental band-like compositions, but this is the first time that such synchronization is exactly paralleled and almost generated by the movement of the spectator. It is the first case where a space/time line is fully exploited.

The treatment of the Panathenaic procession on the Parthenon frieze is partly a consequence of the designer's realization of the peculiar problem of perception posed by a long frieze which cannot be seen all together at one moment; it also depends on his appreciation of the peculiar qualities of the procession. For a procession can, more easily than any other art form, persuade us of the similarity of space and time as linear dimensions. Whoever took the decision to represent the Panathenaic procession may thus have played an essential role in generating the new treatment of time and space on the Parthenon frieze. It is interesting to observe that the new insight into the space/time operation of both frieze and procession revealed in the Parthenon is precisely contemporary with Zeno's popularization of the problem of Achilles and the tortoise. Zeno was also a teacher of Pericles who was

164 Horsemen of the Panathenaic procession, from the frieze of the Parthenon, Athens, 447–432 BC.

largely responsible for the creation of the Parthenon.

Although we do not have examples of a frieze being used in the same way until the Telephus frieze of the Zeus altar at Pergamum we do have evidence of how, by the third century, space and time could be exploited in the iconography of processions. The Ptolemaic procession, possibly of 276, has already been referred to when personifications were discussed. If the account of the procession is studied further the principle of arrangement of its different sections can be more fully understood. Both in the overall layout of the procession and in the arrangement of individual sections we find allusions to the passage of time. The first section was dedicated to the Morning Star and the last to the Evening Star in expression of the procession's duration from morning to evening. Within the part of the procession devoted to Dionysus a series of carts bore tableaux illustrating the successive scenes of the god's life. In the same section were repre-

sentations of the Seasons with their attributes commemorating Dionysus as god of regeneration. This example of the passing of the procession marking the passing of the seasons provides a direct link with the Neo-Attic friezes where the Four Seasons are also found in Dionysiac troupes. 102 The movement of the procession was, in fact, used to illustrate the passage of time on several different scales. A primary purpose of the procession was that of reinforcing the Ptolemies' dynastic claims. Hence, Alexander, who had raised the first Ptolemy above his fellows, was placed both among the gods and next to the image of Ptolemy II himself. Also, early sections of the procession were dedicated to Ptolemy's parents. Ptolemy's position was thus seen to derive from his position at the culmination of a historical sequence. Another way in which the Ptolemies strengthened their dynastic authority was by always taking the name of the dynasty's founder, Ptolemaios, so that the same stock seemed endlessly regenerated. The god who personified

cyclical recurrence above all others was Dionysus, who embodied the principle of regeneration
in the yearly vintage. One of the reasons why
Hellenistic rulers associated themselves with
Dionysus was because they wished also to be
identified with the divine control of natural
forces. Hence the combination of reference to
both Dionysiac and dynastic regeneration in the
Ptolemaic procession. Indeed, this general similarity of theme between Dionysiac and dynastic
imagery, the fact that both are concerned with the
representation of cycles and sequences, and the
assertion that continuity underlies apparent
change explains why the study of time and the
development of narrative are chiefly associated
with these two contexts. This is seen in the series
of scenes of Dionysus' life displayed in the
Ptolemaic procession and in the series of scenes of
the Telephus story on the Pergamene frieze. It is
also visible in the continuity of the tradition of
illustrating the life of Dionysus in the Roman
period and in the development out of this of the

narrative of Christ's life. It was, of course, in the
treatment of Christ's life, with its associations,
both dynastic and Dionysiac, that the great
tradition of European narrative art grew up.

The stages of Dionysus' life were marked in the
Ptolemaic procession by a series of tableaux; the
dynastic sequence was illustrated by single
statues. Plato, in the *Critias*, had already shown
how a continuous series of portrait statues could
be used by a dynasty to document its descent
from divine ancestors; images of the rulers of
Atlantis surrounded the great temple of Poseidon
there. Like Herodotus Plato knew of the existence
of such statues in ancient Egypt, and the Egyptian
examples must also have influenced the Ptolemies. Rather surprisingly, at almost the same time
that the *Critias* was being composed a similar
practice actually appeared on Greek soil. Shortly
after 369 a semicircular base was constructed at
Delphi supporting a series of statues of the early
kings and queens of Argos. The figures seem to
have been put only on the left-hand side of the

157

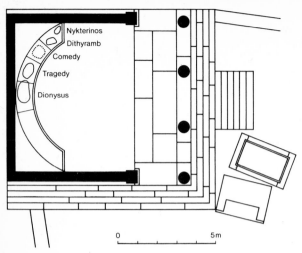

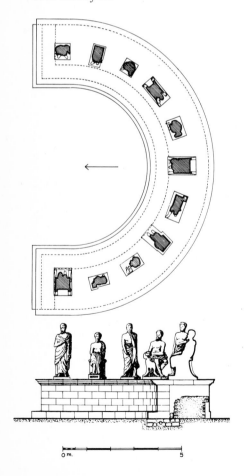

165 Plan of the shrine of Dionysus, Thasos, c. 300–275 BC.

166 Reconstruction of the group of philosophers and poets from the Serapeum, Memphis, first half of the third century BC.

exhedra and were arranged in a chronological order from right to left. The purpose of the monument was to glorify Argos rather than the dynasty, which was extinct, but the monument does show that a row of statues could by this time be seen to suggest a chronological sequence. For, although there had been earlier monuments at Delphi containing groups of statues, these had brought together the heroes of one moment. The Argive monument is the first example where a line of statues acquires temporal value; moreover it was erected not long before the time that Aristotle was laying stress on the temporal problems involved in surveying large objects. The idea was soon taken up by contemporary dynasties. In the 330s, also at Delphi, Daochus of Thessaly put up nine statues on a long straight base to represent his genealogical line. At Olympia Philip of Macedon erected a circular shrine, the Philippeion, with his own statue in the centre, his parents on his right and his wife and son, Alexander, on the left. In the third century at Delos an even longer series of at least twenty-one statues of the ancestors of the then ruler of Macedon, Antigonus Gonatas, were set up in front of a long portico. The first statue on the left was apparently larger than the rest, to judge by its feet, and so probably represented the divine founder of the family, suggesting that a chronological series ran from left to right as in the Philippeion group. This apparently was the normal way a group would be 'read' when the movement of the spectator could not be predicted. For when, as in the two monuments at Delphi, the normal movement of the spectator was along a processional way from right to left, the statues are arranged to succeed each other chronologically in that direction too. It appears that in these monuments, as in the Parthenon, the lapse of time is suggested by the motion through space.

A feature of the Argive monument at Delphi is that it takes the form of a hemicycle, evidently responding to the earlier Argive dedication opposite. As a number of Hellenistic groups are also arranged in semicircles it is worth inquiring into the function of this form. One of the ways in which such an arrangement of figures differs from a group in a straight line is that the spectator is made clearly aware that he is looking at a group and not at a series of individual statues which may seem to run on into adjoining series. In

167 Seven Sages. Roman mosaic of the first century BC, perhaps recording a Hellenistic composition.

Aristotle's terms it makes possible a 'periodic' rather than a 'continuous' arrangement, having a clear beginning and an end. Another important point is that the spectator can stand still and enjoy an equally close relation with each statue, while if they were arranged in a straight line he would need to move along in order to confront each statue individually. This last point, of course, makes a semicircular arrangement less appropriate for groups where the movement of the spectator was intended to reflect the passing of time. Hence it is not surprising that, after the semicircular monument to the Argive kings where the arrangement was necessary to balance an earlier exhedra across the path, in the later groups of this kind the straight line is preferred. By contrast, the hemicycle is used where it is most appropriate, that is for groups where no temporal distinction is intended. This was the case at 165 Thasos where a small building of the early third

century contained a curved podium on which stood statues of Dionysus and the personifications of different types of theatrical performance, Tragedy, Comedy, Dithyramb and Nykterinos. Four other statues from the same group are lost; presumably they represented similar personifications. Later in the third century a full semicircle of philosophers and poets was set up, probably around a figure of Dionysus, at the Memphis Serapeum. Here the statues have 166 survived, though some are unidentifiable, and while they run in time from Homer to the almost contemporary Demetrius of Phalerum, no attention ever seems to have been given to a chronological sequence. A similar group may have adorned the Alexandrian Serapeum and either this or the Memphis group may have inspired a semicircular grouping of the Seven Sages illustrated in numerous Roman mosaics. In all these 167 groups the spectator seems intended to forget

168 Roman perspective wall-painting from Boscoreale, first century BC.

temporal factors as he stands in front of the curve, just as he was expected to be aware of them when moving along the rectilinear arrangements mentioned earlier.

One difference between the group at Thasos and those at Delphi and Memphis is that it is arranged in an arc which is far from being a complete semicircle. This means that the centre of the circle of whose circumference the arc is an approximate, if depressed, section is a considerable distance in front of the group. This must be related to the situation of the typical observer. For the group at Thasos is the only one enclosed in a sort of temple where, presumably, the observer could not approach the group closely. This difference draws our attention to the main factor governing the design of such groups, that is the visual relationship between the spectator and the individual figures. The basic function of the curved arrangement is to allow all

the statues to be at the same distance from the spectator. This was critical in Greek visual theory, as not only would disparity of distance mean that some figures were larger and more clearly defined than others, but also the experience of vision would not be synchronized; according to all Greek theories – whether rays went out from the eye, whether images were given off by the object or whether the object was thought to affect the medium progressively until the eye was reached – it was assumed that there was movement between the eye and the object, which took time to occur.

The central figure at Thasos, and probably also at Memphis, was the god Dionysus, and such groups are thus connected with the world of the theatre. *Theatron* means a 'place for seeing' and there is evidence that the theatre was a centre for the study of the principles of visual perception. Scenography, or scene-painting, which Aristotle said was first introduced by Sophocles, came to be used as the normal term for perspective. Vitruvius tells how the architect uses *ichnographia* (ground plans), *orthographia* (elevations) and *scaenographia* (perspective views). This last he characterized as showing buildings with receding sides and all the lines responding to a 'compass point', an expression which may or may not refer to the vanishing-point of the Renaissance. Certainly the development of perspective coincides with the heyday of the ancient theatre in the fifth and fourth centuries, and the most magnificent examples of ancient perspective are the wall decorations of first-century Italy, 168 many of which may derive from stage designs. There remains a doubt as to whether a full linear perspective system was in use in antiquity, but clearly any system would have demanded just such a consideration of the position of the typical spectator as we have suggested is evident in the semicircular groups.

Sound and Space in the Theatre

If the argument about the relation between such groups and the science of optics lacks ancient documentation, this is not true of the relation between theatre design and the science of acoustics. Vitruvius gives us an extended account of how theatres should be laid out and equipped. The Greek theatre, as established in the fourth century and described later by Vitruvius, con-

169 Greek theatre, Epidaurus, begun *c.* 350 BC.

sisted basically of a steep curved auditorium extending for slightly more than a semicircle around a circular *orchēstra*, or dancing area, with the *skēnē*, or combined stage and scene, tangential to the open part of the circle. The theatre of Dionysus at Athens developed slowly to acquire this form by the mid-fourth century and the theatre at Epidaurus, newly built at that date by Polyclitus the Younger, includes all these features. The circular form of the orchestra matched the circular form of the original dithyrambic dance in honour of Dionysus. The shape of this orchestra obviously affected the shape of the auditorium. Yet, although there is this obvious coherence between the shape of the dancing place and the auditorium, and although the circular arrangement produced excellent visibility for all, it is not in terms of these properties that Vitruvius explains the form of the Greek theatre. For him the main considerations are acoustic. According

to his account the ancient architects observed that sound moved outwards in circles like the waves around the spot where a stone enters the water, with the modification that the rings rise as they move outwards through the air. 'Therefore the ancient architects, following (in their investigations) the path of nature, made the gradients of their theatres follow the rising sound.'

Vitruvius is here referring to an extension of Aristotle's theory of acoustics, one such as that attributed to the Stoics by Plutarch, that sound moves out spherically from its source. The fact that he states specifically that this was the theory of ancient architects makes it almost certain that he is referring to an oral or written tradition associated with theatre design. The rising circular seats of the Greek theatre were thus designed to ensure that a voice coming from the orchestra was received in the most effective way, being at the

169

maximum strength possible at each given distance. As the period of development of the Greek theatre between 450 and 300 was that at which there was the maximum concentration on the words and music of the performance rather than on the dancing, the notion that acoustic considerations were paramount seems quite acceptable. The later development of the theatre up to Roman times can also be seen as reflecting the increasingly rigorous application of acoustic theory. For the early Greek theatres frequently have a gradient which increases towards the top, while it is chiefly Late Hellenistic and Roman theatres where Vitruvius' regulation is followed exactly and where one line can be drawn from the front of the lowest seat to the front of the highest one touching those in between. It is also only in the later theatres that allowance is made for the fact that the most important sounds came from the stage, with the result that the stage itself begins to cut across the orchestra and the section of seating which extended beyond the semicircle

was either opened out or curtailed, until the perfection of the Roman theatre as described by Vitruvius was achieved, with the stage forming the diameter of a semicircular auditorium. The actors would then be at the centre of the rings of seating.

Further evidence of the way Greek theatre designers thought about sound is provided by Vitruvius' lengthy discussion of the use of musical vases in theatre. He describes how in the Greek theatre vases tuned to particular notes could be arranged in the auditorium to pick up and amplify the music. These were to be arranged in three different rows at regular intervals up the seating. Generally the highest notes of the octave would be placed at the extreme edges and then the notes would be progressively lowered towards the centre. The lowest row would be tuned to the enharmonic scale, the middle to the chromatic and the highest to the diatonic. Knowledge of Greek musical theory enables us to see that this whole system provides a musical

170 Reconstruction of the Hellenistic theatre, Priene, begun second century BC.

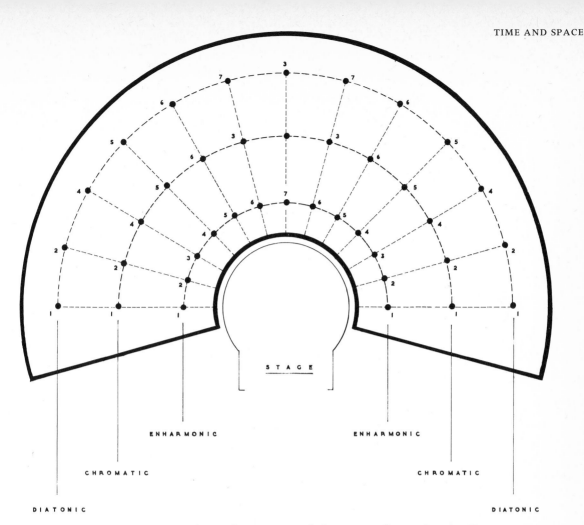

STAGE

ENHARMONIC

ENHARMONIC

CHROMATIC

CHROMATIC

DIATONIC

DIATONIC

171 Plan showing the arrangement of musical vases in a Greek theatre according to Vitruvius. Notes are numbered from the highest (*1*) to the lowest (*7*).

commentary on the shape of the theatre. The arrangement of the notes with the lower towards the centre and the higher towards the edges is probably intended to relate to the varying distance between the stage and the individual vase. The distance between the vases and stage would progressively increase from the edges towards the centre. This may seem insignificant to us, but for the Greeks, who were fascinated by the relationship between the pitch of a note and the length of a string, and who described their notes in terms of the length of strings on the lyre, so that the 'highest' note for them was that produced by the 'highest' or 'longest' string and thus the lowest in our terms, it would have been natural to think of the increasing length of

distance between the vase and the stage as tending to favour lower notes.

How these distances were measured can be understood by the use of a diagram. This shows that in the Greek theatre the central area of the stage used for acting was actually closest to the edges of the auditorium and furthest from the centre. The fact that this was particularly true for the lowest row of vases perhaps explains why that is the only one to be completely consistent, with the lowest note in the centre. In the upper rows, where the difference diminishes, although the same principle applies, the notes closest to the centre are taken from the middle of the scale rather than from the bottom. A consciousness of the difference in position of the three rows of

171

vases probably also explains why the enharmonic scale was the lowest, the chromatic in the middle and the diatonic the highest. For the enharmonic scale operates with the smallest intervals, that is quarter tones, the chromatic with semitones and the diatonic with the largest intervals, that is full tones. It can be seen from the diagram that the physical intervals between the vases would also increase from enharmonic to diatonic. The intervals between the vases thus match the type of musical interval appropriate to the different scales. A secondary consideration may have been that the placing of the different scales could also be seen as appropriate to the section of the audience in which it was placed. In general the more sophisticated part of the audience would sit low in the theatre and the less sophisticated further up. Thus the enharmonic scale characterized by Vitruvius as 'serious and of a distinguished authority' would be situated among the priests and notables, while the 'easy and natural' diatonic scale would be placed in the area occupied by the general populace.

Further evidence of how the Greeks related linear distance to musical notes is found in another passage in Vitruvius, at the beginning of book six of *De Architectura*. There Vitruvius explains how peoples who live to the north of Italy tend to have low voices and those to the south, as far as the equator, high voices. This, according to Vitruvius, is because the earth and the heavens are so related that the peoples who live at the equator are closest to the sky and those at the North Pole furthest from it. The relationship between the surface of the earth and the sky is thus that of an approximately triangular musical instrument. Just as the long strings produce low and the short strings high notes, so the people who live in corresponding positions have high or low voices. The underlying theory of the musical relationships of distances is the same as that applied to theatre design.

Unfortunately we do not know the date at which any of these ideas found in Vitruvius were formulated. No reliable evidence on the use of musical vases in theatres has come down to us. However, the fact that Vitruvius says that such vases were brought to Rome by Mummius after he had sacked Corinth in 146 suggests that the use of vases was certainly Hellenistic. Admittedly, the basic notion of the relation between distance

and music goes back to Pythagoras and had received one of its first embodiments in the Pythagorean theory of the music of the spheres, with each planet emitting a different sound in proportion to its distance from the earth, but the easy way in which Vitruvius relates science, geography and art is much more characteristic of his own period.

Geometry, Geography and Space

One of the concepts underlying all the theories described in the preceding pages is that of imaginary lines extending between objects, or between people and objects. From the beginning of measurement lines had been imagined between objects, and in geometry a whole science had been constructed using such notional lines. With the enormous expansion of both measurement and geometry in the Hellenistic period the imaginary line became accepted as essential for the conceptualization of much of reality. The sciences of seeing and hearing, perspective and acoustics, assumed linear contact between man and his environment and the application of this assumption had a striking effect on the development of art. Complicated networks of lines were posited in order to facilitate the study of three-dimensional solid figures such as cylinders, spheres and cones, especially in the work of Archimedes. This solid geometry enabled scientists like Eratosthenes to see the world clearly as a sphere of the correct size and clearly subdivided by horizontal and vertical lines so that a flat projection could be made of the known world using lines of longitude and latitude. The application of solid geometry combined with the use of a theory of perspective enabled astronomers like Aristarchus to attempt calculations of the sizes and distances of the heavenly bodies and even to plot their paths in complex curving lines; though in this area the persistence of the idea that the earth was the centre of the universe inhibited advance. The significance of these developments is that the educated man – and general education made great progress at this time – not only conceived of the surface of the earth and any other solid he wished to understand as covered with a net of lines, but even projected straight and curved lines into the void.

An increasing awareness of these conceptual lines affects art in different ways. Some examples

160

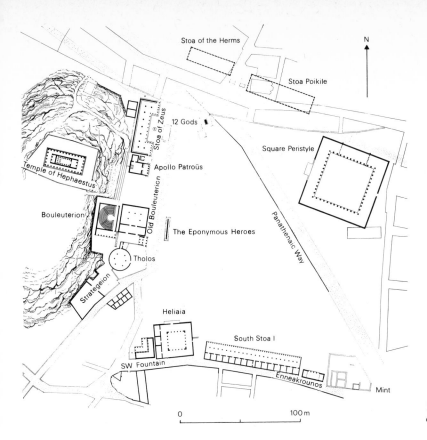

172 Plan of the Athenian Agora at the end of the fourth century BC.

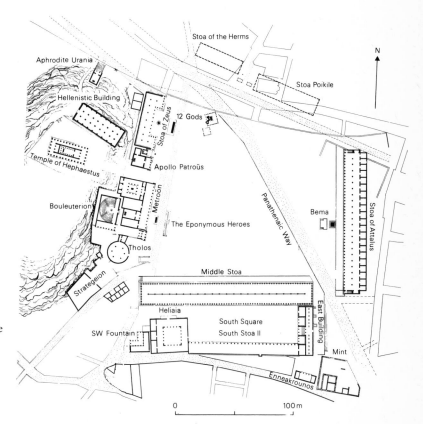

173 Plan of the Athenian Agora after Hellenistic remodelling in the second century BC.

172
173 of this on the largest scale, that of architectural planning, can be seen in the Athenian Agora. In the second century two parallel stoas were built on the south side of the traditional central open space of the city. Surprisingly they were oriented, unlike any earlier buildings in the area, exactly on an east-west axis. At the same time, around 150, a great two-storey stoa was built by Attalus II running exactly north-south on the east side of the Agora. Individual temples had been

174 Tower of the Winds, Athens, *c.* 40 BC.

built roughly facing east and west from the earliest times and, indeed, whole cities, such as Priene, or extensions to cities of the fifth and fourth centuries, had been laid out with their streets, and consequently their buildings, oriented on the cardinal points. In Athens, however, the destruction of the most celebrated city centre of the ancient world and the imposition of a new and jarring principle reveals a new awareness of the system of geographical geometry. The passing nature of this mood is revealed by the fact that the great buildings of the Roman agora at Athens return to the traditional irregular plan. Another direct connection between the development of Hellenistic science and Athenian architectural activity is established by the erection, a century after the Stoa of Attalus, of the Tower of the Winds in the area that was to become the Roman 174 agora. This was an octagonal building with its eight sides aligned on the four cardinal points and the four intermediate points from which the eight main winds were supposed to blow. Each side was accordingly decorated with a relief representation of the relevant wind, and a triton weather-vane above pointed with an indicator at the figure of the wind then blowing. Sundials were also engraved on the relevant faces of the building and inside there was a water-clock. Citizens were thus able by using this building to orient themselves in space and time. Architecture, sculpture and the new science were perfectly integrated.

If the reorganization of the Athenian Agora can be related to the development of the technique of using lines of latitude and longitude to organize the surface of the earth and to record geographical knowledge, it is not surprising that a similar grid of lines came increasingly to be imposed on buildings and their environments at the same time. It has been observed earlier that temples in the fourth century tended to have regularized plans. The temple of Athena Polias at Priene, for 117 example, employs a standard unit of three feet to determine the size of paving slabs, spacing of columns, arrangement of cella walls and other features. However, there remained one area in which architects still failed to achieve complete regularity. As in earlier buildings, the temples of around 300, such as the temple of Artemis at Sardis or the Didymaeum at Miletus, all reveal a lack of correspondence between the columns or pilasters inside the cella and the exterior side colonnades. Apparently architects felt no need to achieve this correspondence because the elements concerned could never be seen at the same time. Only when the architect begins to think of his ground-plan in terms of 'conceptual' lines linking interior and exterior is it natural for him to develop a correlation between inner and outer elements. The first temple where this seems to have happened is the temple of Artemis Leuko-phryene at Magnesia-on-the-Maeander, built by Hermogenes in the later second century. Here all interior columns are aligned on the centre two columns of the façades while half of them are also aligned on flank columns. Hermogenes' obsession with geometrical coherence is documented by Vitruvius who tells how he entirely rejected the Doric order because of the inevitable irrationality of the relation of triglyph and metope at the corner of the frieze. In the temple of Artemis Leukophryene simple geometrical proportions abound. But two features in particular confirm Hermogenes' application of a framework of conceptual lines. Although the dimensions of the temple platform and cella would allow for the use of a double colonnade on the exterior, only the outer ring was actually built, thus leaving a large space between this and the cella. This arrangement, called pseudodipteral, had occasionally been used before, as in temple G at Selinus (sixth century) and in the temple of Artemis at Sardis, but no earlier temple provided such a convincing impression of space around the cella. It is indeed clear that the capacity of both artist and spectator to imagine conceptual lines passing through the void and linking corresponding objects enabled them, finally, to see space as an ordered three-dimensional volume. Equally, the three large openings that Hermogenes made in the pediments of his temple, perhaps with a view to lightening the weight on the architraves below, would have probably been unacceptable earlier because they would have seemed to destroy the solid container-like quality of the roof; now the spectator may have been able to more readily imagine the line of the wall continuing conceptually across the aperture and could thus accept the novelty of the interrupted wall.

It is difficult for us to conceive the imaginative effort involved in first making windows in walls. The ritual and functional origins of walls as barriers and enclosing surfaces meant that man could only really accept apertures other than the

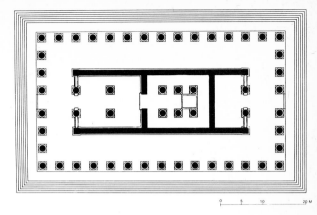

175 Plan of the temple of Artemis Leukophryene, Magnesia-on-the-Maeander, mid-second century BC.

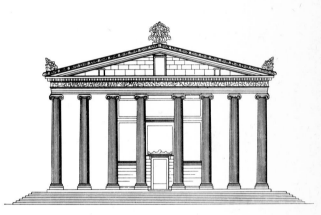

176 Elevation of the temple of Artemis Leukophryene, Magnesia-on-the-Maeander.

necessary door if he could see the containing function of the wall still continuing unaffected by the opening. Certainly, windows, which had appeared only rarely in Greek monumental buildings previously, now begin to appear regularly. The Ecclesiasterion or Assembly Hall of Priene, built around 200, had a large arched window and was indeed one of the first structures to introduce the arch at all. The Bouleuterion of Miletus of twenty years later had a whole range of windows on a large scale. The wall of the Bouleuterion is also one of the first examples of

167

the extensive use of half-columns. As well as walls being opened by the use of windows, colonnades could be closed by walling up the intercolumniations. These are startling departures in the Greek world where the column and the wall had retained their integrity unmodified since the first emergence of stone architecture. Earlier architects had normally thought directly in terms of columns and walls when planning buildings. Now, in the second century, architects apparently started to lay out their buildings first as a geometrical arrangement of lines. Architectural forms thus became secondary instead of being absolute and the designer could treat them with a much greater flexibility. Only such an assumption as this can explain why columns which had previously been free-standing now are often linked by walls or low screens as, for example, at the entrances to Hermogenes' temple at Magnesia or why corner columns are now made into heart-shaped forms as in the gymnasium of Miletus, clearly expressing the junction of the two lines at a right angle. Both these developments could easily arise from an architect superimposing columns on a network of lines. Curiously, there is an exactly parallel shift of architectural styles at the time of the Renaissance when Alberti abandons Brunelleschi's exploitation of the pure forms of wall and column in favour of the pier and the half-column attached to the wall, and we know from his book *De Re Aedificatoria* that Alberti's greatest pride was in the *lineamenta* or conceptual lines which were the foundations of all his designs. While there is no such explicit evidence that linear geometry had already taken on a new importance in architectural practice in the second century too, such a change could explain at once both the new rationalization of large-scale planning and the fondness for a new vocabulary of architectural details.

One of the main features of the new architecture is the control of the void. Void, in fact, takes on dimensions and becomes space. No temples before those of Hermogenes could be so easily read in terms of measurable and commensurable volumes. Another example of the new approach to the void is again provided by the Athenian Agora. In the later Hellenistic period a garden was laid out around the temple of Hephaestus, above the Agora. Two rows of trees were set in holes along the sides and along the back of the building

and these trees were aligned exactly on the columns of the temple, so that the geometrical organization of the fifth-century structure was extended into the surrounding environment. The real colonnade of the temple is surrounded by what amounts to a double colonnade of trees, which immediately integrates the architecture with the enveloping space.

The development described above is a shift rather than a sudden change and to define it more precisely presents considerable problems of vocabulary and word usage. We can however perhaps gain some further insight into the change by examining the vocabulary of antiquity itself. The Greeks had apparently no word to describe the notion of space here emerging. Their *topos* (place) and *chōra* (space) both only allude to the point or area where something is or may be situated. For the Greeks the void (*to kenon*) was a negative experience, being almost by definition lacking in order. The universe (*kosmos*) was ordered matter. Admittedly, distances could be measured on the ground, as by the *stadion*, a fixed unit of 600 feet, and in the Hellenistic period attempts could be made at calculating absolute distances across space between the heavenly bodies, but there was no word which the Greek could use to express the notion of two-dimensional area, still less three-dimensional volume, as we can through the word space. Our term space derives in fact from the Latin *spatium*, and already in Roman times this word had come to refer to two-dimensional and perhaps even three-dimensional extension; more important, however, is that it always has measurable connotations. This is because it derives from the Greek *stadion*, or rather a dialect spelling *spadion*, and was applied regularly to the colonnaded walks of the houses of the Roman Republic which were used for exercise as was the Greek stadium. From first meaning a measured distance in one dimension it came to refer to measured extension in two dimensions and then, as it slowly became more general in reference through its derivative *spatiosus*, it came to refer to three-dimensional size. The Romans thus had a word which enabled them to think positively about architectural space while the Greeks did not; the particular character of this word derived from its use to describe the open exercise colonnades of Republican, that is essentially Late Hellenistic, architecture. The development of our word space from the Latin *spatium* and the Greek *stadion* establishes that the first application of the word to measurable voids is linked to the use of colonnades in the Late Hellenistic world.

This ties in well with the arguments advanced above about the temple of Artemis at Magnesia and the garden of the temple of Hephaestus at Athens. Presumably the character of the colonnade as a structure moulding part of the earth's atmosphere into a measurable quantity, and especially the function of the intercolumnar distances as a means of measurement, taught people that any open area surrounded by rows of columns could be seen to possess the desirable attribute of measure; and the planting of trees at regular intervals in gardens could even extend measurability to areas not surrounded by architecture. An interesting parallel to this awakening consciousness of space is provided by fifteenth-century Italian art where the rediscovery of perspective as a means of describing space is associated with a great enthusiasm for open arcades and also with the disposition of trees in measured rows like so many columns.

Optics and Architectural Planning

Changes of consciousness are not sudden and in the Hellenistic period the stoa only slowly developed to the point where it could provide the Romans with the concept of measured space. The first stoas were just long porticos with walls at the back designed to provide shelter. Only later as they were extended and several fitted together did they come to enclose and control the open areas of Greek cities. The fifth-century Stoa of Zeus at Athens already had projecting wings at either end, so that the approaching visitor, as also on the path to the Propylaea on the Acropolis, 189 was for a brief moment actually surrounded by colonnades on his sides before he entered the building. At Miletus in the fourth century, as part of a reconstruction of the whole city on regular lines, an 'L-shaped stoa was built round one 177 corner of the port. The U-shaped grouping of stoas is found in the late fourth century at Priene 179 and in the following century in the south agora of Miletus where it is composed of two adjoining L- 177 forms. At Magnesia-on-the-Maeander in the third

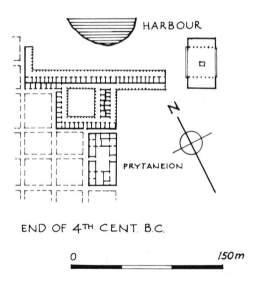

END OF 4TH CENT. B.C.

0   150m

177 Plan of the commercial centre, Miletus, at the end of the fourth century and at the middle of the second century BC.

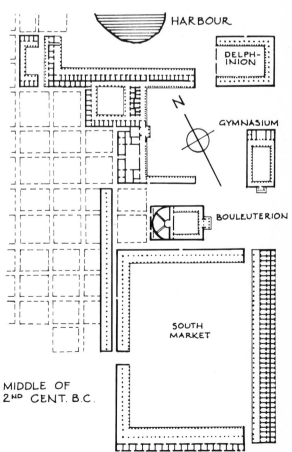

MIDDLE OF
2ND CENT. B.C.

178 century the wings take on a greater importance as they are longer than the base of the U. This means that the effect of enclosure is considerably increased. Several of the U-forms also appear to have had separate stoas closing their open ends, though often, as at Priene, these were found to be too weak and insignificant and had to be rebuilt. At Priene the great Sacred Stoa was accordingly 179 rebuilt around 150. As rebuilt, it not only closed the open end of the U but was also extended eastward along the street that bordered the agora. The eastern arm of the U was also extended at right angles along this street and then at the end the two stoas were linked by a light semicircular arch spanning the street. The agora area was thus almost completely surrounded by masonry and turned into an open-air interior space. The same was true of the small court laid out south of the main south stoa in the Athenian Agora, while the Lower agora at Pergamum built by Eumenes II in the first half of the second century was a large completely enclosed court.

In fact this last work should be associated with another set of Hellenistic colonnaded courts because it is not penetrated by the street plan as is normal with a true agora. Probably it derived from a tradition of complete buildings with interior courts rather than from that of urban open spaces. Most Greek houses of any size were built round courtyards, usually with a colonnade in front of the main room on one side. It is not clear when the full peristyle developed. Macedonian houses and palaces at Pella and Palatitsa of the Early Hellenistic period possess the form already fully developed. Larger peristyles are found in the third-century gymnasia (buildings for physical recreation), as at Epidaurus and Olympia. Complex gymnasia of the second century are found at Priene and Miletus, but there new planning ideas break up the regularity of the peristyle.

The new organization is seen most clearly in the gymnasium on the east side of the north agora at Miletus. The peristyle is here attenuated, so that it becomes a long rectangle instead of approximating to a square. It is entered on one short side by a propylon or portico and on the opposite short side there is a room for teaching 74 with its entrance also emphasized by a pair of columns. In this feature it seems related to the house type mentioned above which was built round a court with a colonnade or row of posts in front of the main room. Indeed, contemporary houses on Delos also have courtyards surrounded by colonnades with the portico in front of the main room higher than the others. But in its full

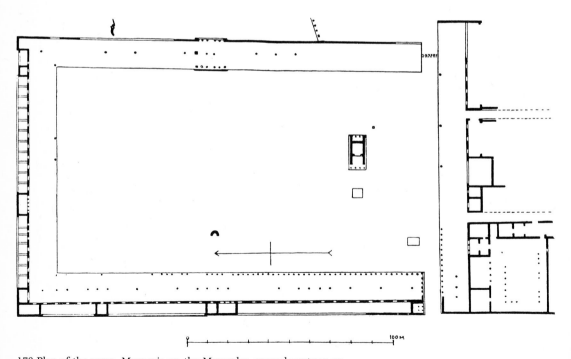

178 Plan of the agora, Magnesia-on-the-Maeander, second century BC.

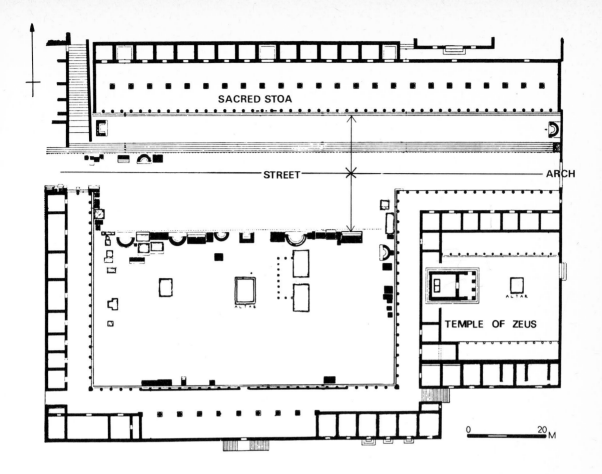

SACRED STOA

STREET   ARCH

ALTAR

TEMPLE OF ZEUS

ALTAR

0   20 M

development around a longitudinal axis the Miletus gymnasium is related rather to a group of public buildings of which other prominent examples are the Artemisium at Magnesia with its axial propylon and the Bouleuterion of Miletus.
75 The latter building also has a propylon leading into a colonnaded court with a taller building on the other side; though in this case there is no central entrance. Instead, as we saw, a shrine in the court may well have terminated the central axis, as it did in the Roman period. There is thus a tendency in the later Hellenistic period to organize complexes of buildings around a single central line. This development may seem at odds with the contemporary tendency in agora design. It is possible to show, however, that the common element behind both developments is a new attention to the visual expectations and interests of the spectator.

This may become clearer if we examine further the second-century extension to the agora of Priene. One aspect of this extension, which

179 Plan of the agora, Priene, second century BC, showing axis of agora arch and symmetry about it.

180 Reconstruction of agora arch, Priene, mid-second century BC.

180 tended to turn the agora into a more closed interior space, was the construction of an arch over the road that entered the agora from the east. This serves to enclose the agora if one views it from the west side. It also frames a view of the

179 agora as one approaches from the east. Because an arch is higher in the centre than at the sides it encourages the spectator to adopt a position from which the arch will appear symmetrical, that is with the two parts to left and right exactly corresponding. A rectangular opening does not have this effect so strongly because it lacks the radii all converging on one central point. It is easy then to see an archway as being divided into two identical halves by a line dropping vertically from the apex. This is all only a possible rather than a necessary consequence of the introduction of an arched opening, but in the case of Priene it is demonstrable that there was a strong concern with symmetry about the axis of the arch described above. For inside the agora, opposite the Sacred Stoa, is a line of bases which is not related directly to existing buildings. Its position is determined instead in relation to a line running through the arch's axis; it is the same distance from this line as is the base of the colonnade opposite. So it is clear that this axis, and symmetry about it, were both important concerns for the planners of Priene in the second century. Such an imposition of symmetry on an inherently asymmetrical environment represents a quite different approach from that which had ensured that most buildings and other smaller works of art produced by earlier cultures exhibited internal symmetry. What we have with the arch at Priene is not the creation of a symmetrical single object, like the temple of Athena higher in the city, but rather the pursuit of symmetrical relationships between different objects. This new pursuit of symmetry is in fact associated with a decline in interest in the symmetry of individual buildings. The rooms and openings at the back of the Sacred Stoa are arranged quite asymmetrically. The U-shaped agora itself which had previously been a symmetrical structure is now put off balance by the addition of a wing running out along the road to the east. The reason for all this is that symmetry, far from being regarded as a goal in itself, is a quality that is only desirable because of the way sight operates. As the majority of visitors to the agora at Priene would approach it from the east or west sides either under or

facing the arch, the latter naturally took on a crucial role in determining their axis of vision.

The same considerations help us to understand the new organization found in such structures as the Bouleuterion and gymnasium at Miletus 73 mentioned above. Earlier gymnasia tended to have a considerable level of symmetry about both axes, that is the colonnades on opposing sides of their courts tended to be identical. This was true although the entrances were not placed on either axis. The symmetry was just a normal characteristic of traditional design. In the gymnasium at Miletus, however, the only two sides of the court which correspond are those to left and right of the entrance; the other two sides not only have columns of different sizes, but are actually of different orders, Doric on the near side and Ionic on the far side. This development coincides with the transformation of the court from a square into a rectangle, which further decreases the internal symmetry of the plan. This general decline in symmetry is compensated for by the moving of the propylon into the centre of the entrance side and also by the placing of the lecture room in the centre of the opposite side of the court. It is clear from this arrangement that the only type of symmetry that interests the architect is that about the line of sight of the approaching and entering visitor, and this is so important for him that he is prepared to break down traditional patterns. Exactly the same traits are found in the Bouleuterion at Miletus.

Another example of the new importance attached to the axis of vision is found in the second-century Athenian Agora. Here too the 181 pursuit of symmetry on the visual axis tends to diminish other types of symmetry. For if we look, not at the two great stoas studied earlier, but at the structures of the Bouleuterion and Metroön as rebuilt in the second century, we note that they in no sense correspond to the other new buildings being built with their co-ordinated geometry. Instead they conform to the old non-cardinal orientation. Yet if we adopt another standpoint, that of someone looking up at the Hephaesteum from a position in the Agora on axis with its façade, it is clear that the new buildings were intended to provide a colonnaded front balancing that of the fifth-century Stoa of Zeus. The length of the new front corresponds to the older stoa almost exactly. Limitations of the site have made it impossible that the symmetry could be exact,

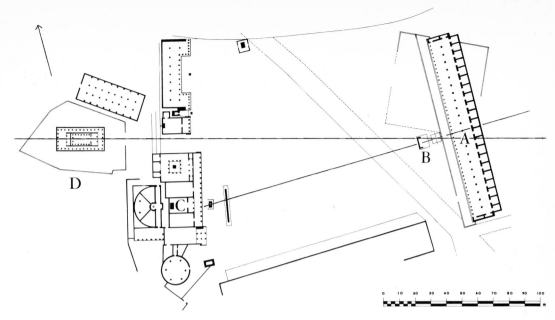

181 Plan of the Athenian Agora in the second century BC, showing axial lines. A = Stoa of Attalus, B = bema, C = Metroön, D = temple of Hephaestus.

just as they did in the case of the colonnades inside the agora arch at Priene. But the importance now attached to the axis of vision of the temple is confirmed in the long straight stairway leading right up to the façade, replacing a much broader shallow stair; and the planting of trees all round the temple, except in the front, further concentrated attention on that view. Moreover, if we go up the steps and look back down the same axis we find that it leads directly to the base which probably supported a statue of Attalus II, 184 builder of the stoa behind. Indeed this base has an even greater importance since it is in turn aligned on the altar of the rebuilt Metroön, while in front of it on this line was built a new bema or speaking platform. The base thus marks the junction of the two lines of vision, just as did the gate of the Altar 163 of Zeus in Attalus' native city. Just as there the typical visitor found himself perfectly situated to enjoy two geometrical relationships with his environment, being placed both at a right angle to the centre of the rear face of the altar and where a line at right angles to the entrance wall would meet the compositional centre of the great frieze, so too Attalus on his pedestal was uniquely placed to enjoy two great axial compositions. In both cases lines of sight have exercised a powerful influence over architectural planning. The Attalus base has an even more complex relation with its setting as it is also placed on the east/west, north/south axes which provide the alignments for the new stoas.

It has been observed that around 170–150 there is a tendency in architecture to develop symmetry about one axis, that of the spectator, and to diminish the other axis which crosses this. The same tendency can be seen in the representational arts in the composition of the crucial group of Zeus and Athena on the great frieze of the Zeus 86 altar at Pergamum. Another field where this is demonstrated, probably at the same date, is that of mosaics. In virtually all earlier examples of mosaics, where they are surrounded by decorative borders they are identical on all sides, 6 preserving relative symmetry. The same is true of the mosaics of most second-century houses in Delos, but in one, the House of the Masks, the decorative borders of the mosaics are divided at 182 the centre on a line bisecting the floor, so that the 183 patterns run outwards in two directions. In painting and sculpture used in architectural contexts, there had been a growing interest in symmetry along a line of vision from the time that the Caryatids first on the Siphnian Treasury and

182 Mosaic floor from the House of the Masks, Delos, *c.* 220–150 BC.

183 Mosaic floor from the House of the Masks, Delos.

then on the Erechtheum put opposed legs forward either side of the centre of their respective groups. More conscious is the use of balancing *lēkythoi* with reversed scenes on the funeral terrace of the Dipylon cemetery at Athens of *c.* 350, and doubtless the growth of such an interest parallels that in perspective. It is, however, clear both from mosaics and from architecture that a decisive step was reached in this development in the second century. What is particularly striking about the mosaics from the House of the Masks is that the way they are each composed of a central element and two flanking elements further emphasizes the axial effect when seen from the doorways of the rooms; while the use of taller columns on one side of the court shows that the whole building documents the new axial approach to architecture. It must have been for a house planned along these lines that the first great pair of matching sculptures, the originals of the Old and Young Centaurs mentioned earlier, were designed.

127
128

How might such an interest have arisen and how might it have been discussed at the time? The most useful Hellenistic discussion of vision is found in Euclid's *Optics*, written in the early third century. There Euclid notes the symmetrical behaviour of objects to the left and right of the eye: 'Of lines which extend forward those on the right seem to swerve to the left and those on the left to the right' (theorem 12). This is apparently a statement about the convergence of receding lines and it establishes that Euclid believed that man has in some sense a centre to his vision and that there is a balance about this between objects to the left and right. He is not, of course, stating that objects either side of the centre should be symmetrically arranged. Nevertheless his statement could certainly encourage a tendency to ensure this, because then the theorem would be more clearly demonstrated. Indeed, it may not be so strange to suggest that the Hellenistic Greeks may have looked for the demonstration of geometrical theorems in their architecture. For it is quite possible that Euclid only established his theory of optics on the basis of his experience of architecture. Theorem 10 states that of planes lying above the eye, the further parts appear lower and of those below the eye, higher. The fact that Euclid talks of *planes* when describing what happens above and below the centre of vision and of *lines* when talking of what happens to right and

184 Interior of lower floor, Stoa of Attalus, Athens, *c.* 150 BC.

left suggests that he had some particular experience in mind. If he had been talking of a pure demonstration he would have noted the identity of what happens above and below and left and right. Certainly one experience that would elicit his observations would be that of looking down a colonnade or stoa. For in such a context there would indeed be a plane above, the ceiling, balanced by a plane below, the floor, while on the side a colonnade could not be called a plane but would rather be seen as a series of lines formed by details such as the receding capitals and bases. The side wall too would be likely to have corresponding mouldings running along its top and footing. Another theorem in the same series would also refer most naturally to a colonnade: theorem 4 states that 'when objects are situated along the same straight line at equal intervals, those seen at the furthest distance appear smaller'.

184

The importance that this particular architectural form appears to have had for Euclid is more understandable if it is remembered that two of the major contemporary schools of philosophy both took their names from such structures, the Aristotelians or Peripatetics from the *peripatos* or covered walk in the Lyceum and the followers of Zeno, the Stoics, from the Stoa Poikile. In the case of Euclid's *Optics* it is only possible to guess at the

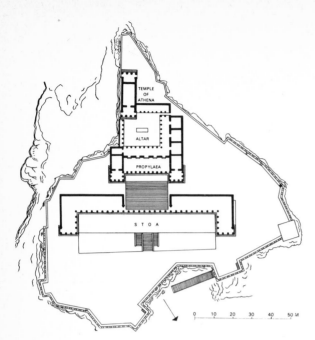

185 Plan of the sanctuary of Athena at Lindos, Rhodes, *c.* 200 BC.

186 Terrace and stair, sanctuary of Athena, Lindos.

importance of the colonnade. By the time of Lucretius in the early first century, however, the stoa is expressly introduced to demonstrate the same optical principles: 'Although a portico may have two parallel sides and be supported on equally spaced columns, nevertheless when the whole length is seen from one end gradually it contracts into the point of a narrow cone; the ceiling meets the floor and the right side the left until the eye is led to the cone's dark apex' (*De Rerum Natura* iv, 426–31). Seneca and Sextus Empiricus also discuss perspective in terms of our perception of receding colonnades and the same phenomenon is referred to by other writers. If such observations were commonplaces of philo-sophical education, and if architecture was the main instrument for instruction about the way we perceive space, architectural planning could well have received a reverse influence from optical theory. The notion of a visual cone found in Lucretius may also have encouraged an interest in arches such as that in the agora gate at Priene, 180 particularly as the diameter of this arch was

apparently almost the same as its height; the archway could thus be seen as a circular section cut through the cone of vision. It is perhaps worth noting that although the literary evidence implies an axis of sight from the eyes to a distant centre of vision, there is never any explicit mention of such an axis. The phenomenon of perspective is defined as yet only in terms of what happens right and left and above and below our eyes. This may explain why, in the examples of architectural planning quoted, the tendency to emphasize the central axis of buildings is much less apparent than that to provide a clear balance between the lateral elements.

Attention has so far been concentrated on the development of architectural organization right and left of the line of vision. It would, however, be reasonable to expect that, if Euclid's comment on lines lateral to the eye had some counterpart in architecture, so too would his observations on planes above and below. If architectural space could be organized to correspond further with the optical theorems, we should expect an increasing tendency to organize the areas between the lateral lines into plane surfaces. It is unfortunately difficult to establish the dating of the levelling and paving of agoras, although this must have been done as their borders became regularized. Nevertheless the organization of important areas into regular plane surfaces is clearly documented in the increasing use of stairways, ramps and terraces. This is best demonstrated in two great sanctuaries which took their present form largely in the second century, that of Athena at Lindos on Rhodes and that of Asclepius on the nearby island of Cos. At Lindos a monumental approach to the existing temple was 185 achieved by laying out first a broad stair leading 186 to a narrow platform bordered by a long portico with projecting wings and then another stair leading to a smaller building of the same type higher up. In this case the stairs predominate over the terraces. At Cos the situation is reversed, with 187 large terraces surrounded by porticos being linked by relatively small stairs and ramps. The best example of a stair as a broad inclined plane

187 Reconstruction of the Hellenistic sanctuary of Asclepius, Cos.

188 leading to a flat terrace is the Zeus altar at Pergamum where, of course, the elevation is completely man-made.

It is therefore clear that in the second century there was a strong movement towards organizing the surfaces 'below our eyes' into geometrically consistent plane surfaces, whether flat or inclined with lines of stoas bounding our field of vision 'to left and right'. This is in contrast with earlier planning on sites such as Olympia, Delphi and Epidaurus where the major buildings were all isolated on their own stereobates and were linked by meandering paths along which were arranged minor structures, each with its own orientation.

189 A building such as the Propylaea at Athens, ancestor to the porticos at Lindos, framed no flat terrace between its wings and was approached by an irregular zigzag path. Significantly, it was only in 174 that a large pedestal was erected to balance the asymmetrical projection of the bastion under the temple of Athena Nike and in the Roman period the surface of the enclosed area so formed was wrought into a regular inclined plane. Yet another architectural complex was thus given coherence in terms compatible with Euclid's visual theories. The significance of the development described here is that while previously only individual buildings had been treated as regular geometrical solids, now the air between them could be described in the same way in terms of regular volumes.

This study of the principles which may have influenced Greek architectural planning in the second century can do little more than suggest possibilities. However, in general terms it does seem justifiable to separate out two diverse influences, as in the Athenian Agora. The new stoas on the south and east seem to integrate the Agora into the geometry of the world, and even of the universe. The reorganization of the west side around the approaches to the temple of Hephaestus seem to accord a new importance to the visual awareness of the spectator. It is typical of the flexibility of Hellenistic man that the two planning approaches are applied virtually simultaneously and that they meet and are united in the Attalus base, which is both on the axis of the temple of Hephaestus and firmly linked by position and association with the great stoa built by the Pergamene monarch behind. Both approaches share an assumption of the importance of measure and measurable geometrical correlation. This is seen to apply both on the macrocosmic scale to geographical and astronomical organization and on the microcosmic scale to the visual experience of the human individual.

188 Altar of Zeus, Pergamum, c. 170 BC.

189 South-western approach of the Propylaea, Athens, *c.* 435 BC.

Greek Epilogue – Roman Prologue

The Hellenistic world was born in pride and soon moved from vanity to delusion. The Greeks of the late fourth century were sure of their superiority to other peoples and to other periods. Aristotle had pressed Alexander to treat the Greeks as equals and the barbarians as slaves. His follower Theophrastus asserted that no one could any longer call the Greeks of the heroic age happy; that term could only be applied to his own contemporaries. When time and space did not suffice to measure their excellence the Greeks turned to other dimensions. From Alexander onwards rulers identified themselves with heroes and gods. Alexarchus, son of one of Alexander's lieutenants, Antipater, even founded a community called Ouranopolis (Heaven City), is credited with inventing his own language, minted coins adorned with sun, moon and stars, and identified himself with the sun. But it was to be the Romans who provided the measure of the Greeks. They defeated Pyrrhus at Beneventum in 275, took Syracuse in 212 and defeated Philip V and Perseus of Macedon in Greece itself in 197 and 168. After defeat came surrender. Attalus III left his kingdom to Rome in 133 and Cleopatra finally yielded her heart and the political credibility of the Ptolemies to Caesar and Antony.

Polybius gives a glimpse of the shattered Greek psyche after 168. The Romans were politically superior to the Greeks, he observes, because they had a mixed constitution in which elements of monarchy, oligarchy and democracy were combined. Polybius was well aware that Greek history had shifted uneasily between these forms, with the first predominant in the Hellenistic period. The differences between the Greek and Roman army camp further demonstrated the Romans' military and organizational superiority. The Greeks, Polybius says, laid out their camps in an irregular way following the lie of the land, while the Romans by excavation and terracing constructed a regular plan which was always the same. The constancy of camp design combined with a consistent use of coloured standards and billet numbering enabled the Roman soldier to know where he had to go while he was still outside the camp. The Greek had to find his own way each time. Another important element of the Romans' moral superiority was due, according to Polybius, to their use of rhetoric, sculpture and painting to communicate the significance of great events to people who could never witness them. Almost everything Polybius says points to the Romans having attained as a result of a natural development the high ideals to which the Greeks had long aspired. The moderation and balance manifest in the Roman constitution had been cardinal values to Greek philosophers such as Aristotle. The sense of order and geometry that was attributed to Roman soldiers had constituted the highest goal of Greek education from the time of Pythagoras. In their use of the arts as an instrument of moral improvement the Romans had achieved what Plato had dreamed of in his *Republic*. What Polybius implies is that the Romans are more Greek than the Greeks.

The Greeks who had set out to chasten the barbarians now found that those whom they had considered their inferiors were in fact their betters. Plato would have recognized in Rome many of the qualities that he had attributed to 'Athens', and in the Hellenistic world the corruption and materialism of 'Atlantis'. The Hellenistic period was the time when the Greeks following Alexander set out to Hellenize the barbarian world, that is to impose on the barbarians their values, attitudes and patterns of life. By the end of the third century they began to waver in their conviction. The Ptolemies of Egypt adopted more and more pharaonic forms and archaeological evidence shows that in the Seleucid kingdom oriental elements increasingly penetrated the Greek way of life. As the Greeks lost the strength and the conviction which were necessary if they were to impose Hellenism, the Hellenistic period drew to a close. Yet even as they faltered they had the presence of mind to recognize their true successors. They thus ensured the continuance of much of what they had achieved.

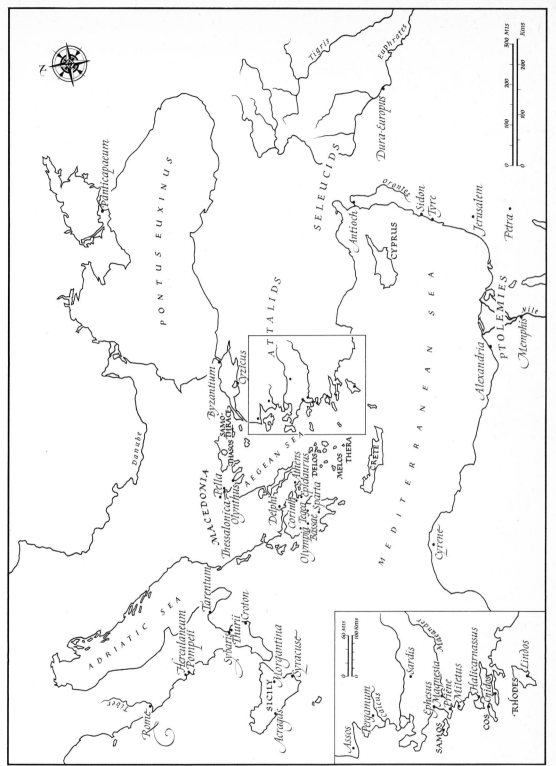

Greece and the Eastern Mediterranean

181

Guide to Further Study

This book is founded on three approaches: the reading of contemporary and later Greek and Latin texts, the study of the Greek and Roman collections in the museums of Europe and America, and familiarity with the sites of the Hellenistic world as they have been exposed by archaeologists. In each case the most direct contact with the material is the best, that is by reading the texts in the original language, by personally visiting the museums and by actually travelling to see the sites themselves. But it is increasingly possible to have access to the three classes of material indirectly, by reading the texts in translation, by using the illustrated catalogues and handbooks of the main museums and by consulting the publications of the archaeological excavations and surveys of the major sites. The following lists are intended to provide a guide to the three different approaches.

Texts

The following are all conveniently available in the original, with a translation on the opposite page, in the Loeb Classical Library published by Harvard University Press and William Heinemann:
Apollonius Rhodius, Aristotle, Athenaeus, Callimachus, Greek Anthology, Herondas, Menander, Plato, Plutarch, Polybius, Theocritus, Theophrastus.

Museums

The most useful museums which are unevenly covered by catalogues and handbooks are:
Athens: Agora Museum; National Museum. Berlin: Staatliche Museen. Boston: Museum of Fine Arts. Cambridge (England): Fitzwilliam Museum. Copenhagen: Ny Carlsberg Glyptothek. Florence: Uffizi; Archaeological Museum. Istanbul: Archaeological Museum. London: British Museum. Munich: Glyptothek. Naples: National Museum. New York: Metropolitan Museum. Oxford: Ashmolean Museum. Paris: Louvre. Rome: Capitoline Museum; National Museum (Baths of Diocletian); Vatican Museum.

Sites

The major sites and their publications are as follows:
Athens: *The Athenian Agora*, Princeton, 1953–.
  J. Travlos, *Pictorial Dictionary of Ancient Athens*, London and New York, 1971.
Cos: R. Herzog and P. Schazmann, *Kos*, I, Berlin, 1932.
Delos: *Exploration archéologique de Délos*, I–, Paris, 1909.
Delphi: *Fouilles de Delphes*, I–, Paris, 1904.
Epidaurus: C. Cavvadias, *Fouilles d'Epidaure*, I–, Athens, 1891—.
  A. Burford, *The Greek Temple Builders at Epidaurus*, Liverpool and Toronto, 1969.
Lindos: C. Blinkenberg *et al.*, *Lindos*, I–III, Berlin and Copenhagen, 1931–60.
Magnesia-on-the-Maeander: C. Humann, *Magnesia am Maeander*, Berlin, 1904.

Miletus: T. Wiegand *et al.*, *Milet, Die Ergebnisse der Ausgrabungen und Untersuchungen*, Berlin, 1906–.
Pergamum: A. Conze *et al.*, *Altertümer von Pergamon*, Berlin 1885–.
Priene: T. Wiegand and H. Schrader, *Priene*, Berlin, 1904.
Samothrace: A. Conze *et al.*, *Archäologische Untersuchungen auf Samothrake*, I and II, Vienna, 1875 and 1880.
  K. Lehmann *et al*, *Samothrace: Excavations*, I–, New York, 1959–.

The other essential approach to the problems dealt with in the book is through the extensive secondary literature, which is here introduced in outline.

General

The Cambridge Ancient History, vols VI–VIII, Cambridge, 1923–39.
J. Ferguson, *The Heritage of Hellenism*, London, 1973.
P. M. Fraser, *Ptolemaic Alexandria*, 3 vols, Oxford, 1972.
E. V. Hansen, *The Attalids of Pergamum*, Ithaca and London, 1971.
A. Lesky, *A History of Greek Literature*, London, 1966.
A. A. Long, *Hellenistic Philosophy*, London, 1974.
R. Pfeiffer, *A History of Classical Scholarship. From the Beginnings to the End of the Hellenistic Age*, Oxford, 1968.
M. Rostovtzeff, *The Social and Economic History of the Hellenistic World*, 3 vols, Oxford, 1953.
F. H. Sandbach, *The Stoics*, London, 1975.
G. Sarton, *A History of Science*, vol. 2, Cambridge, Mass., 1959.
T. B. L. Webster, *Hellenistic Poetry and Art*, London, 1964.

Art

GENERAL
J. D. Beazley and B. Ashmole, *Greek Sculpture and Painting to the End of the Hellenistic Period*, Cambridge, 1966.
G. M. A. Richter, *A Handbook of Greek Art*, 4th ed., New York, 1965.
M. Robertson, *A History of Greek Art*, 2 vols, Cambridge, 1975.
K. Schefold, *Die Griechen und ihre Nachbarn*, Frankfurt and Berlin, 1967.

HELLENISTIC
J. Charbonneaux, R. Martin and F. Villard, *Hellenistic Art: 330–50 BC*, London, 1973.
C. M. Havelock, *Hellenistic Art*, London, 1971.
T. B. L. Webster, *The Art of Greece: The Age of Hellenism*, New York, 1964.

ARCHITECTURE
M. Bieber, *The History of the Greek and Roman Theatre*, Princeton, 1961.

J. J. Coulton, *The Architectural Development of the Greek Stoa*, Oxford, 1976.

W. B. Dinsmoor, *The Architecture of Ancient Greece*, New York, 1975.

A. W. Lawrence, *Greek Architecture*, Harmondsworth, 1962.

W. A. McDonald, *The Political Meeting Places of the Greeks*, Baltimore, 1943.

R. Martin, *L'urbanisme dans la Grèce antique*, Paris, 1956.

D. S. Robertson, *A Handbook of Greek and Roman Architecture*, 3rd ed., Cambridge, 1959.

G. Roux, *L'architecture de l'Argolide aux IVe et IIIe siècles avant J.-C.*, Paris, 1961.

J. B. Ward-Perkins, *Cities of Ancient Greece and Italy: Planning in Classical Antiquity*, New York, 1974.

R. E. Wycherley, *How the Greeks Built Cities*, London 1962.

PAINTING

B. Brown, *Ptolemaic Paintings and Mosaics and the Alexandrian Style*, Cambridge, Mass., 1957.

R. M. Cook, *Greek Painted Pottery*, London, 1960.

L. Curtius, *Die Wandmalerei Pompejis*, Hildesheim, 1960.

W. J. T. Peters, *Landscape in Romano-Campanian Mural Painting*, Assen, 1963.

E. Pfuhl, *Malerei und Zeichnung der Griechen*, 3 vols, Munich, 1923.

M. Robertson, *Greek Painting*, Geneva, 1959.

K. Schefold, *Pompeianische Malerei: Sinn und Ideengeschichte*, Basel, 1952.

J. White, *Perspective in Ancient Drawing and Painting*, London, 1956.

SCULPTURE

S. Adam, *The Technique of Greek Sculpture in the Archaic and Classical Period*, London, 1966.

M. Bieber, *The Sculpture of the Hellenistic Age*, New York, 1961.

J. Charbonneaux, *Greek Bronzes*, London, 1962.

R. Carpenter, *Greek Sculpture, A Critical Review*, Chicago, 1960.

R. A. Higgins, *Greek Terracottas*, London, 1967.

A. W. Lawrence, *Later Greek Sculpture and its Influence on East and West*, London, 1927.

R. Lullies and M. Hirmer, *Greek Sculpture*, London, 1960.

G. M. A. Richter, *The Sculpture and Sculptors of the Greeks*, New Haven, Conn., 1950.

G. M. A. Richter, *The Portraits of the Greeks*, 3 vols, New York, 1965.

INDIVIDUAL MONUMENTS

P. H. von Blanckenhagen, 'Laokoon, Sperlonga und Vergil', *Archäologischer Anzeiger*, 1969, pp. 256–75.

H. Kähler, *Der Grosse Fries von Pergamon*, Berlin, 1948.

D. Pinkwart, *Die Relief des Archelaos*, Kallmünz, 1965.

K. Schefold and M. Seidel, *Der Alexander-Sarkophag*, Berlin, 1968.

OTHER ARTS

J. Boardman, *Greek Gems and Finger Rings*, London, 1971.

R. A. Higgins, *Greek and Roman Jewellery*, London, 1961.

C. M. Kraay, *Greek Coins*, London, 1966.

D. E. Strong, *Greek and Roman Gold and Silver Plate*, London, 1966.

THEORY

J. A. Overbeck, *Die antiken Schriftquellen zur Geschichte der Bildenden Künste bei den Griechen*, Leipzig, 1868.

J. J. Pollitt, *The Art of Greece 1400–31 BC. Sources and Documents*, Englewood Cliffs, New Jersey, 1965.

J. J. Pollitt, *The Ancient View of Greek Art: Criticism, History and Terminology*, New Haven, Conn. and London, 1974.

F. W. Schlikker, *Hellenistische Vorstellungen der Schonheit des Bauwerks nach Vitruv*, Berlin, 1940.

E. Sellers, *The Elder Pliny's Chapters on the History of Art*, Chicago, 1966.

List of Illustrations

1 Quartz ringstone engraved with head of Alexander the Great, late fourth century BC. Department of Antiquities, Ashmolean Museum, Oxford

2 Plan of the Acropolis, Athens, c. 480 BC. After drawing from John Travlos, *A Pictorial Dictionary of Ancient Athens*, London and New York, 1971

3 Reconstructed plan of Atlantis, after Plato. After *Plato: Timaeus, Critias . . . Epistulae*, with an English translation by R. G. Bury, The Loeb Classical Library, Harvard University Press: William Heinemann, Cambridge, Mass. and London, 1929

4 Reconstruction of east cella of the Parthenon, Athens, with Phidias' colossal gold and ivory statue of Athena Parthenos, 447–432 BC. Copyright Royal Ontario Museum, Toronto

5 Lion hunt. Pebble mosaic, late fourth century BC. From Pella, Macedonia. Photo V. and N. Tombazi, Athens

6 Winged Dionysiac infant riding a lion. Mosaic from the House of the Faun, Pompeii, second century BC. Museo Nazionale, Naples. Photo Anderson

7 Reconstruction of section of the House of the Hermes, Delos, second century BC. From *Exploration archéologique de Délos, faite par l'Ecole française d'Athènes*, VIII, Paris, 1922

8 Agias, from the monument of the Thessalians erected at Delphi by Daochus II, c. 340–330 BC. Probably contemporary copy of bronze original by Lysippus. Marble. Delphi Museum. Photo Marburg

9 Greek fighting Amazons. Detail of frieze from the

Mausoleum, Halicarnassus, mid-fourth century BC. Marble. British Museum, London

10 Dedicatory inscription of Alexander the Great from the temple of Athena Polias, Priene, 334 BC. Marble. British Museum, London

11 Reconstruction of section of the Arsinoeion, Samothrace, 289–281 BC. After A. Conze *et al.*, *Archäologische Untersuchungen auf Samothrake*, Vienna, 1875

12 West front of the Parthenon, Athens, 447–432 BC. Photo Marburg

13 West front of the Erechtheum, Athens, after 421–406 BC. Photo Marburg

14 Nike undoing her sandal, from the balustrade of the temple of Athena Nike, Athens, late fifth century BC. Marble. Acropolis Museum, Athens. Photo Alinari

15 Plato. Roman copy of an original, probably of the fourth century BC. Marble. Fitzwilliam Museum, Cambridge

16 Doryphoros, after Polyclitus. Roman copy of an original of the mid-fifth century BC. Marble. Museo Nazionale, Naples. Photo Deutsches Archäologisches Institut, Rome

17 Diagram of Ionic order of the temple of Athena Polias, Priene, mid-fourth century BC. From Rhys Carpenter, *The Architects of the Parthenon*, London, 1970, after T. Wiegand and H. Schrader, *Priene*, Berlin, 1904

18 Apulian volute krater, fourth century BC. Ruvo, Jatta Collection. Photo Deutsches Archäologisches Institut, Rome

19 Grave stele of Thraseas and Euandria, from Athens, third quarter of the fourth century BC. Marble. Staatliche Museen zu Berlin

20 Aristotle. Roman copy of an original, probably of the fourth century BC. Marble. Museo Nazionale delle Terme, Rome. Photo Deutsches Archäologisches Institut, Rome

21 Reconstruction of elevation of the Stoa of Athena, Pergamum, first half of the second century BC. From A. Conze, C. Humann and R. Bohn, *Die Ergebnisse der Ausgrabungen zu Pergamon*, 1880–81, no. 2, Berlin, 1882

22 Battle between Greeks and Amazons. Detail of frieze from the temple of Artemis, Magnesia-on-the-Maeander, *c.* 140 BC. Marble. Louvre, Paris. Photo Giraudon

23 Detail of grave stele from Attica, *c.* 360 BC. Marble. National Museum, Athens. Photo S. Adam

24 Aphrodite, after Praxiteles. Roman copy deriving from the Aphrodite of Cnidos of *c.* 350–330 BC. Marble. Vatican Museums. Photo Deutsches Archäologisches Institut, Rome

25 Aphrodite, after Praxiteles. Rear view of plaster cast of previous statue (Pl. 24). Photo Alinari

26 Battle between Greeks and Persians. Detail of the Alexander Sarcophagus, *c.* 310 BC. From Sidon. Marble. Archaeological Museum, Istanbul. Photo Hirmer Fotoarchiv

27 Hellenistic bronze statuette of a hunchback beggar. Staatliche Museen zu Berlin

28 Barberini Faun. Roman copy of an original of perhaps *c.* 200 BC. Marble. Staatliche Antikensammlungen, Munich. Photo Hirmer Fotoarchiv

29 Zeno. Roman copy of a Hellenistic original. Marble. Museo Nazionale, Naples. Photo Anderson

30 Epicurus. Roman copy of a Hellenistic original. Marble. Metropolitan Museum of Art, New York, Rogers Fund, 1911. Photo Deutsches Archäologisches Institut, Rome

31 Crouching Aphrodite. Roman copy of an original usually attributed to Doidalsas of Bithynia (*fl.* mid-third century BC). Marble. Museo Nazionale delle Terme, Rome. Photo Deutsches Archäologisches Institut, Rome

32 Hellenistic terracotta group of two knucklebone players. From Capua, third century BC. British Museum, London

33 Drunken Old Woman. Roman copy of an original, perhaps by Myron of Pergamum, of *c.* 200 BC. Marble. Staatliche Antikensammlungen, Munich

34 Boy servant tending fire. Roman adaptation of a Hellenistic original, possibly a painting. Marble. Museo Nazionale, Naples. Photo Deutsches Archäologisches Institut, Rome

35 Mithridates III (*c.* 220–185/3 BC). Obverse of tetradrachm. Photo Hirmer Fotoarchiv

36 Pharnaces I (185/3–170 BC). Obverse of tetradrachm. Photo Hirmer Fotoarchiv

37 Mithridates IV (170–150 BC). Obverse of tetradrachm. Photo Hirmer Fotoarchiv

38 Alexander the Great. Roman copy of a Hellenistic original. Marble. Museo Capitolino, Rome. Photo Alinari

39 Apoxyomenos, after Lysippus. Roman copy of an original of *c.* 330 BC. Marble. Vatican Museums. Photo Deutsches Archäologisches Institut, Rome

40 Fallen Persian and his reflection. Detail of the Battle of Darius and Alexander mosaic (see Pl. 52). Museo Nazionale, Naples. Photo Deutsches Archäologisches Institut, Rome

41 Thetis in the workshop of Hephaestus. Wall-painting from Pompeii. Roman copy of a Hellenistic original perhaps by Theon of Samos. Museo Nazionale, Naples. Photo Alinari

42 Pericles. Roman copy perhaps of an original by Cresilas of the fifth century BC. Marble. Vatican Museums. Photo Deutsches Archäologisches Institut, Rome

43 Socrates. Roman copy perhaps of an original of the fourth century BC. British Museum, London

44 Demosthenes. Roman copy of an original, probably by Polyeuctus, set up in the Athenian Agora *c.* 280 BC. Marble. Vatican Museums. Photo Deutsches Archäologisches Institut, Rome

45 Polyphemus receiving the letter of Galatea. Wall-painting from Pompeii. Roman copy of a Hellenistic original. Museo Nazionale, Naples. Photo Anderson

46 Achilles recognized by Odysseus at the court of Lycomedes. Wall-painting from Pompeii. Roman copy of a Hellenistic original perhaps by Theon of Samos. Museo Nazionale, Naples. Photo Anderson

47 Hermaphrodite. Roman copy of a Hellenistic original. Marble. Museo Nazionale delle Terme, Rome. Photo Anderson

48 Relief showing grotto with Pan, Apollo and nymphs, from the sacred cave at Vari in Attica, c. 340 BC. Marble (restored). National Museum, Athens. Photo Marburg

49 Dionysus and the Tyrrhenian pirates. Detail of frieze (cast) from the Choragic Monument of Lysicrates. Athens, c. 330 BC. Cast in the British Museum, London

50 Votive relief showing Asclepius, Hygieia and worshippers, fourth century BC. Marble. National Museum, Athens. Photo Alinari

51 Pothos, after Scopas. Roman copy of an original of the mid-fourth century BC. Marble. Uffizi, Florence. Photo Deutsches Archäologisches Institut, Rome

52 Battle of Darius and Alexander. Mosaic from the House of the Faun, Pompeii. Work of the second century BC probably based on an original painting, perhaps by Philoxenus of Eretria, of c. 300 BC. Museo Nazionale, Naples. Photo Deutsches Archäologisches Institut, Rome

53 Aphrodite Kallipygos. Roman copy of a Hellenistic original. Marble (restored). Museo Nazionale, Naples. Photo Alinari

54 Satyr admiring his hindquarters. Roman copy of a Hellenistic original. Marble. Museo Nazionale delle Terme, Rome. Photo Anderson

55 Hellenistic head. Marble. Royal Ontario Museum, Toronto. Photo Deutsches Archäologisches Institut, Rome

56 Comic scene, perhaps from Menander's *Synaristōsai*. Detail of mosaic from the Villa of Cicero, Pompeii, signed by Dioscorides of Samos (*fl.* 100 BC), and probably based on an original of the third century BC. Museo Nazionale, Naples. Photo Anderson

57 'Strangford' shield. Roman adaptation of the shield of Phidias' Athena Parthenos. Marble. British Museum, London

58 Electra and Orestes at the tomb of Agamemnon. Work of the first century BC signed by Menelaus. Marble. Museo Nazionale delle Terme, Rome. Photo Alinari

59 Athena, from the library at Pergamum, early second century BC. Marble. Staatliche Museen zu Berlin

60 Glass goblet from Begram, Afghanistan, with painted decoration illustrating the abductions of Ganymede and Europa, Roman period. Musée Guimet, Paris

61 Satyr and Nymph. Roman copy of an original probably of the second century BC. Marble. Museo Capitolino, Rome. Photo Alinari

62 Aphrodite, Eros and Pan, from the Establishment of the Posidoniasts on Delos, c. 100 BC. Marble. National Museum, Athens. Photo Marburg

63 Greek musical instruments. Drawing by A. D. Johnson

64 Contest between Apollo and Marsyas. One of three reliefs from the base of a statuary group, attributed by Pausanias to Praxiteles, from the shrine of Leto at Mantinea, c. 330 BC. Marble. National Museum, Athens. Photo Marburg

65 Temple of Isis, Philae, Egypt, third century BC and later. Photo Deutsches Archäologisches Institut, Rome

66 Green basalt bust of Serapis. Roman adaptation of an original by Bryaxis of c. 300 BC. Museo di Villa Albani, Rome. Photo Anderson

67 Head of an Egyptian princess, Ptolemaic period. Marble. Museo Capitolino, Rome. Photo Alinari

68 Reconstruction of interior of the temple of Apollo, Bassae, later fifth century BC. After F. Krischen

69 Tholos, Epidaurus, mid-fourth century BC. Photo Marburg

70 Plan of Tholos, Epidaurus, showing arrangement of orders. Drawing by A. D. Johnson

71 Plans of Epidaurian buildings of the fourth century BC, showing arrangement of orders. Drawing by A. D. Johnson

72 Temple of Olympian Zeus, Athens, begun in 174 BC in partial fulfilment of a plan by the sons of Pisistratus in the late sixth century BC. Photo Marburg

73 Plans of buildings of the second century BC, showing arrangement of orders. Drawing by A. D. Johnson

74 Reconstruction of lecture room of the Lower gymnasium, Priene, c. 130 BC. After F. Krischen

75 Reconstruction of the Bouleuterion, Miletus, c. 170 BC. From T. Wiegand, *Milet*, I, 2, Berlin, 1908

76 Reconstruction of elevation and section of the Stoa of Attalus, Athens, 159–138 BC. After drawing from John Travlos, *A Pictorial Dictionary of Ancient Athens*, London and New York, 1971

77 Reconstruction of capital from the inner colonnade of the upper storey of the Stoa of Attalus, Athens, 159–138 BC. Drawing by Ian Mackenzie-Kerr

78 Reconstruction of capital from a temple at Neandria, early sixth century BC. Drawing by Philip Ward

79 Model of the upper city, Pergamum. Staatliche Museen zu Berlin

80 Plan of the upper city, Pergamum. After Pauly-Wissowa, *Real-Encyclopaedie d. class. Altertumswissenschaft*, XIX, I, Stuttgart, 1937

81 Dead Giant. Roman copy of an original of c. 200 BC. Marble. Museo Nazionale, Naples. Photo Soprintendenza alle Antichità, Naples

82 Dead Amazon. Roman copy of an original of c. 200 BC. Marble. Museo Nazionale, Naples. Photo Soprintendenza alle Antichità, Naples

83 Dying Persian. Roman copy of an original of c. 200 BC. Marble. Museo Nazionale, Naples. Photo Anderson

84 Dying Gaul. Roman copy of an original of c. 200 BC. Marble. Museo Nazionale, Naples. Photo Anderson

85 Poseidon and Athena competing for Attica, from the west pediment of the Parthenon, Athens, c. 440–435 BC. Drawing by Jacques Carrey, c. 1674. Bibliothèque Nationale, Paris

86 Zeus and Athena in combat with giants, from the large frieze of the Altar of Zeus, Pergamum, c. 170 BC. Marble. Staatliche Museen zu Berlin

87 Battle between Lapith and centaur. Metope from the Parthenon, Athens, 447–432 BC. Marble. British Museum, London

88 Battle between Apollo and giant, from the large frieze of the Altar of Zeus, Pergamum, c. 170 BC. Marble. Staatliche Museen zu Berlin

89 Head of a centaur. Detail of metope from the Parthenon, Athens, 447–432 BC. Marble. British Museum, London

90 Head of a giant, from the large frieze of the Altar of Zeus, Pergamum, c. 170 BC. Marble. Staatliche Museen zu Berlin

91 Marsyas. Roman copy of a Hellenistic original forming part of a group with Apollo and the Scythian slave (see Pl. 92). Marble. Uffizi, Florence. Photo Alinari

92 Scythian slave. Roman copy of a Hellenistic original forming part of a group with Apollo and Marsyas (see Pl. 91). Marble. Uffizi, Florence. Photo Anderson

93 Farnese Bull (the punishment of Dirce). Roman adaptation of an original by Apollonius and Tauriscus of Tralles of c. 150 BC. Marble. Museo Nazionale, Naples. Photo Alinari

94 The punishment of Laocoön and his two sons. Hellenistic original by Agesander, Polydorus and Athenodorus of Rhodes of c. 150 BC, or Roman adaptation. Marble. Vatican Museums. Photo Fototeca Unione

95 Son of Niobe. Roman copy of a probably Late Hellenistic original group. Marble. Uffizi, Florence. Photo Alinari

96 Face of Laocoön (detail of Pl. 94). Marble. Vatican Museums. Photo Deutsches Archäologisches Institut, Rome

97 Face of Old Centaur (detail of Pl. 127). Roman copy probably deriving from one of a pair of statues made in the mid-second century BC. Marble. Louvre, Paris. Photo Deutsches Archäologisches Institut, Rome

98 Marriage chamber of Alexander and Roxane, by Giovanni Antonio Bazzi ('Il Sodoma'). Early sixteenth-century fresco. Renaissance reconstruction of a painting by Aëtion (fl. c. 325 BC). Villa Farnesina, Rome. Photo Anderson

99 Calumny of Apelles, by Botticelli. Late fifteenth-century painting on panel. Renaissance reconstruction of a painting by Apelles of the late fourth century BC. Uffizi, Florence. Photo Alinari

100 Eirene and Ploutos, after Cephisodotus. Roman copy of an original of c. 370 BC. Marble. Staatliche Antikensammlungen, Munich. Photo Deutsches Archäologisches Institut, Rome

101 Tyche of Antioch, after Eutychides. Roman copy of an original of c. 295 BC. Marble. Vatican Museums. Photo Alinari

102 Roman relief showing Dionysus with Spring, Summer and Autumn. Probably adaptation of an original of c. 200 BC. Marble. Louvre, Paris

103 Detail of frieze from the temple of Hecate, Lagina, showing the personifications of Rome and various local Carian cities, c. 100 BC. Marble. Archaeological Museum, Istanbul

104 Reconstruction of the symposium tent of Ptolemy II, c. 275–270 BC. From F. Studniczka, Das Symposion Ptolemaios II, Leipzig, 1914

105 Wall-painting from the House of Obellius Firmus, Pompeii, first century BC. Photo Deutsches Archäologisches Institut, Rome

106 Homer crowned by Time and the World (detail of Pl. 107). Marble. British Museum, London

107 Relief showing the apotheosis of Homer, signed by Archelaos of Priene, c. 150 BC. Marble. British Museum, London

108 Drawing of a relief from a clay cup of c. 200 BC illustrating scenes from Euripides' Iphigenia in Aulis. Metropolitan Museum of Art, New York

109 Propylon of the temple of Athena Polias, Pergamum, c. 170 BC. Staatliche Museen zu Berlin

110 Artist's signature on a mosaic from the palace at Pergamum, c. 200 BC (see also Pl. 136). Staatliche Museen zu Berlin

111 The Egg, by Simias. From The Greek Anthology, with English translations by W. R. Paton, The Loeb Classical Library, Harvard University Press: William Heinemann, Cambridge, Mass. and London, 1918

112 The Pipes of Theocritus. From The Greek Anthology, with English translations by W. R. Paton, The Loeb Classical Library, Harvard University Press: William Heinemann, Cambridge, Mass. and London, 1918

113 The Altar, by Dosiadas. From The Greek Anthology, with English translations by W. R. Paton, The Loeb Classical Library, Harvard University Press: William Heinemann, Cambridge, Mass. and London, 1918

114 Funeral stele of Menophila, from Sardis, second century BC. Marble. From W. H. Buckler and W. M. Calder (eds), Anatolian Studies Presented to Sir William Mitchell Ramsay, Manchester, 1923

115 Funeral stele of Pythagoras, from Philadelphia, first century BC. Marble. From J. Keil and A. von Premerstein, Bericht über eine Reise in Lydien . . ., Vienna, 1908

116 Greek song with notation marks, from the stele of Seikilos, Tralles, c. 100 BC. Marble. From Bulletin de correspondance hellénique, Paris, 1894

117 Plan of the temple of Athena Polias, Priene, mid-fourth century BC. From T. Wiegand and H. Schrader, Priene, Berlin, 1904

118 Ground-plan of Miletus in the first century BC. After Gerhard Kleiner, 'Die Ruinen von Milet' in Mitteilungen des

Deutschen Archäologischen Instituts, Abteilung Istanbul, Berlin, 1968

119 Inscription from Potidaea with lettering arranged *stoichēdon*, late fifth century BC. Marble. British Museum, London

120 Themis, by Chaerestratus, from the shrine of Nemesis at Rhamnus in Attica, *c.* 300 BC. Marble. National Museum, Athens. Photo Alinari

121 Mausolus, from the Mausoleum, Halicarnassus, *c.* 350 BC. Marble. British Museum, London

122 Hercules Farnese, after Lysippus. Roman copy signed by Glycon of Athens after an original of the later fourth century BC. Marble. Museo Nazionale, Naples. Photo Anderson

123 Hercules Epitrapezios, after Lysippus. Roman copy of an original of the later fourth century BC. Marble. British Museum, London

124 Hercules and Omphale. Wall-painting from the House of Siricus, Pompeii. Roman copy of a probably Hellenistic original. Photo Brogi

125 Infant Hercules strangling the snakes. Roman copy of a probably Hellenistic original. Marble. Hermitage, Leningrad. Photo Deutsches Archäologisches Institut, Rome

126 Hermes holding the Infant Dionysus, after Praxiteles. Copy, probably of *c.* 100 BC, after an original of *c.* 330 BC. Marble. Olympia Museum. Photo Deutsches Archäologisches Institut, Rome

127 Old Centaur. Roman copy probably deriving from one of a pair of statues made in the mid-second century BC (see also Pls. 97, 128). Marble. Louvre, Paris. Photo Alinari

128 Young Centaur (detail). One of a pair of statues from Hadrian's villa at Tivoli. These are signed by Aristeas and Papias and are Roman copies probably deriving from an original pair of the mid-second century BC (see also Pls. 97, 127). Grey marble. Museo Capitolino, Rome. Photo Deutsches Archäologisches Institut, Rome

129 Hellenistic gold earrings with figures of Eros. British Museum, London

130 Pan and Satyr. Roman, probably copy of a Hellenistic original. Louvre, Paris. Photo Alinari

131 Cupids playing with Hera's peacock. Wall-painting from the House of the Bronzes, Pompeii, first half of the first century AD. Photo Deutsches Archäologisches Institut, Rome

132 Cupids with lion. Roman mosaic. Museo dei Conservatori, Rome. Photo Alinari

133 Roman silver cup with a design of leaves, birds and insects. British Museum, London

134 Doves at a bowl of water. Roman mosaic deriving from an original composition by Sosus of the second century BC. Museo Capitolino, Rome. Photo Anderson

135 Unswept Room. Detail of Roman mosaic, after an original by Sosus of the second century BC. Museo Laterano, Vatican Museums. Photo Anderson

136 Foliate scroll with grasshopper. Detail of mosaic from the palace at Pergamum, *c.* 200 BC (for signature of this mosaic, see Pl. 110). Staatliche Museen zu Berlin

137 Marine life. Detail of Roman mosaic from Pompeii, after a Hellenistic original of perhaps *c.* 200 BC. Museo Nazionale, Naples. Photo Anderson

138 Garland with tragic mask, fruit and flowers. Detail of Roman mosaic from Pompeii, after an original of the second century BC. Museo Nazionale, Naples. Photo Alinari

139 Circular altar with masks and garlands, from the theatre of Dionysus, Athens, *c.* 100 BC. Marble. Photo Deutsches Archäologisches Institut, Athens

140 Homer. Roman copy after an original of probably *c.* 200 BC. Marble. Museo Nazionale, Naples. Photo Hirmer Fotoarchiv

141 Aeschylus. Roman copy of a probably Hellenistic original. Marble. Museo Archeologico, Florence. Photo Alinari

142 Sophocles. Roman copy of a probably Hellenistic original. Marble. Museo Archeologico, Florence. Photo Alinari

143 River god. Roman adaptation of a Hellenistic type. Marble. Vatican Museums. Photo Deutsches Archäologisches Institut, Rome

144 River god, from the left corner of the west pediment of the Parthenon, Athens, 447–432 BC. Marble. British Museum, London

145 Tazza Farnese (detail). Sardonyx cameo from Alexandria. Probably Hellenistic. Museo Nazionale, Naples. Photo Deutsches Archäologisches Institut, Rome

146 Nike, by Paeonius, after 420 BC. From Olympia. Marble. Olympia Museum. Photo Hirmer Fotoarchiv

147 Plan of original setting of the Nike of Samothrace. Drawing by A. D. Johnson

148 Nike of Samothrace, by Pythocritus, early second century BC. Marble. Louvre, Paris. Photo Alinari

149 Birth of Athena. Drawing from a marble relief in Madrid adapted from the east pediment of the Parthenon, Athens, 447–432 BC. After R. Schneider, *Die Geburt der Athena*, Vienna, 1880

150 Head of the Titan Anytus. From a colossal group at Lycosura, by Damophon of Messene, mid-second century BC. Marble. National Museum, Athens. Photo Marburg

151 Zeus, by Eucleides, *c.* 150 BC. From Aegira. Marble. National Museum, Athens. Photo Deutsches Archäologisches Institut, Athens

152 Poseidon, *c.* 150 BC. From Melos. Marble. National Museum, Athens. Photo Alinari

153 Roman relief deriving from the parapet of the temple of Athena Nike, Athens, late fifth century BC. Marble. Uffizi, Florence. Photo Alinari

154 Building of Auge's boat, from the small frieze of the Altar of Zeus, Pergamum, *c.* 170 BC. Marble. Staatliche Museen zu Berlin

155 Teuthras running to receive Auge, from the small frieze of the Altar of Zeus, Pergamum, *c.* 170 BC. Marble. Staatliche Museen zu Berlin

156 Amphitrite, from the large frieze of the Altar of Zeus, Pergamum, *c.* 170 BC. Marble. Staatliche Museen zu Berlin

157 Nike of Samothrace, by Pythocritus, early second century BC. Marble. Louvre, Paris. Photo Marburg

158 Sacrifice of Iphigenia, from the 'Medici' vase, first century BC. Marble. Uffizi, Florence. Photo Alinari

159 Roman sundial, after Hellenistic type. Marble. British Museum, London

160 Reconstruction of map of the world by Eratosthenes. After *Lexikon der Alten Welt*, Zurich and Stuttgart, 1965

161 Reconstruction of gearing from a Hellenistic astronomical calculator. From Derek J. de Solla Price, 'Gears from the Greeks. The Antikythera Mechanism—A Calendar Computer from *c.* 80 BC', in *Transactions of the American Philosophical Society*, new series, 64.7, 1974

162 Dionysiac procession with Silenus, satyrs and maenads. Drawing from a vase of the second century AD, itself a copy of a Neo-Attic original of the first century BC. Campo Santo, Pisa

163 Plan of the Altar of Zeus, Pergamum, showing axial lines. Drawing by A. D. Johnson

164 Horsemen of the Panathenaic procession, from the frieze of the Parthenon, Athens, 447–432 BC. Marble. British Museum, London

165 Plan of the shrine of Dionysus, Thasos, *c.* 300–275 BC. Drawing by Peter Bridgewater

166 Reconstruction of the group of philosophers and poets from the Serapeum, Memphis, first half of the third century BC. After J. P. Lauer and C. P. Picard, *Les Statues ptolémaïques du Sarapieion de Memphis*, Paris, 1955

167 Seven Sages. Roman mosaic of the first century BC, perhaps recording a Hellenistic composition. From Boscoreale. Museo Nazionale, Naples. Photo Alinari

168 Roman perspective wall-painting from Boscoreale, first century BC. Metropolitan Museum of Art, New York

169 Greek theatre, Epidaurus, begun *c.* 350 BC. Photo Hirmer Fotoarchiv

170 Reconstruction of the Hellenistic theatre, Priene, begun second century BC. From A. von Gerkan, *Das Theater von Priene*, Munich, 1921

171 Plan showing the arrangement of musical vases in a Greek theatre according to Vitruvius. Drawing by A. D. Johnson

172 Plan of the Athenian Agora at the end of the fourth century BC. After drawing from John Travlos, *A Pictorial Dictionary of Ancient Athens*, London and New York, 1971

173 Plan of the Athenian Agora after Hellenistic remodelling in the second century BC. After drawing from John Travlos, *A Pictorial Dictionary of Ancient Athens*, London and New York, 1971

174 Tower of the Winds, Athens, *c.* 40 BC. Photo Marburg

175 Plan of the temple of Artemis Leukophryene, Magnesia-on-the-Maeander, mid-second century BC. After C. Humann, *Magnesia am Maeander*, Berlin, 1904

176 Elevation of the temple of Artemis Leukophryene, Magnesia-on-the-Maeander. From C. Humann, *Magnesia am Maeander*, Berlin, 1904

177 Plan of the commercial centre, Miletus, at the end of the fourth century and at the middle of the second century BC. From G. Kleiner, *Die Ruinen von Milet*, Berlin, 1968

178 Plan of the agora, Magnesia-on-the-Maeander, second century BC. From C. Humann, *Magnesia am Maeander*, Berlin, 1904

179 Plan of the agora, Priene, second century BC, showing axis of agora arch and symmetry about it. After J. B. Ward-Perkins, *Cities of Ancient Greece and Italy: Planning in Classical Antiquity*, George Braziller, Inc., New York, 1974

180 Reconstruction of agora arch, Priene, mid-second century BC. After F. Krischen

181 Plan of the Athenian Agora in the second century BC, showing axial lines. Drawing by A. D. Johnson

182 Mosaic floor from the House of the Masks, Delos, *c.* 220–150 BC. From *Exploration archéologique de Délos, faite par l'Ecole française d'Athènes*, XXIX, Paris, 1972

183 Mosaic floor from the House of the Masks, Delos, *c.* 220–150 BC. From *Exploration archéologique de Délos, faite par l'Ecole française d'Athènes*, XXIX, Paris, 1972

184 Interior of lower floor, Stoa of Attalus, Athens, *c.* 150 BC. Photo Agora Excavations, American School of Classical Studies, Athens

185 Plan of the sanctuary of Athena at Lindos, Rhodes, *c.* 200 BC. After G. Gruben, *Die Tempel der Griechen*, Munich, 1966

186 Terrace and stair, sanctuary of Athena, Lindos, Rhodes, *c.* 200 BC. Photo Deutsches Archäologisches Institut, Rome

187 Reconstruction of the Hellenistic sanctuary of Asclepius, Cos. From P. Schazmann and R. Herzog, *Asklepieion, Kos*, I, Berlin, 1932

188 Altar of Zeus, Pergamum, *c.* 170 BC. Staatliche Museen zu Berlin

189 South-western approach of the Propylaea, Athens, *c.* 435 BC. Photo Marburg

Index

Numbers in italics refer to the illustrations

Academus 50
Achilles, recognized by Odysseus 49, *46*; and the tortoise 151, 155
acoustics, and theatre design 160–4
Acragas, Olympieum 21, 69, 103
Acropolis, Athens 8, 9, 14, 63, 81, 85, 155, 169, *2*
Adonis 64
Aegira *151*
Aegistheus 109
Aeolian mode 64
Aeolians 18, 21
Aeolic capitals 80, *78*
Aeschylus 23, 134, 135, 138, 140, 146, *141*; *Persae* 15, 16, 57; *Suppliant Women* 56
Aëtion 95–6, 126, *98*
Agamemnon 109
Agatharcus of Samos 10, 23
Agathe Tyche 36
Agathon 36, 38
Agesander of Rhodes 90, *94*
Agias 13, 42, *8*
Agora, Athens 34, *44*; planning of 166, 170, 178, *172, 173*; Stoa Poikile 33; and temple of Hephaestus 168, 169, 178; visual axes 172–3, *181*
Alberti, Leon Battista 168
Alcaeus of Messene 112, 115, 148
Alcibiades 10, 46
Alcmaeon of Croton 115
Alexander I of Macedon 7
Alexander the Great 7, 8, 10, 12, 13, 14, 15, 23, 26, 30, 31, 34, 35, 38, 64, 67, 69, 100, 103, 107, 115, 128, 142, 180, *1, 10, 38*; Plutarch on 32, 35–6; political philosophy 31–3; portrayals of 41–2, 48, 55, 95–6, 98–9, 156, 158, *98*; title 123–5
Alexander Sarcophagus 33, *26*
Alexandria 31, 32, 50, 61, 64, 69, 70, 71, 80, 88, 99, 135, *145*; library 68, 98, 118, 151; literature in 38, 105, 134, 142; Museum 31, 69, 98, 118, 133; Serapeum 159
Alexarchus 180
allegory 88–9, 95–105
Altar of Zeus, Pergamum 84–5, 87, 90, 92, 94, 106, 140, 144–6, 173, 178, *163, 188*; large frieze of 144–6, 147, 153–5, *86, 88, 90, 156*; small frieze of 144–5, 156, *154, 155*; *see also* Gigantomachy; Telephus story
Amazons 14, 81, 84, *9, 22, 82*
Amphion 90
Amphitrite 85, 145, 155, *156*
Amun Ra 13
Antidotus 121
Antigone 56
Antigonus of Carystus 155
Antigonus Gonatas 15, 158
Antioch 36, 99; library 118
Antiochus III 123, 144, *148*
Antiochus IV 140
Antiope 90, *93*
Antipater of Sidon 111, 112, 114, 132, 180
Antiphilus 57
Anyte of Tegea 66, 128
Anytus, head of 140, *150*
Apelles 29–30, 38, 40–1, 54, 55, 57, 60, 97–8, 120, 126, *99*
Aphrodite 70; of Cnidos 30, 37, 57, 58, *24, 25*; of Cos 58; of Doidalsas 30, 37, *31*; with Eros and Pan 62, 92, *62*; Kallipygos 57, *53*; on Pergamum frieze 155
Apis 71
Apollo 133, *48*; Colossus of Rhodes 123; and children of Niobe 91; from Delos 98, 108; Lyceius 50; and Marsyas 66, 89, 90, 91, *64, 91, 92*; and the Muses 105, 132, 135; on Pergamum

frieze 85, *88*; Sauroktonos 50
Apollo, temple of, Athens 73
Apollodorus, painter 121
Apollodorus, pupil of Aristarchus 88, 94, 155
Apollonius of Alexandria, *eidographos* 68
Apollonius Rhodius 61, 105, 133–4, 147; *Argo-nautica* 133, 140, 146
Apollonius of Tralles 90, *93*
Apoxyomenos 37, 42, *39*
Apulia *18*
Aratus 62
Arcadia 66, 123
Archelaos of Priene, relief signed by 103–6, 107, 108–9, *106, 107*
Archilochus of Paros 132
Archimedes 164
architecture, commentaries on 53; decoration 10–12, 13, 24, *7*; evolution of temples 27; and mathematical proportion 23; orders 79–81, *77, 78*; sculpture, architectural, and naturalism 102–3; and stylistic choice 72–9; vegetable forms in 73, 80, 103; *see also* Corinthian order; Doric order; Egypt; geometry; Ionic order; optics
aretē 21, 24
Argive base, Delphi 157–9, 160
Argos 23, 157–8
Aristarchus of Samos 164
Aristarchus of Samothrace 61
Aristeas *128*
Aristides Ponticus 64
Aristides of Thebes, painter 55, 56
Aristophanes of Byzantium 61
Aristophanes, playwright 23, 57, 58, 64
Aristotle 7, 23, 26–31, 32, 34, 38, 50, 62, 114, 160, *20*; acoustic theory 161; on barbarians 32, 64, 180; and chronological classification of art 58–60; on cities 52; definition of art 36, *37*; distinction between comedy and tragedy 38, 54, 55–6; emotional and psychological effects of art 27–9, 53, 68; on language 94, 96, 116–18; *On Memory and Recollection* 116; *Metaphysics* 26, 53, 60, 115, 116, 120; *Nicomachean Ethics* 120, 121; on perception, thought and the senses 96, 97, 115, 116, 120, 151, 152–3; *Parts of Animals* 27; *Physics* 151; *Poetics* 27, 28, 38, 40, 53, 58–9, 120; *Politics* 68, 78; on the pleasure of imitations 38, 40, 58–9, 102; on prose style 72, 147; on public oratory 143; *Rhetoric* 27, 28, 53, 58, 97, 120–1, 122, 152; on rhythm and metre 147, 152, 153, 155, 159; *On Sense and Sensible Objects* 115, 116, 120; on size in art 121–2, 123, 133, 146, 151, 155, 159; on social classes 78; *On the Soul* 116, 151, 152; use of symbols 118
Aristotelians 45, 46, 94, 175
Aristoxenus 31, 68
Arsinoë, wife of Ptolemy IV 103
Artemis 51; on Pergamum frieze 85
artistic creation, attitudes to 133–5, 146–8
Asclepiadae 26
Asclepius 50, 51, *50*
Asia Minor 72, 99, 114, 144
astronomical calculator, gearing from *161*
Athena 8, 9, 81, 88, 90, 122; invents flute 66; from library, Pergamum 84, 88, *59*; and Panathenaic procession on Parthenon frieze 155–6; on Parthenon pediments 84–5, 140, *85, 149*; on Pergamum frieze 84–5, 140, 155, 173, *86, 163*
Athena Nike, temple of, Athens 63, 142, 178, *14, 153*
Athena Parthenos 10, 60, 63, 73, 85, 108, 142, *4, 57, 59*
Athenaeus 27, 67, 69, 99

Athenodorus of Rhodes 90, *94*
Athens 15, 26, 50, 64, 69, 84, 103, 144, 155; architectural planning of 166, *172, 173*; and Atlantis 7–16; and Ionians 18–19, 20; and stylistic choice in architecture 72; war with Sparta 16, 17, 18, 19; *and see* Acropolis; Agora; Apollo, temple of; Athena Nike, temple of; Bouleuterion; Dipylon cemetery; Erechtheum; Hephaesteum; Lysicrates; Metroön; Olympieum; Parthenon; Peiraeus; Propylaea; Stoa; theatre of Dionysus; Tower of the Winds
Athos, Mount 14, 125
Atlantis, myth of 7–16, 157, *3*
Atlas 103
Atomists 34, 152
Attalids 62–3, 69, 145, 155; buildings of 80, 84, 108
Attalus I 81
Attalus II 88, 89, 106, 173; Stoa of 15, 79–80, 166, 173, *76, 77, 181, 184*
Attalus III 180
Attic grave art 25, 29, *19, 23*
Attic Hellenism, cult of 15; style of sculpture 29, 143, 155, *23*
Attica 8, 9, 15, *48, 85*
Auge *154, 155*
Augustine, St 16
Augustus 15

Babylon 9
barbarians, Greek attitudes to 7, 9–10, 14–26, 32–3, 64, 180
Barberini Faun 33, *28*
Bassae, temple of Apollo 23, 73, 78, 119, *68*
baths 9, 13, 14
Battiadae of Cyrene 146
Battle of Darius and Alexander, painting and mosaic 37, 45, 56, *40, 52*
beasts 50–1, 87, 92; *and see* mosaics, animal subjects
Begram, Afghanistan *60*
Beneventum 180
black-figure pottery 18
boats 69–72
Boethus 50
books 115, 118
Boscoreale *168*
Botticelli, Sandro 97, *99*
Bouleuterion, Athens 172
boy with a goose 50
Bronze Age 7, 15
Brunelleschi, Filippo 168
Bryaxis *66*
Byblos 114

Caesar, Julius 180
Calates 57
Caligula 14
Callimachus of Cyrene 49, 98, 105, 110; *Aetia* 133, 134, 147; and dispute on size and excellence in art 133–4, 140, 142, 146, 147, 148; *Hymns* 68, 133; *Iambi* 68; *Pinakes* 61; variety of language 68–9, 81
Callimachus, sculptor 73
Calumny of Apelles 55, 97–8, *99*
Caria *103*
Carneades 50
Carrey, Jacques *85*
Carthage 16
Caryatids 103, 173
Cato 16
Catullus 148
centaurs 14, 87, *87, 89*; Old and Young Centaurs 92, 126, 175, *97, 127, 128*

Cephisodotus 30, 36, 98, *100*
Chaerestratus 123, *120*
Chaeronea 15
chance and art 35–8
character, in visual arts 55–6
Chares of Lindos 123
Christianity 16, 157
Chrysippus 34, 94, 96, 114
Cicero 62, 142, 143; *De Officiis* 94; *Orator* 142
circuses 13
civil engineering 14
classic literature and art, and Hellenistic imitativeness 61–2
classification and criticism of art, chronological
  58–63; geographical 63–9
Cleanthes 34, 88, 92, 97, 98
Cleopatra 180
Cnidos, Aphrodite of 30, 37, 57, 58, *24, 25*;
  treasury of 21
coins 41, 48, *35–7*
colossi 122–3, 125
comedy 28, 38, 54, 59, 61, 105, 159, *165*;
  character and emotion in 54, 55; New Comedy
  38, 97; in visual arts 57–8, *53–6*
Constantine 10
Corinth 18, 64, 69, 100, 164
Corinthian order 70, 103, 140; and boat of
  Ptolemy IV 70–1; and stylistic choice in
  architecture 72–9, 80, *70, 71, 73*
Cos 68, 69; Aphrodite of 58; sanctuary of
  Asclepius 126, 177–8, *187*
country *see* town and country
Crates of Mallos 88, 89, 91, 94
Cresilas *42*
Croesus 107
Croton 16
Ctesicles 46, 58
Ctesilochus 57
cults, rural 50–2; of Zeus 140–1
cupids 95–6, 126, 129, *98, 131, 132*
Cynics 34–5
Cyzicus, shrine of Apollonis 89, 90, 92, 106, 108,
  155

Damophon of Messene 123, 140, *150*
Daochus II of Thessaly 13, 158, *8*
Darius III 56
deception and the deceiving eye 40–6
Delian confederacy 73
Delos 10, 12, 51, 60, 158, 170; Aphrodite from *62*;
  Apollo from 98, 108; House of the Hermes 7;
  House of the Masks 173, 175, *182, 183*;
  hypostyle hall 79; Sanctuary of the Bulls 15
Delphi 25, 73, 103, 123, 178; Argive base 157–9,
  160; monument of the Thessalians 13, *8*;
  temple of Apollo 14; tholos 73
Demeter 133
Demetrius of Alopece, sculptor 62
Demetrius I of Macedonia 38
Demetrius of Phalerum 31, 159
Democritus 34, 38
Demosthenes 10, 46, 52, 142, *44*
Diana 91
Didyma, temple of Apollo 73
Dinocrates 14, 125
Diodorus 113
Diogenes of Babylon 88
Diogenes, Cynic 34–5
Diogenes, Epicurean 38
Dionysiac rites 50, 97, 99–100, 148, *102, 162*
Dionysius II, tyrant of Syracuse 10
Dionysus 50, 51, 57, 113, 126, 128, 133, *49, 126*;
  cult of 50, 51, 97, 99–100, 103, 148, *102, 162*; on
  Pergamum frieze 85, 155; and procession of
  Ptolemy II 99–100, 156–7; shrine of, on boat of
  Ptolemy IV 13, 70; shrine of, Thasos 105, 159,
  160, *165*; and the theatre 132–3, 160, 161, *139*
Dioscorides of Samos 134, 135, 146, *56*
Dipylon cemetery, Athens 175
Dirce 90, 92, *93*
Dithyramb 105, 159, *165*
Doidalsas of Bithynia 37, *31*

Domitian 15
Dorian mode 24, 64, 67, 68
Dorians 17–21, 64, 68–9; and comedy 38–40
Doric order 21, 27, 69, 71, 167, 172; and boat of
  Hiero II 69–71, 72, 80; and stylistic choice in
  architecture 72–9, 80–1, *70, 71, 73*
Doryphoros 23, 42, 53, 119, *16*
Dosiadas 109; *The Altar* 110, *113*
Douris 31, 60, 63
Dresden 92
Drunken Old Woman 33, 40, *33*
dualism in art 46–50
Dying Iocasta 41
dynastic portraiture 9, 13, 41, 48, 70, 157–8, *35–7*

Egypt 16, 112, 113; art and architecture 9, 13,
  71–2, 79, 114, 157, *65–7*; hieroglyphics 112–13,
  114; papyrus production 115; in Plato's
  dialogues 9, 15, 21–2, 24, 113, 116
Eirene and Ploutos 98, 99, *100*
Electra and Orestes 62, *58*
Eleusis 12; hall of the Mysteries 50
Eos 155
Ephesus, Artemisium 14, 15, 107
epic 59, 61, 105, 133, 138, 140, 146
Epicureanism 33, 34, 36, 38, 45, 46, 58, 97, 152
Epicurus 34, 37, 38, 50, 58, 96, *30*
Epidaurus 50, 178; gymnasium 170; Propylaea
  71; temple of Artemis 73, *71*; temple of
  Asclepius *71*; temple L (temple of Aphrodite)
  71; theatre 161, *169*; tholos 73, *69, 70*
epigrams 128, 129, 133, 134, 155; and picture
  poems 109–10, *111–13*; on shrine of Apollonis,
  Cyzicus 89, 106, 108, 155; on statues 98–9, 108
epitaphs 110–11, 134
Eratosthenes 151, 164, *160*
Erechtheum, Athens 19, 21, 72, 73, 175, *13*
Erechtheus 19
Eros 92, 126–8, *62, 129*
erotic art 29–30
ēthos and *pathos* 54–8
Etruria 9
etymology 52, 96, 98, 105
Eucleides *151*
Euclid 45, 175, 177, 178; *Optics* 45, 175
Eumenes II 84, 88, 89, 106–7, 108; builder of
  Lower agora, Pergamum 170; Stoa of 15
Eunica 64
Euphranor 121, 123
Eupompus of Sicyon 42, 64
Euripides 19, 50, 106, 115; *Bacchae* 50; *Iphigenia
  in Aulis* 108; *Ion* 19
Europa 60
Eutychides 36, 99, 101, *101*

Farnese Bull 90, *93*
Fates, the 155

Galatea 48, 49, 64, *45*
Galaton 105, 134, 135, 146
Ganymede 60
garlands 129–33, *138, 139*
Gauls 80, 81, 84, 107, 145, *84*
geometry, and architectural planning and art
  164–8, 175
Germans 14, 16
Giant 84, *81*
Gigantomachy, on Altar of Zeus, Pergamum 29,
  84–5, 87, 88–9, 91, 94, 95, 145–6, *86, 88, 90*; on
  Parthenon metopes 81
glass 128, *60*
Golden Age 66
Gordion 12
Gorgias 54, 72
Gothic architecture 79
Greek Anthology 110; *and see* epigrams; Palatine
  Anthology
Gryllos 57
gymnasia 9, 50, 70, 80; *and see* Epidaurus;
  Miletus; Olympia; Priene

Hadrian's villa, Tivoli *128*

Hagia Sophia 15
Halicarnassus, Mausoleum 53, 119, 123, 147, *9,
  121*
hearing, theories of 152, 161; *and see* acoustics
Hegesias 72
Helicon, Mount 133
Helios 155
Hellenism, philosophy of, and Hellenistic philo-
  sophies 31–5
Hephaesteum, Athens 168, 169, 172, 173, 178,
  181
Hephaestus 8, 45, *41*
Hera 96, 98, *131*
Heraclitus 26, 38
Hercules 125, 128, 145; 'Choice of' 17, 21, 24, 72,
  95, 114; colossus of Tarentum 123; Epi-
  trapezios 125–6, *123*; Farnese 125, *122*; Infant
  126, *125*; and Omphale 49, 126, *124*
Hermaphrodite 49, 64, 92, *47*
Hermes 51, 114, *126*
Hermogenes 76, 167, 168
Herodotus 16, 17, 59, 157
Herondas 40, 68, 69, 71, 126; *The Dream* 68, 69
Hesiod 24, 105, 146; *Theogony* 96
Hiero II of Syracuse 10, 13, 80; boat of 69–71, 72
Hippocrates of Cos 27
Hippodamus of Miletus 23, 119
hippodromes 9, 13
Hipponax 68
history 59–60, 94, 105
Homer 46, 48, 58, 66; and allegory 96; Apotheosis
  of, by Archelaos 103–6, 107, 108–9, *106, 107*;
  hexameters 68; *Iliad* 24, 59, 70, 103, 106, 133;
  Margites 59; and *megethos* (greatness) 122, 140;
  Odyssey 24, 59, 103, 133; portrayed in visual
  arts 103–5, 134, 135, 137, 138, 146, 159, *106,
  107, 140*; tradition of 8, 24
Homereion 103, 105, 134, 135
horses 13–14
Hygieia *50*

Ictinus 23
India 32, 99
inscriptions 15, 119–20, *10, 119*; on Archelaos
  relief 105–6, 107; on buildings 106–7, 108, *109*;
  on clay cups 106, *108*; on Gigantomachy,
  Pergamum 89, 106, 145–6
Ion 19
Ionia 8, 26, 114
Ionian mode 24, 64
Ionian philosophy 9, 24, 35, 120
Ionians 17–21, 64, 68, 69
Ionic order 19, 21, 27, 71, 80, 103, 172; and
  stylistic choice in architecture 72–9, *71, 73*
Iphigenia *158*
Iron Age 15
Isis 24, 113, 114; Euthenia-Isis *145*
Isocrates 31, 54
Italy 10, 15, 16, 23

Jerusalem 9
jewellery 128, *129*
Jewish tradition 16
Jockey 40
Justinian 15
Juvenal 16

Kairos 36, 98, 101
Kings 9
kritikoi 60–1

Lagina, temple of Hecate *103*
language, theories of 94, 96, 115–16
Laocoön 90, 91, 92, 96, *94, 96*
Lapiths 85, 87, *87*
Larisa 80
Leonidas of Tarentum 110
Leucippus 34
libraries, growth of 118; *and see* Alexandria;
  Antioch; Pergamum
Lindos, sanctuary of Athena 177, 178, *185, 186*
Longinus 122

Lucian 95, 96, 98, 126
Lucretius 50, 176
Lyceum 27, 50, 175
Lycomedes 49, *46*
Lycosura, sculptural group by Damophon of Messene 123, 140, *150*
Lydian mode 24, 64
lyric poetry 61, 68, 129–32
Lysias 142
Lysicrates, Choragic Monument of 51, 73, *49*
Lysimachus 38
Lysippus 41–2, 46, 54, 55, 60, 62, 99, 123, 125–6; Agias 42, *8*; Apoxyomenos 37, 42, *39*; Hercules Epitrapezios 125–6, *123*; Hercules Farnese 125, *122*; Kairos 36, 98, 101, 108
Lysistratus, brother of Lysippus 41

Macedon 7, 15, 71, 80, 142, 158
Macedonia 26, 31; houses and palaces 170
Madrid 85, *149*
maenads 50, 97, 147, *162*
Magnesia-on-the-Maeander, architectural planning 169–70, *178*; temple of Artemis Leukophryene 29, 167, 168, 169, 171, *22, 175, 176*
male and female dualism 64–6, *60*; *and see* Hermaphrodite
Manetho 112
Mantinea, shrine of Leto *64*
maps 151, *160*
Mark Antony 180
Marriage of Alexander and Roxane 95–6, 126, *98*
Marsyas 66, 67, 68, 89–90, *64*; Flaying of 33, 89–90, 92, *91, 92*
Mausolus 123, *121*
measure, scale and perception 119–21; and friezes on Altar of Zeus, Pergamum 144–6
'Medici' vase *158*
medicine 26, 27
Megalopolis 123
Meleager 111–12, 114, 129–33
Melos 140, *152*
Memphis, Serapeum 71, 159, 160, *166*
Menander 35, 38, 46, 55, 57; *Arbitrants* 35; *Synaristōsai 56*
Menecrates of Rhodes 91
Menelaus 62, *58*
Menoeceus 58
Menophila, tomb of, Sardis 112, 114, *114*
Metrodorus 142
Metroön, Athens 172, *181*
Middle East 8
Miletus, Bouleuterion 76, 78, 167–8, 171, 172, *73, 75*; Didymaeum 166–7; ground plan of 119–20, *118*; Hellenistic gymnasium 76, 78, 168, 170, 171, 172, *73*; town-planning 169, *177*
mimiambi 68
mimos 38, 40
Mithridates III *35*
Mithridates IV *37*
Morgantina 10, 12
mosaics 10–12, 37, 40, 45, 51, 56, 70, *5, 6, 52, 132, 138*; Battle of Darius and Alexander 45, 56, *40, 52*; comic *56*; fish and animal subjects 129, *134, 136, 137*; from House of the Masks, Delos 173, 175, *182, 183*; from palace at Pergamum 110, *136*; Seven Sages 159, *167*; Unswept Room 129, *134, 135*; visual axes 173, 175, *182, 183*
Mummius 164
Muses, the 88, 105, 132–3, *107*; 'birdcage of' 133; and poetic inspiration 134, 135, 146
music 23, 24–5, 31, 110, 119, 120; geographical classification of 24, 64, 66–8; instruments 66–7, 109–10, *63*; notation 118, *116*; psychological effects of 53–4
Mycenaean period 18
Myron of Pergamum 67, 89, *33*
Mysteries 50
myths 16; allegorical interpretation of 88–9, 96, 98, 105

Naples 81, 84, 125

narrative art 157
naturalism 38–42, 62, 101–3
Neandria 80, *78*
Neo-Attic art 60, 62, 63, 142, 145; and oratory 142–4; reliefs and friezes 142, 143, 147–8, 153, 156, *153*; rhythm in 147–8; vases 147–8, 153, *158, 162*
Neo-Platonism 116
Nicias, painter 121
Nike 85, *14*; of Paeonius 138, *146*; of Samothrace 37, 137–8, 140, 141, 147, *147, 148, 157*
Nile 135–7, 138, *145*
Niobid sculpture group 91–2, *95*
Nykterinos 105, 159, *165*
nymphs 51, 64, 92, *48, 61*
Nyx 155

Odysseus 46, 49, *46*
Old Testament 16, 17
Olympia 12, 178, *146*; gymnasium 170; Philippeion 15, 73, 158; temple of Zeus 135
Olympieum, Athens 14, 76, 140, 144, *72*
Olynthus 10–12
Omphale 49, 126, *124*
optics 45; and architectural planning 169–78; *and see* Euclid
Orestes 62, *58*
Osiris 71, 113–14
Ouranopolis 180

Paeonius 138, *146*
painting 31, 40, 46, 48, 49, 121, 129, *41, 45, 46, 105, 124, 131, 168*; and allegory 95–6, 134, 135, *98*; criticism and classification of 53; and ideas of Aristotle 28, 40; and mathematical order 23–4; and personification 97–8, *99*
Palatine Anthology 66, 89; *and see* epigrams; *Greek Anthology*
Palatitsa 170
Pamphilus of Amphipolis 24, 53, 72, 119
Pan 50, 51, 64, 66, 68, 109, *48, 130*; and Aphrodite 92, *62*
Panaetius of Rhodes 88, 89, 91, 92, 94
Panathenaea 155; procession of, on Parthenon frieze 155–6, *164*
Pancaspe 30
Panionium 21
Papias *128*
Parrhasius of Ephesus 24, 25, 40, 55
Parthenon, Athens 10, 18–19, 72, 73, 80–1, 84–5, 137, *4, 12*; frieze 29, 138, 155–6, 158, *164*; metopes 81, 87, 138, *87, 89*; pediments 85, 87, 138–40, 143, *85, 144, 149*
Pasiteles 62, 63, 148
pathos see *ēthos*
patronage of art 62–3, 69
Paullus, Macedonicus 142
Pausanias *64*
Pausias 53
Pauson 55
Peiraeus 119
Pella 10–12, 170, *5*
Peloponnesian War 16, 17, 50, 59
Pergamum 15, 62, 69, 103, 142, 79, *80*; Heroön 78, *73*; and influence of Stoics on art 94; library 80, 84, 87, 88, 118, *59*; Lower agora 170; mosaics 12, 129, *110, 134–6*; and parchment 115; sculpture 62, 69, 81–8, 90–2, 143, 148, 155, *81–4, 86, 88, 90*; Stoa of Athena 21; stylistic choice at 79–88; temple of Athena Polias 80, 106–7, 108, *109*; *and see* Altar of Zeus
Pericles 9–10, 46, 69, 73, 85, 108, 142, 155–6, *42*
period form, in literary composition 152–3; in visual arts 153, 159, *162*
Peripatetics 175
Perseus of Macedon 180
Persian Wars 7, 16, 17–18, 59, 67, 81, 142
Persians 9, 14, 84, 103, 123, *26, 83*
personification 97–8, 99–100, 103, 156, *99–103*
perspective 23, 160, 164, 176–7, *18, 168*
phantasia 62, 116
Pharnaces I *36*

Phidias 10, 60, 62, 63, 73, 84, 108, 122, 140, 142, *4, 57*
Philadelphia 114, *115*
Philae, temple of Isis *65*
Philetaerus 80
Philip II of Macedon 7, 10, 13, 15, 158
Philip V 180
Philippeion, Olympia 15, 73, 158
Philocion 56
Philoxenus of Eretria *52*
Phoebe 155
Phoenicia 113–14, 119
Phrygian mode 24, 64, 66, 67
Phryne 25
physiognomics 55
Pindar 67
Pisistratus, sons of 14, *72*
Plato 7, 19, 32, 34, 35, 50, 60, 113, 144, 152, *15*; Academy of 50, 120; *Cratylus* 96, 115; *Critias* 7, 8, 10, 17, 157; on dance 147; on goodness and beauty in art 21–6, 115, 116, 119; ideas on art, contrasted with Aristotle 26, 27, 28, 29, 30, 53, 59; on language and speech 115–16, 118; *Laches* 24, 64; *Laws* 24, 67, 116; on measure 120; on music 54, 67, 68; and myth of Atlantis 7–9, 10, 12, 13–17, 26, 64, 180, *3*; *Phaedrus* 21–2; *Philebus* 120; *Philodemus* 22; *Republic* 22, 24, 64, 120, 180; on sight 97, 115–16; *Sophist* 120; *Symposium* 50; *Timaeus* 7; word and image, in thought of 97, 106
Pliny the Elder 24, 36, 41, 42, 55, 57, 60, 63, 64, 91, 105, 120, 126, 129; *Natural History* 36, 60, 64, 120, 123
Plotinus 116
Ploutos 36, 98, 99, *100*
Plutarch 32, 33, 35, 41–2, 62, 113, 114, 121, 161; *On the Fortune or Virtue of Alexander* 32, 35–6
Pluto 71, 113
poetry 28, 31, 88, 129–33; classification of 68, 72; metre and rhythm 118, 147, 148, 152; originality and inspiration 133–5, 146–7; in shape of the subject 109–110, *111–13*; *and see* epic; epigram; lyric
Polus 36
Polybius 16, 94, 142, 180
Polycles 60, 142
Polyclitus 23, 42, 53, 72, 119, 120, 161, *16*; *Kanōn* 23, 53
Polycrates of Samos 9
Polydorus of Rhodes 90, *94*
Polyeuctus 46, *44*
Polygnotus 51, 55, 63
Polyphemus 46, 48, 49, 64, *45*
Pompeii, House of the Bronzes *131*; House of the Faun 6, *40, 52*; House of Obellius Firmus *105*; House of Siricus *124*; mosaics 57, *6, 40, 52, 56, 137, 138*; Villa of Cicero *56*; wall-paintings 45, 49, 126, *41, 45, 46, 105, 124, 131, 168*
Poseidon 9, 10, 14, 16, 21, 64, 157; from Melos 140, *152*; on Parthenon pediment 85, 140, *85*
Posidonius 92, 94
Pothos 55, *51*
Potidaea *119*
Pratinas 67
Praxiteles 25, 30, 38, 60, 62, 142; Agathe Tyche 36; Aphrodite of Cnidos 30, 37, 58, *24, 25*; Aphrodite of Cos 58; Contest between Apollo and Marsyas 67, 90, *64*; Hermes with Infant Dionysus 50, 126, *126*; Weeping Matron and Smiling Courtesan 58
Priene 10, 166, 169; agora 170, 171–2, 173, 176–7, *179, 180*; Ecclesiasterion 167; Hellenistic theatre 170; Lower gymnasium 76, 78, 170, *74*; Sacred Stoa 170, 172; temple of Athena Polias 15, 23, 53, 80, 107, 119, *10, 17, 117*
private houses 10, 12, 13, 170
Problems 121, 152
Probus 68
Prodicus 17, 19, 21, 72, 95
Prophthasia, Sogdiana 32
Propylaea, Athens 72, 73, 107, 155, 169, 178, *189*

Protogenes of Rhodes 36, 126
Ptolemies 13, 14, 80, 113, 115, 156–7, 180
Ptolemy I 15, 71, 97, 100, 113
Ptolemy II 68; procession of 99–100, 156–7; symposium tent of 103, *104*
Ptolemy III 62, 64
Ptolemy IV 103; boat of 13, 69–71, 72
Ptolemy VI 137
Pyrrhus 105, 180
Pythagoras 16, 22–3, 34, 113, 164, 180
Pythagoras, tomb of, Philadelphia 114, *115*
Pythagoreans 9, 16, 50; and Egyptian ideas 114–15; on letters 116
Pythius 23, 53
Pythocritus *148, 157*

Quintilian 61, 62, 142

Renaissance 41, 46, 160, 168
Rhamnus, shrine of Nemesis *120*
Rhea 100
rhetoric 27, 31, 54, 64, 119; Attic and Asiatic in, and sculpture 142–6; and stylistic choice 72; *see also* Aristotle, *Rhetoric*
Rhodes 91, 94, 177, *148*; colossus of 123; sanctuary of Athena, Lindos 177, 178, *185, 186*; sculpture 69, 90, 140
Rhoecus 53
river gods 135–7, *143, 144, 145*
Rome 94, 142, 168, *103*; and Hellenistic art 141–2; informative content of Roman art 102; moral and physical defeat of the Greeks by 142, 180; and Plato's Atlantis 7, 8, 10, 13, 14, 15, 16, 180
Romulus and Remus 106
Roxane 95–6, *98*

Sais 113
Samos, temple of Hera 53
Samothrace, Arsinoeion 15, *11*; Kabeirion 12, *148*; Nike of 37, 123, 137–8, 140, 141, 147, *147, 148, 157*
Sappho 132, 148
Sardis, temple of Artemis 166, 167; tomb of Menophila 112, 114, *114*
satire 57–8
satyrs 50, 57, 64, 66, 90, 92, 147, *54, 61, 130, 162*
scene-painting 23, 160
Sceptics 35, 46, 50
science and technology 27, 46, 166
Scipios, the 16
Scopas 23, 50, 55, *51*
Scythia 32
Scythian slave 89, 90, *92*
Seikilos, stele of, Tralles *116*
Selene *155*
Seleucia 36
Seleucids 80, 180
Seleucus 99
Selinus, temple G 167
Semele 99
Semiramis 9
Seneca 125, 176
Serapis 71, 113, *66*
Seven Sages 159, *167*

Sextus Empiricus 176
Sicily 10, 13, 69, 72
Sicyonian school 60, 62, 64
Sidon, sarcophagi from 114
sight, power of 97, 115–18; theories of 152, 160, 164; *and see* optics
Silanion 37, 41
Silenus *162*
silver 69, 106, 128, *133*
Simias, *Double Axe* 109; *The Egg* 109, *111*; *Wings of Eros* 109
Simonides of Ceos 110
Siphnos, treasury of 21, 173
Siwa 13
size, and artistic merit 121–33; and linear organization of works of art 152; and literary quality 133–4, 135; and painting 134, 135; and rhetoric 142–6; and sculpture 135–42, 142–6
skiagraphia 28, 120–1, 144, 145
social classes 78–9
Socrates 7, 16, 17, 19, 35, 46, 54, 55, *43*; on goodness and beauty in art 21–6, 119
'Sodoma, Il' (Giovanni Antonio Bazzi) *98*
Solomon, temple of 9, 15
Solon 7, 15
Sophists 17, 21, 36
Sophocles 56, 135, 160, *142*
Sophron 68
Sositheus 134
Sosus 129, *134, 135*
sound 115, 116, 118, 152; and space in the theatre 160–4
space, and architectural planning 167, 168–9; and time 151–3; and linear movement in visual arts 153–60; and sound in the theatre 160–4
Sparta 16, 17, 18, 19, 69, 103
Stephanus, pupil of Pasiteles 62
stoa, as architectural concept 34, 175–6; and architectural planning 166, 169–70, 172, 173, *178, 179, 181*; and orders 79–80
Stoa, of Athena, Pergamum 21; of Attalus, Athens 15, 79–80, 166, 173, 178, *76, 77, 181, 184*; of Eumenes, Athens 15; of Zeus, Athens 169, 172
Stoa Poikile, Athens 33, 175
Stobaeus 53
Stoicism 16, 33–4, 36, 38, 50, 58, 62, 175; and allegory 96–7, *98*; and artistic style 88–94, 106; theory of acoustics 161
'Strangford' shield 57
Stratonice 46, 58
sundials 151, 166, *159*
Sybaris 15–16
symbols 111, 116–18
Syracuse 10, 13, 46, 69, 71, 80, 180
Syria 69

Tacitus 16
Tarentum 123, 125
Tauriscus of Tralles 90, *93*
Tazza Farnese 137, *145*
technē, technai 53, 146
Tegea, temple of Athena Alea 23, 73
Telephus story, on small frieze of Altar of Zeus, Pergamum 145, 146, 156, 157
Telestes 67

Teuthras 145, *155*
Thamous 22
Thasos, shrine of Dionysus 105, 159, 160, *165*
theatre, sound and space in the 160–4, *169, 170, 171*
theatre of Dionysus, Athens 132, 161, *139*
Themis 123, *120*
Theocritus 40, 48, 50, 64, 68, 69, 71, 81, 128; *The Pipes of Theocritus* 109, 110, *112*
Theodorus of Samos 53
Theon of Samos *41, 46*
Theophrastus 27, 38, 55, 97, 180; *Characters* 38, 55
Thermopylae 110
Thersites 46
Thessaly 13
Thetis in the workshop of Hephaestus 45, *41*
Theuth 21–2, 113
Thucydides 16, 18, 59
Thurii 16, 119
Tiberius 15
time *see* space, and time
Timocles 142
Titan 140, *150*
tombstones 110–15, *114, 115*
Tower of the Winds, Athens 166, *174*
town and country 33, 49, 50–2, 64, 68
town-planning 23, 119, 166, *118*
tragedy 56, 61, 105, 159, *165*; Aristotle on 28, 29, 54, 55, 59; in painting and sculpture 56, 62; and Stoicism 38
Triptolemus-Horus *145*
tychē 36–7
Tyche of Antioch 36, 99, 101, *101*

ugliness and deformity, subject of art 33, 40, *27*; and comedy 54, 58, *55*

Vari, Attica *48*
vase painting 23, 50, 51, *18*; and inscriptions 105; and personification 97
vases, musical 162–4, *171*; Neo-Attic 147–8, 153, *158, 162*
Venus de Milo 140
verbal images, and Pergamene art 92–4, 95
Virgil 135; *Aeneid* 62
Vitruvius 21, 23, 45, 73, 125, 144, 148, 167; *De Architectura* 164; on theatre 160–4, *171*

word and image 105–8, 110–15
writers and images 108–10

Xenocrates 60, 62, 63
Xenophon 24, 25, 52, 55; *Memorabilia* 17; *Oeconomicus* 22
Xerxes 15, 56

Zeno of Elea 151, 155–6
Zeno, Stoic 33–4, 38, 50, 58, 175, *29*
Zenodotus 118
Zethus 90
Zeus 15, 57, 88, 96, 99, 107, 145; Ammon *1*; colossi by Phidias and Lysippus 62, 122, 123; cult of, and large-scale sculpture 140–1, *151*; on Pergamum frieze 85, 88, 140, 153–5, 173, *86, 163*
Zeuxis 38, 40, 67, 121, 126; Aphrodite of 25